The Supreme Court

The Supreme Court

Seventh Edition

Lawrence Baum
Ohio State University

CQ PRESS

A Division of Congressional Quarterly Inc.
Washington, D.C.

CQ Press
A Division of Congressional Quarterly Inc.
1414 22nd St. N.W.
Washington, DC 20037
(202) 822-1475; (800) 638-1710

www.cqpress.com

Printed in the United States of America

05 04 03 02 01   5 4 3 2 1

♾ The paper used in this publication meets the minimum requirements of
the American National Standard for Information Sciences—Permanence of
Paper for Printed Library Materials, ANSI Z39.48-1992.

Photo credits: frontispiece, CQ photo / Ken Heinen; p. 16, Reuters /
U.S. Senate; p. 19, Reuters / Tony Ranze; p. 44, Reuters / Win McNamee;
p. 73, Reuters / Win McNamee; p. 83, AP Wide World Photos / Leslie E.
Kossoff; p. 103, Reuters / Win McNamee; p. 131, courtesy the Supreme
Court Historical Society; p. 163, CQ photo; p. 189, CQ photo; p. 190, cour-
tesy the Supreme Court Historical Society; p. 242, © Bettmann / CORBIS.

Library of Congress Cataloging-in-Publication Data

Baum, Lawrence.
    The Supreme Court / Lawrence Baum.—7th ed.
        p. cm.
    Includes bibliographical references and index.
    ISBN 1-56802-524-6 (cloth)—ISBN 1-56802-523-8 (pbk.)
        1. United States. Supreme Court. 2. Constitutional law—United States.
3. Courts of last resort—United States. 4. Judicial review—United States.
I. Title.

KF8742.B35 2000
347.73'26—dc21   00-063078

In memory of my father,
Irving S. Baum

Contents

Preface

The annual Supreme Court term that ended in June 2000 was eventful. The Court surprised many observers by upholding its 1966 *Miranda* decision on police questioning of criminal suspects. It ruled that public schools could not permit student-led prayers at football games. It concluded that the federal Food and Drug Administration could not regulate cigarettes under existing law. It held that states could not give grandparents a right to visitation with their grandchildren. It addressed other contentious issues ranging from gay rights to rationing of medical services by health maintenance organizations. And it continued a recent trend by using several decisions to cut back on the power of Congress to regulate state and private activities.

Not all terms of the Court are so eventful, but the Court regularly rules on major issues in government and society. By doing so, it exerts considerable impact. While the Court is limited in its power, it nonetheless helps to shape important aspects of American life.

The Court's importance is well understood by people in politics and by the public at large. Certainly it receives its share of attention from the mass media. Major decisions are reported on front pages of newspapers and at the beginning of newscasts, and appointments to the Court garner enormous coverage.

Yet the Court itself is not understood as well as Congress or the president. One reason is that information about the Court's workings is scarce. Although the Court's decisions are readily available, the process by which it reaches those decisions is not so apparent. The justices do most of their work in private, and their public sessions can be seen only by the small number of people who attend them. Another reason is the Court's role as interpreter of law, a role that adds a degree of complexity to its work. Thus, even people with a strong interest in politics and government may know little about how the Court functions or about the forces that shape its behavior and impact.

This book represents an effort to improve understanding of the Supreme Court. It is intended to serve as a short but comprehensive guide to the Court, for those who already know a good deal about it as well as for those who have a more limited sense of it.

The book's first chapter serves as an introduction. It discusses the Court's role in general terms, examines the Court's place in the judicial system, analyzes the Court as an institution, and presents a brief summary of its history.

Each of the other chapters deals with an important aspect of the Court. Chapter 2 focuses on the justices: their selection, their backgrounds and careers, and the circumstances in which they leave the Court. Chapter 3 discusses how cases reach the Court and how the Court selects the small portion of those cases that it will hear.

Chapter 4 looks at decision making in the cases that the Court accepts for full decisions. After outlining the Court's decision-making procedures, I turn to the chapter's primary concern: the factors that influence the Court's choices among alternative decisions and policies. Chapter 5 examines the content of the Court's work: the kinds of issues on which the Court concentrates, the policies it supports, and the extent of its activism in policy making. I give special attention to changes in the Court's role as a policy maker and the sources of those changes.

The final chapter examines the ways in which other government policy makers respond to the Court's decisions as well as the Court's impact on American society as a whole. The chapter concludes with an assessment of the Court's significance as a force in American life.

This edition of the book reflects the substantial help that many people gave me with earlier editions. In revising the book for this edition, I made use of information provided by Richard

Pacelle, Eric Heberlig, and the Office of the Solicitor General in the Justice Department. I received useful suggestions for revisions from Brian Fife, Christine Harrington, Timothy Lenz, and Stephen Roberds.

This edition, like the sixth edition, has been strengthened considerably by the work that Tracy Villano did as copyeditor. I appreciate the help I received from Tom Roche, Gwenda Larsen, and Brenda Carter of CQ Press. CQ continues to be the model of what an author wants from a publisher: its people make my job easier and the results better. I am very pleased to acknowledge the contributions that they and others have made to this book.

The
Supreme
Court

Chapter 1

The Court

For many people, the future of the United States Supreme Court was a major concern in the presidential election of 2000. Candidates, interest groups, and commentators emphasized the potential impact of the next president's appointments to the Court. This concern reached the Court itself: after describing several questions whose outcome in the Court might depend on future appointments, one justice told a visiting group of college students to "vote carefully."[1]

But the prospect of presidential appointments was not the Supreme Court's most important role in the election. Its decisions in *Buckley v. Valeo* (1976) and later cases had struck down much of a body of regulations that Congress had enacted in 1974 to control campaign finance. As a result, George W. Bush was able to spend as much money as he could raise on his campaign for the Republican nomination, and his financial advantage over his rivals helped to secure his nomination. In the general election, both Bush and Al Gore benefited from lavish spending on their behalf by political parties and interest groups, because the Court had invalidated strict limits on such spending.[2]

The Court also played a key role in the impeachment of President Bill Clinton. Its 1997 decision in *Clinton v. Jones* rejected Clinton's argument that proceedings in a lawsuit against the president should be delayed until the president left office. Thus it removed a potential barrier to the deposition that provided the primary basis for Clinton's impeachment. And in *Morrison v. Olson* (1988) the Court ruled that the existence of an independent counsel to investigate executive-branch officials did not violate the constitutional separation of powers. If the Court had taken the opposite position, Kenneth

1

Starr would not have served as special prosecutor, the role in which he pursued a series of investigations of Clinton and ultimately presented to Congress the evidence on which impeachment was based.

In recent years the Court has made other major rulings on issues that help to shape society. It has tilted the balance of constitutional power away from the federal government in favor of the states. It has helped to determine when people can bring lawsuits for sexual harassment and for withholding of medical services by health maintenance organizations. Its decisions have established rules for the death penalty, abortion, and assisted suicide.

None of this is new. The Supreme Court has frequently been an issue in presidential elections.[3] A quarter century before the Clinton impeachment, the Court's ruling in *United States v. Nixon* (1974) forced President Richard Nixon to turn over tape recordings of some of his conversations to a federal court, thereby ensuring that he would leave office early. And the Court has always addressed major issues in American government and society, from the powers of president and Congress to the scope of protection for freedom of speech. Whatever their reactions to the Court's decisions on these issues, most people agree that the Court plays a central role in American life.

For this reason, those who seek to understand government and politics in the United States must inquire into the Supreme Court. Who are the people who serve on it, and how do they get there? What determines which cases and issues the Court decides? In resolving the cases before it, how does the Court choose between alternative decisions? In what policy areas is it active, and what kinds of policies does it make? Finally, what happens to the Court's decisions after they are handed down, and what impact do they actually have?

This book is intended to contribute to an understanding of the Supreme Court by answering these questions. Each question is the subject of one of the book's chapters. Chapter 1 introduces the Court and provides background information for the remainder of the book.

A Perspective on the Court

The Court in Law and Politics

The Supreme Court as a Legal Institution. The Supreme Court is, first of all, a court—the highest court in the federal judicial system. Like other courts, it has a specified *jurisdiction,* the power to hear and decide particular kinds of cases. And, like other courts, it can decide legal issues only in those cases that are brought to it.

As a court, the Supreme Court makes decisions within a legal framework. While Congress simply writes new law, the policy choices that the Court faces are framed as interpretations of existing law. In this respect the Court operates within a constraint from which legislators are free.

In another respect, however, the Supreme Court's identity as a court reduces the constraints on it. The widespread belief that courts should be insulated from the political process has given the Court a certain degree of actual insulation. The lifetime appointments of Supreme Court justices allow them some freedom from concerns about approval by political leaders and voters. Justices usually stay out of partisan politics, because open involvement in partisan activity is perceived as inappropriate. And because direct contact between lobbyists and justices is generally deemed unacceptable, interest group activity in the Court is basically restricted to the formal channels of legal argument.

The Supreme Court as a Political Institution. The insulation of the Supreme Court from politics should not be exaggerated. People sometimes speak of courts as if they are, or at least ought to be, "nonpolitical." In a literal sense, of course, this is impossible: as part of government, courts are political institutions by definition. What people really mean when they refer to courts as nonpolitical is that courts are separate from the political process and that their decisions are unaffected by nonlegal considerations. This is also impossible—for courts in general and certainly for the Supreme Court.

The Court is political chiefly because it makes important decisions on major issues; people care about those decisions and want to influence them. As a result, appointments to the Court are frequently the subject of political battles. Similarly, interest groups bring cases and present arguments to the Court in an effort to affect what it does. Because members of Congress pay attention to the Court's decisions and hold powers over the Court, the justices may take Congress into account when they decide cases. And their own political values affect the votes they cast and the opinions they write in the Court's decisions.

Thus the Supreme Court should be viewed as both a legal institution and a political institution. What it does and how it operates are influenced by both the political process and the legal system. This ambiguous position makes the Court more complex in some ways than most political institutions; it also makes the Court an interesting case study in political behavior.

The Court as a Policy Maker

This book is concerned with the Supreme Court in general, but I give particular emphasis to the Court's role in the making of public policy—the authoritative rules by which government institutions seek to influence the operation of government and to shape society as a whole. Legislation to provide subsidies for wheat farmers, a judge's ruling in an auto accident case, and a Supreme Court decision laying down rules to govern police procedure are all examples of public policy. The Court may be viewed as part of a policy-making system that includes lower courts as well as the other branches of government.

Policy Making through Legal Interpretation. As I have noted, the Supreme Court makes public policy by interpreting provisions of law. Issues of public policy come to the Court in the form of legal questions that the Court is empowered to resolve. In this respect the Court's policy making differs fundamentally in form from that of Congress.

The Court does not face legal questions in the abstract. Rather, it addresses these questions in the process of settling specific controversies between parties (sometimes called litigants) that bring cases to it. In a sense, then, every decision by the Court has three aspects: it is a judgment about the specific dispute brought to it, an interpretation of the legal issues in that dispute, and a position on the policy questions that are raised by the legal issues.

These three aspects of the Court's rulings are illustrated by its decisions on police powers to search automobiles. In recent years the Court has decided a number of cases involving the circumstances under which car searches are acceptable and the permissible scope of those searches.[4] In each case it rules on the specific dispute, determining whether the evidence obtained from a search could be admitted in the trial of a particular defendant. If a state supreme court or federal court of appeals ruled against the defendant, the Supreme Court may affirm that judgment and thus allow the defendant's conviction to become final. Alternatively, the Court may reverse the conviction and remand the case—sending it back to the lower court for further action in line with the Court's ruling.

The Court's decision in each case is also a judgment on the law of search and seizure. The Court determines how the Fourth and Fourteenth Amendments should be interpreted in relation to the situation involved in each case. Lower courts then are obliged to apply the Court's interpretation of the Constitution to any other case that involves the same kind of auto search.

Finally, the Court's decisions shape policy on police powers to engage in searches for evidence. In the last decade the Court generally has given broad interpretations to those powers, in turn giving law enforcement agencies more freedom to engage in searches. Because the legal limits on police searches are determined primarily by the courts, the Supreme Court's expansions of search powers are an important component of government policy in this field.

The Court's Significance in Policy Making. The Supreme Court's substantial role in government policy on police searches is not unusual. Through its individual decisions and lines of decisions, the Court contributes a great deal to policy on a variety of important issues. The Court's assumption of this role has been facilitated by several circumstances. For one thing, as the French observer Alexis de Tocqueville noted more than a century ago, "scarcely any political question arises in the United States that is not resolved, sooner or later, into a judicial question."[5] One reason that policy disputes tend to reach the courts is the existence of a written Constitution whose provisions offer a basis for challenging the legality of government actions.

Because so many policy questions come to the courts, the Supreme Court has the opportunity to rule on a large number that are significant. And during much of its history the Court has welcomed that opportunity, first insisting on its supremacy as legal arbiter and later making frequent use of its chances to rule on major issues. In doing so the Court has engaged in a good deal of what is often called *judicial activism.* That term can have many meanings. But its key element is that a court makes significant changes in public policy, particularly in policies established by other institutions.[6]

At the same time, the Court's role in policy making is limited by three conditions. First, the Court can do only so much with the relatively few decisions that it makes in a year. In the past decade, the Court has issued decisions with full opinions in an average of fewer than 90 cases each year. In deciding such a small number of cases, the Court addresses only a select group of policy issues. Inevitably, there are whole fields of policy that it barely touches. Even in the areas in which the Court does act, it can deal with only a limited number of the issues that exist at a given time.

Second, the Court exercises considerable judicial restraint, which is the avoidance of activism. This behavior stems in part from judges' training in a legal tradition that emphasizes the value of restraint, and in part from a desire to avoid controversy and attacks on the Court. Judicial restraint is reflected in the Court's refusal to hear some important and controversial cases, such as the legal challenges brought against U.S. participation in the war in Vietnam.[7] It is also reflected in the frequent—though not consistent—practice of deciding cases on relatively narrow grounds where possible.

Third, even a highly activist Court is limited in its impact by the actions of other policy makers. The Court is seldom the final government institution to deal with the policy issues that it addresses. Its decisions usually must be implemented by lower court judges and administrators, who often retain considerable discretion about how they will put a ruling into effect. The impact of a decision concerning police searches for evidence depends largely on how police officers react to it. Congress and the president influence the ways that the Court's decisions are carried out, and they can overcome its interpretations of federal statutes simply by amending those statutes. There may be a considerable difference between what the Court rules on an issue and the public policy that ultimately results from government actions on that issue.

For these reasons, those who see the Supreme Court as the dominant force in the U.S. government almost surely are wrong. But if not dominant, the Court is a very important policy maker. Certainly the extent of its role is extraordinary for a court.

The Court in the Judicial System

Structure of the System

The Supreme Court works within a system of courts, and its place in that system structures its role. Strictly speaking, it is inaccurate to refer to a single court system in the United States. Rather, there is both a federal court system and a separate court system in each state. The federal system can be distinguished from the state systems in terms of jurisdiction: federal courts can hear only those cases that Congress has put under their jurisdiction. Most of the jurisdiction of the federal courts can be placed in three categories. First are the criminal and civil cases that arise under federal laws, including the Constitution. A prosecution for bank robbery, which is a violation of federal criminal law, is brought to federal court. So are civil cases based on federal patent and copyright laws.

Second are cases to which the U.S. government is a party. When the federal government sues an individual to recover what it claims to be owed from a student loan, or when an individual sues the federal government over disputed social security benefits, the case almost always goes to federal court.

Third are civil cases involving citizens of different states, if the amount in question is at least $75,000; if this condition is met, either party may bring the case to federal court. If a citizen of New Jersey sues a citizen of Texas for $100,000 as compensation for injuries resulting from an auto accident, the plaintiff (the New Jersey resident) might bring the case to federal court, or the defendant (the Texan) might have the case "removed" from state court to federal court. If neither does so, the case will be heard in state court—generally, in the state where the accident occurred.

Only a small proportion of cases fall into these categories. The most common kinds of cases—criminal prosecutions, personal injury suits, divorces, debt collection actions—typically are heard in state court. The trial courts of a single populous state such as Illinois or Florida hear far more cases than do the federal trial courts. But federal cases are more likely than state cases to raise major issues of public policy.

State Court Structure. There is considerable variation in the structures of state court systems, but some general patterns exist (see Figure 1-1). Each state system has courts that are primarily *trial courts,* which hear cases initially as they enter the court system, and courts that are primarily *appellate courts,* which review lower court decisions that are appealed to them. Most states have two sets of trial courts, one to handle major cases and the other to deal with minor cases. Major criminal cases usually concern what the law defines as felonies; major civil cases are those involving large sums of

Figure 1-1
Most Common State Court Structures

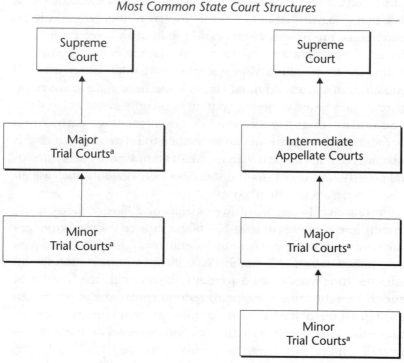

Note: Arrows indicate most common routes of appeals.

[a] In many states, major trial courts or minor trial courts (or both) are composed of two or more different sets of courts. For instance, minor trial courts in California include municipal courts and justice courts.

money. Most often, appeals from decisions of minor trial courts are heard by major trial courts.

Appellate courts are structured in two ways. In about one-quarter of the states, generally the less populous states, there is a single appellate court—usually called the state supreme court. All appeals from major trial courts go to this supreme court. About three-quarters of the states have a set of intermediate appellate courts below the supreme court. These intermediate courts initially hear most appeals from major trial courts. State supreme courts are required to hear certain appeals brought directly from the trial courts or from the intermediate courts, but for the most part they have discretionary jurisdiction over appeals from the decisions of intermediate courts. The term *discretionary jurisdiction* means simply that a court can choose to hear some appeals and refuse to hear others; cases that a court is required to hear fall under its *mandatory jurisdiction*.

Federal Court Structure. The structure of federal courts is shown in Figure 1-2. At the base of the federal court system are the federal district courts. There are ninety-four district courts in the United States; each state has between one and four, and there is one district court in the District of Columbia and in some of the territories such as Guam. The district courts hear all federal cases at the trial level, with the exception of a few types of cases that are heard in specialized courts.

Above the district courts are the twelve courts of appeals, each of which has jurisdiction over appeals in one of the federal judicial circuits. The District of Columbia constitutes one circuit; each of the other eleven circuits includes three or more states. The Second Circuit, for instance, includes Vermont, New York, and Connecticut. Appeals from the district courts in one circuit generally go to the court of appeals for that circuit, along with appeals from the Tax Court and from some administrative agencies. Patent cases and some claims against the federal government go from the district courts to the specialized Court of Appeals for the Federal Circuit, as do appeals from three specialized trial courts. The Court of Appeals for the Armed Forces hears cases from lower courts in the military system.

The Court's Jurisdiction

The Supreme Court stands at the top of the federal judicial system. Its jurisdiction, summarized in Table 1-1, is of two types. First, the Constitution gives the Court jurisdiction over certain specified classes of cases as a trial court—what is called *original jurisdiction*. Those cases may be brought directly to the Court. The Court's original jurisdiction includes some cases to which a state is a party and cases involving ambassadors. Most cases within the Court's original jurisdiction can be heard alternatively by a district court. Lawsuits between two states can be heard only by the Supreme Court, and these lawsuits—often involving disputed state borders—account

FIGURE 1-2
Basic Structure of the Federal Court System

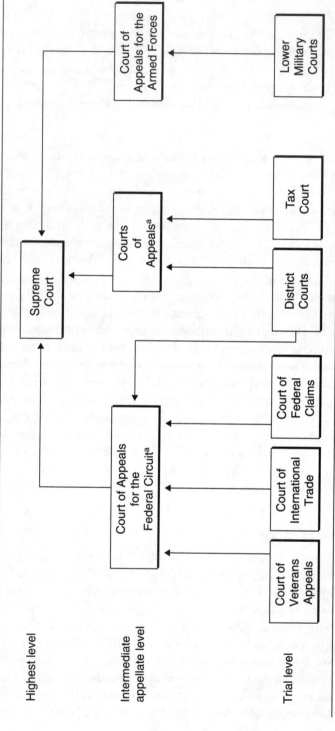

Note: Arrows indicate most common routes of appeals. Some specialized courts of minor importance are excluded.

[a] These courts also hear appeals from administrative agencies.

TABLE 1-1

Summary of Supreme Court Jurisdiction

A. Original jurisdiction
   1. Disputes between states[a]
   2. Some types of cases brought by a state
   3. Disputes between a state and the federal government
   4. Cases involving foreign diplomatic personnel

B. Appellate jurisdiction[b]
   1. All decisions of federal courts of appeals and specialized federal appellate courts
   2. All decisions of the highest state court with jurisdiction over a case, concerning issues of federal law
   3. Decisions of special three-judge federal district courts (mandatory)

[a] It is unclear whether these cases are mandatory, and the Court treats them as discretionary.
[b] Some minor categories are not listed.

for most of the decisions based on the Court's original jurisdiction. The Court frequently refuses to hear cases under its original jurisdiction—even some lawsuits by one state against another. In part for this reason, full decisions in original jurisdiction cases are not plentiful; there have been about 175 such decisions in the Court's entire history.[8] When the Court does accept an original case, it usually appoints a "special master" to gather facts and propose a decision to the Court.

A recent original case was *New Jersey v. New York* (1998). This case involved a dispute between the two states over Ellis Island, the famed port of entry for millions of immigrants to the United States and currently a major tourist attraction. The Court appointed Paul Verkuil, dean of Cardozo School of Law, to take evidence. Verkuil did so and proposed where to draw the line on the island between the two states. The Court then heard the case itself and modified Verkuil's proposal, giving New Jersey most of the island, to the great displeasure of some New Yorkers.

Second, the Court has *appellate jurisdiction* to hear cases brought by parties dissatisfied with certain lower court decisions. In the federal system, such cases can come from the federal courts of appeals and from the two specialized appellate courts. Cases may also come directly from special three-judge district courts that hear a few classes of cases. Most cases that reach the Court from the three-judge district courts concern voting and election issues.

Cases can come to the Supreme Court after decisions by the state supreme courts if they involve claims arising under federal law, including the Constitution. More precisely, a case can come to the Court from the highest state court with the power to hear it—in one instance, from the police court of Louisville, Kentucky.[9] Table 1-2 shows that a substantial majority of the cases that come to the Court, and an even larger majority of the cases that it hears, originated in federal court rather than in state court.

The rule by which state cases come to the Supreme Court may be confusing, because cases arising under federal law ordinarily start in federal court. But cases brought to state courts on the basis of state law sometimes contain issues of federal law as well. This situation is common in criminal cases. A person who is accused of burglary under state law will be tried in a state court. But during the state court proceedings, the defendant may argue that his rights under the Constitution were violated in a police search. The case eventually can be brought to the Supreme Court on that issue. If it is, the Court will have the power to rule only on the federal issue, not on the issues of state law involved in the case. For instance, the Court cannot rule on whether the defendant actually committed the burglary.

Nearly all cases brought to the Court are under its discretionary jurisdiction, so it can choose whether or not to hear them. They come to the Court primarily in the form of petitions for a writ of certiorari, a legal device by which the Court calls up a case for decision from a lower court. Some cases, called appeals, must be heard by the Court. In a series of steps culminating in 1988, Congress converted the Court's jurisdiction from mostly mandatory to almost entirely discretionary. Today, appeals can be brought in only the few small classes of cases that come directly from three-judge district courts.

The Supreme Court hears only a fraction of 1 percent of the cases brought to federal and state courts. As this figure suggests, courts other than the Supreme Court have ample opportunity to make policy on their own. Moreover, their decisions help to determine the ultimate impact of the Court's policies. Important though it is, the Supreme Court is hardly the only court that matters.

TABLE 1-2

Sources of Supreme Court Cases in Recent Periods (in percentages)

	Federal courts			
	Courts of appeals	District courts	Specialized courts	State courts
Cases brought to the Court[a]	76.4	0.0	1.4	22.2
Cases heard by the Court[b]	76.5	3.7	6.2	13.6

Note: Original jurisdiction cases are not included.

[a] Cases in which the Court granted or denied hearings, October 4, 1999 (1,685 cases).

[b] Cases in which the Court heard oral argument, 1998 term (81 cases).

A First Look at the Court

The Court's Physical Structure

The Supreme Court did not move into its own building until 1935. During its first decade the Court met first in New York and then in Philadelphia. The Court moved to Washington, D.C., with the rest of the federal government at the beginning of the nineteenth century. For the next 130 years it sat in the Capitol, as a "tenant" of Congress.

The Court's accommodations in the Capitol were not entirely adequate. Among other things, the lack of office space meant that justices did most of their work at home. After an intensive lobbying effort by Chief Justice William Howard Taft, Congress appropriated money for a Supreme Court building in 1929. The five-story structure, completed in 1935, occupies a full square block across from the Capitol. Because the primary material in the impressive building is marble, it has been called a "marble palace."

The building houses all the facilities necessary for the Court's operation. The Court's formal sessions are held in the courtroom on the first floor. The justices sit behind their bench at the front of the courtroom; other participants and spectators sit in sections in the back of the room and along the sides. Behind the courtroom is the conference room, where the justices meet to decide cases. Also near the courtroom are the chambers that contain offices for the associate justices and their staffs. (Reflecting the chief justice's special status, the chief's chambers are attached to the conference room.)

The Court's Personnel

The Justices. Under the Constitution, members of the Supreme Court must be nominated by the president and confirmed by a majority vote in the Senate. The Constitution establishes that they will hold office "during good behavior"—that is, for life unless they relinquish their posts voluntarily or are removed through impeachment proceedings. Beyond these basic rules, such questions as the number of justices, their qualifications, and their duties have been settled by federal statutes and by tradition.

We are accustomed to a Court of nine members, but the number of justices was changed several times during the Court's first century. The Judiciary Act of 1789 provided for six justices. Subsequent statutes changed the number successively to five, six, seven, nine, ten, seven, and nine. The changes were made in part to accommodate the justices' duties in the lower federal courts, in part to serve partisan and policy goals of the president and Congress. The most recent change to nine members was made in 1869; any further changes in size appear quite unlikely.

In 2000 each of the associate justices received a salary of $173,600; the chief justice received $181,400. Substantial as these salaries are, they are not much higher than what some law firms pay new attorneys and less than what some firms give to new hires who served as Supreme Court clerks. According to one report, this disparity has become increasingly annoying to the justices.[10] Some justices also have considerable personal wealth on which they can draw: Sandra Day O'Connor, John Paul Stevens, Ruth Bader Ginsburg, David Souter, and Stephen Breyer apparently are millionaires.[11]

The primary duty of the justices, of course, is to participate in the collective decisions of the Court: determining which cases to hear, deciding cases, and writing and contributing to opinions. Ordinarily, the Court's decisions are made by all nine members, but there are several exceptions. There are periods when the Court has only eight members because a justice has left the Court and a replacement has not been appointed. A justice's illness may leave the Court temporarily short-handed. And a justice may decide not to participate in a case because of a perceived conflict of interest; this self-disqualification is called a recusal.

Recusals may occur for several reasons. (These reasons usually must be inferred, because the justices do not make them public.) Clarence Thomas did not participate in *United States v. Virginia*

(1996), in which the all-male status of the Virginia Military Institute was challenged, because his son was a student at VMI. Justices sometimes recuse themselves when a relative's law firm participates in a case. But the most common reason for recusal is the stock holdings of justices and their spouses. Some current justices have substantial holdings, and such holdings have resulted in frequent recusals for Stephen Breyer and Sandra Day O'Connor.

When only eight justices participate in a decision, the Court may divide 4–4. Such a vote occurred in a 1999 case arising from a dispute over the practices of a company in which Justice O'Connor owned stock. O'Connor recused herself, and the Court split evenly. In that case, as in others, a tie vote affirmed the lower court decision, the votes of individual justices were not announced, and no opinions were written. Frustrated by the lack of a decision, one lawyer whose interest group had filed a brief in the case said, "I think the time has come when we need to take appropriate measures to reduce the number of instances where stock ownership causes recusal."[12]

In rare instances, the Court fails to achieve a quorum of six members. In 1995, a federal court of appeals ruled that a 1983 federal statute requiring federal judges to pay social security and Medicare taxes had diminished their salaries in violation of the Constitution. The federal government asked the Court to hear the case. Four of the justices potentially were affected financially by the outcome, so they recused themselves and the Court fell one member short of a quorum.[13] Failure to achieve a quorum, like a tie vote, results in affirmance of lower court decisions.

In addition to their participation in collective decisions, the justices make some decisions individually, as circuit justices. The United States has always been divided into federal judicial circuits. Originally, most appeals within a circuit were heard by ad hoc courts composed of a federal trial judge and two members of the Supreme Court assigned to that area as circuit justices. The circuit duties were arduous, particularly in the days when long-distance travel was very difficult, and they damaged the health of some justices.[14] The justices' "circuit-riding" responsibilities were reduced in several stages and eliminated altogether when Congress created the courts of appeals in 1891.

The twelve judicial circuits continue to have circuit justices assigned to them, with three justices doing double duty. The circuit

Chief Justice William Rehnquist presides over the Senate impeachment trial of President Clinton in January 1999.

justices deal with applications for special action, such as a request to stay a lower court decision (prevent it from taking effect) until the Court decides whether to hear a case. Ordinarily, such an application must go first to the circuit justice. That justice may rule on the application as an individual or refer the case to the whole Court. If the circuit justice rejects an application, it can then be made to a second justice. That justice ordinarily refers it to the whole Court.

This process is illustrated by a 1998 case in which several tobacco companies sought a stay of an order requiring them to turn over internal documents to the state of Minnesota. They went first to Justice Thomas, circuit justice for the Eighth Circuit where the case arose. After Thomas refused to issue a stay, the companies turned to Justice Scalia. Scalia referred their request to the full Court, which also refused to issue a stay.[15]

The most common subject of stay requests is the death penalty. The Court is confronted with numerous requests to grant or vacate (remove) stays of execution, many of which come very close to the scheduled execution time. These requests put considerable pressure on the justices, and they sometimes result in close votes, dissenting opinion, and what one commentator called "hard feelings among the Justices."[16]

For the most part, the nine justices are equal in formal power. The exception is the chief justice, who is the formal leader of the Court and of the federal judicial system. The official title, "Chief Justice of the United States," symbolizes the chief's responsibilities for the federal judicial system as a whole. In this role, the chief chairs the Judicial Conference and conveys to Congress the views of the conference on legislative issues. The chief also delivers an annual "state of the judiciary" message, directed primarily at Congress.[17]

The Constitution requires that the chief justice preside over Senate trials in impeachment proceedings against presidents, a duty that added considerably to William Rehnquist's workload in January 1999. It also attracted attention to Rehnquist's distinctive robe with four gold stripes on each sleeve, modeled on the costume of the British lord chancellor in a theater production that he attended in 1995.[18]

Within the Court, the chief justice presides over the Court's public sessions and conferences. The chief also supervises administration of the Court, with the assistance of committees of justices such as the Committee for the Budget and the Cafeteria Committee. One justice serves as "social secretary."[19]

Law Clerks and Other Support Staff. The justices are supported by a staff of more than 300 people. A large majority of those staff members carry out custodial and police functions under the supervision of the marshal of the Court. About thirty people work for the clerk of the Court, who is responsible for the clerical processing of all the cases that come to the Court. The reporter of decisions supervises preparation of the official record of the Court's decisions, *United States Reports*. The librarian is in charge of the libraries in the Supreme Court building.

Of all the members of the support staff, the law clerks have the most direct impact on the Court's decisions.[20] Justices can employ four clerks each, though John Paul Stevens and William Rehnquist choose to use only three. (Rehnquist likes to play tennis with his clerks, and one reporter pointed out that his three clerks are "just enough to fill a doubles team."[21]) The typical clerk is a recent, high-ranked graduate of a prestigious law school (over the past quarter century, 40 percent have come from Harvard and Yale) who clerked in a federal court of appeals before coming to the Supreme Court. Clerks are disproportionately white and male, a fact that has led to criticism of the Court in recent years and to a 1998 demonstration at the Court that was organized by the National Association for the Advancement of Colored People (NAACP).[22]

Clerkships are prized positions, and more than 1,000 people apply for them each year.[23] Most apply to several justices. Clerks usually work with a justice for only one year. After leaving the Court, clerks have little difficulty obtaining good positions at high salaries. Many go on to distinguished careers. Indeed, William Rehnquist, John Paul Stevens, and Stephen Breyer were once law clerks in the Court.

What clerks do differs from justice to justice. They typically spend much of their time on the petitions for hearings by the Court, digesting information in the petitions and the lower court records and summarizing it for the justices. Clerks also work on cases that have been accepted for decision, analyzing case materials and issues and drafting opinions. And they participate in the informal communication that helps the justices work toward collective decisions.

The extent of law clerks' influence over the Court's decisions is a matter of considerable interest and, not surprisingly, wide disagreement.[24] Observers who depict the clerks as highly powerful seem to underestimate the justices' ability to maintain control over their decisions. Still, the jobs that justices give to their clerks ensure significant influence. One former clerk estimated that "well over half of the text the Court now produces was generated by law clerks," and he concluded that "delegation of the initial drafting task inevitably entails a substantial transfer of responsibility over the final content of an opinion."[25] The same is true of the other work that clerks do.

The Court and the Outside World

Busy as Supreme Court justices are with their judicial work, they engage in a good deal of outside activity. Most common are speeches and lectures at law schools and legal conferences. This activity is heaviest in summer, when the Court's workload is lightest. This work often provides opportunities for free travel. The justices' 2000 financial disclosures indicated that in the preceding

Justice Clarence Thomas speaks with NASCAR driver Dale Earnhardt at the Daytona 500 race in 1999. Thomas, an auto racing fan, served as grand marshal of the race.

year they had traveled to such nations as Greece, Japan, and New Zealand.[26]

The justices engage in a variety of other activities. In 1997 William Rehnquist and Sandra Day O'Connor served as judges in a re-enactment of the murder trial of Lizzie Borden for the 1892 murders of her father and stepmother.[27] Rehnquist may be the most active of the current justices, with off-the-Court pursuits that range from writing three books about law and courts to solving a newspaper puzzle about the meaning of an obscure personalized license plate.[28] As suggested by the photo of Clarence Thomas at the Daytona 500, shown above, not all the justices' activities are closely related to the legal system.[29]

The justices' outside activities can have implications for policy or politics. Their speeches and lectures sometimes convey a sense of their views on public issues. Indeed, their choices of forums in which to speak shed light on their ideological leanings. For instance, Justice Thomas has shown a preference for conservative groups.[30]

Some justices have become involved in the political process more directly, primarily by consulting with presidents. This was true of President Lyndon Johnson's appointees Abe Fortas and Thurgood Marshall. Fortas, a long-time adviser to Johnson, continued to serve in that role after his appointment. He dealt with some issues that could have come before the Court, and he disclosed to an FBI official information on the Court's deliberations in two cases.[31] Warren Burger, appointed chief justice by President Nixon, later talked with Nixon about pending cases.[32] Since Burger and Nixon, however, it appears that no justice has engaged in that kind of presidential consultation.

Few of the justices are famous as individuals. In a 1995 survey 31 percent of the respondents could name Sandra Day O'Connor, and 30 percent recalled Clarence Thomas; none of the other justices achieved even 10 percent recognition. Among the respondents, 17 percent could name three justices—compared with 59 percent who could name the Three Stooges.[33] When asked who the chief justice was, one in six survey respondents in 1998 named William Rehnquist, about the same number named someone else, and two-thirds said that they did not know.[34] (Awareness of Rehnquist's status undoubtedly increased a few months later, when he presided over the Clinton impeachment trial.)

The justices seem to like their anonymity, which allows them a freedom more visible public figures lack. During a parade of antiabortion marchers in front of the Court, Harry Blackmun, author of the 1973 opinion legalizing abortion, was able to stand nearby and watch unnoticed.[35] As one biographer said of William Brennan, who exerted great influence on civil liberties law, "he enjoyed all the benefits of power with none of the annoyances." [36]

This degree of anonymity results in part from the justices' own choices. Most important, they have refused to allow televising of oral arguments and announcements of decisions. Justice Souter said that "the day you see a camera coming into our courtroom, it's going to roll over my dead body." [37] The release of audiotapes of arguments is delayed, so excerpts cannot be played on same-day newscasts. The justices are also much less willing than their counterparts in the other branches of government to grant on-the-record interviews to journalists.

The Court reveals little about its decision-making processes, which its public information officer once said "are cloaked in a security . . . possibly rivaled only by the National Security Agency or the CIA." [38] This suggests that the justices' efforts to keep out of the public eye have another purpose as well. By limiting the flow of information about themselves and the Court, the justices may be trying to maintain an impression that the Court is outside and above ordinary politics. Indeed, Barbara Perry has argued that the justices and the Court's staff engage in a careful strategy to give the Court an exalted image among the general public. [39]

If there is such a strategy, it has achieved considerable success. While the Court receives some criticism in the mass media, on the whole it is treated far more deferentially than Congress or the president. One scholar has said that the reporters who cover the Court "are in essence tools of the Court." [40] And the Court's public approval ratings are usually more positive than those of the other branches. In a 1998 national survey, 50 percent of the respondents had a high level of confidence in the Court, compared with 26 percent for the federal executive branch and 18 percent for Congress. [41] Such a high level of approval may provide the Court with some protection from criticism and from more concrete attacks by other policy makers.

The Court's Schedule

The Schedule by Year. The Court holds one term each year, lasting from the first Monday in October until the beginning of the succeeding term a year later. The term is designated by the year in which it begins: the 2000 term began in October 2000. Ordinarily, the Court does its collective work from late September to late June. This work begins when the justices meet to dispose of the petitions for hearings that have accumulated during the summer and ends when the Court has issued decisions in all the cases it heard during the term.

Most of the term is divided into sittings of about two weeks, when the Court holds sessions to hear oral arguments in cases and to announce decisions, and recesses of two weeks or longer. The justices meet in conference during the sittings and, less frequently, during recesses. After the Court begins its last sitting in mid-May, it hears no more cases and holds one or more sessions each week to announce decisions.

The Court issues few decisions early in the term because of the time required after oral arguments to write opinions and reach final positions. Typically, about one-third of the decisions are announced in June, as the justices scramble to finish their work by the end of the term. This deadline creates considerable pressure. At the end of the term, reported one former law clerk, "marriages got put on hold. Friendships disappeared."[42] Another said, "I still have nightmares" about the end of the term.[43]

When the Court has reached and announced decisions in all the cases it heard during the term, the summer recess begins. Cases that the Court accepted for hearing but that were not argued during the term are carried over to the next term. In summer the justices generally spend some time away from Washington but continue their work on the petitions for hearings that arrive at the Court. During that time the Court and individual circuit justices respond to applications for special action. When the justices meet at the end of summer to dispose of the accumulated petitions, the cycle begins again.

The Schedule by Week. The schedule of weekly activities, like the annual schedule, is fairly regular. During sittings, the Court generally holds sessions on Monday through Wednesday of two weeks and Monday of the third week.

The sessions generally begin at ten o'clock in the morning. Oral arguments usually are held during each session except on the last Monday of the sitting. They may be preceded by several types of business. On Mondays the Court announces the filing of its order list, which is a report of the Court's decisions on petitions for hearing and other actions taken at its conference on the preceding Friday. Justices announce their opinions in cases that the Court has resolved. New members are admitted to the Supreme Court bar (thus becoming eligible to argue cases before the Court).

The oral arguments consume most of the time during sessions. Most often one hour is allocated for argument in a case, divided equally between the two sides. With the reduced numbers of cases accepted by the Court in recent years, sessions have become shorter; the Court hears two cases on most argument days.

During sittings the Court holds two conferences each week. The Wednesday afternoon conference is devoted to discussion of the cases that were argued on Monday. In a longer conference on Friday, the justices discuss the cases argued on Tuesday and Wednesday, as well as all the other matters that must be taken up by the Court. The most numerous of these matters are the petitions for hearing.

The Court also holds a conference on the last Friday of each recess to deal with the continuing flow of business. The remainder of the justices' time during recess periods is devoted to their individual work: study of petitions for hearing and of cases scheduled for argument, writing of opinions, and reaction to other justices' opinions. That work continues during the sittings.

The Court's History

This book is concerned primarily with the Supreme Court at present and in the recent past. But I will frequently refer to the Court's history in order to better understand the current Court. It is useful at this point to take an overview of that history to provide context for the excursions into history later in the book.

The Court from 1790 to 1865

The Constitution explicitly created the Supreme Court, but it said much less about the Court than about Congress and the president. In the Judiciary Act of 1789, which set up the federal court system, the Court's jurisdiction under the Constitution was used as the basis for granting the Court broad powers. Still, what it would do with its powers was uncertain, in part because their scope was ambiguous.

The Court started slowly, deciding only about fifty cases and making few significant decisions between 1790 and 1799.[44] Several candidates rejected offers of nominations to the Court, and two justices—including Chief Justice John Jay—resigned to take more attractive positions in state government. But the Court's fortunes improved considerably under John Marshall, chief justice from 1801 to 1835. Marshall, who was appointed by President John Adams, dominated the Court to a degree unmatched by any other justice. He used his dominance to advance the policies that he favored and the position of the Court itself.

The Court's key assertion of power under Marshall probably was its decision in *Marbury v. Madison* (1803), in which the Court struck down a federal statute for the first time. In his opinion for the Court, Marshall argued that when a federal law is inconsistent with the Constitution, the Court must uphold the supremacy of the Constitution by declaring the law unconstitutional and refusing to enforce it. A few years later, the Court also claimed the right of judicial review over state acts.

The Court's aggressiveness resulted in denunciations and threats, including an effort by President Thomas Jefferson to have Congress remove at least one justice through impeachment. But Marshall's skill in avoiding confrontation helped to protect the Court from a successful attack. Gradually the powers that he claimed for the Court and the Court's central role in the policy-making process came to be accepted by the other branches of government and by the general public.

This acceptance was tested by the Court's decision in *Scott v. Sandford* (1857), generally known as the *Dred Scott* case. Prior to that decision the Court had overturned only one federal statute, the minor law involved in *Marbury v. Madison*. In *Dred Scott,* however, Marshall's successor, Roger Taney (1836–1864), wrote the Court's opinion holding that Congress had exceeded its constitutional powers in prohibiting slavery in some territories. That decision was intended to resolve the legal controversy over slavery. Instead, the level of controversy increased, and the Court was vilified in the North. The Court's prestige suffered greatly, but the Court and its basic powers survived without serious challenge.[45]

During this period the Court was concerned with more than its own position; it was addressing major issues of public policy. The primary area of its concern was federalism, the legal relationship between the national and state governments. Under Marshall, the Court gave strong support to national powers. Marshall wanted to restrict state policy where that policy interfered with activities of the national government, especially its power to regulate commerce. Under Taney, the Court was not as favorable to the national government. But Taney and his colleagues did not reverse the direction the Court had taken under Marshall. As a result, the constitutional power of the federal government remained strong; the Court had subtly altered the lines between the national government and the state governments in support of the former.

The Court from 1865 to 1937

After the Civil War, the Court increasingly focused on government regulation of the economy. By the late nineteenth century, all levels of government were adopting new laws to regulate business activities. Among them were the federal antitrust laws, state regulations of railroad practices, and federal and state laws concerning employment conditions. Inevitably, much of this legislation was challenged in the courts on constitutional grounds.

Although the Supreme Court upheld a great many government policies regulating business in this period, it gradually became less friendly to those policies. That position was reflected in the development of constitutional doctrines limiting government power to control business activities. Those doctrines were used with increasing frequency to attack regulatory legislation; in the 1920s, the Supreme Court held unconstitutional more than 130 regulatory laws.[46]

In the 1930s, the Supreme Court's attacks on economic regulation brought it into serious conflict with the other branches. President Franklin Roosevelt's New Deal program to combat the Great Depression included sweeping statutes to control the economy, measures that enjoyed widespread support. In a series of decisions in 1935 and 1936 the Court struck down several of these statutes, including laws broadly regulating industry and agriculture, generally by 6–3 and 5–4 margins.[47]

Roosevelt responded in 1937 by proposing legislation under which an extra justice could be added to the Court for every sitting justice over the age of seventy. The result would have been to increase the Court's size temporarily to fifteen justices, thus allowing Roosevelt to "pack" the Court with justices favorable to his programs. While this plan was being debated in Congress, however, the Court took away most of the impetus behind it. In a series of decisions in 1937, the Court upheld New Deal legislation and similar state laws by narrow margins, taking positions contrary to its collective views in recent cases.[48] Most observers have concluded that this shift was a deliberate effort to end an increasingly dangerous conflict with the other branches, though some disagree.[49] In any event, the Court-packing plan died.

During the congressional debate, one of the conservative justices retired. Several other justices left the Court in the next few years, giving Roosevelt the ideological control of the Court that he had sought through the Court-packing legislation. The new Court created by his appointments fully accepted the economic regulation that had been viewed unfavorably by its predecessor, giving very broad interpretations to the constitutional powers to tax and to regulate interstate commerce.

The Court from 1937 to the Present

A Shift to Civil Liberties Concerns. Since its retreat in the late 1930s, the Court has continued to uphold major economic policies of the federal government. The Court hears many cases concerning economic regulation, but this field has become less important as part of its work and as a source of major decisions. Instead, the Court's primary emphasis in the current era is on civil liberties. More precisely, the Court gives most attention to the interpretation of legal protections for freedom of expression and freedom of religion, for the procedural rights of criminal defendants and others, and for equal treatment of racial minorities and other disadvantaged groups.

The Court's general position on civil liberties issues has varied a good deal during this period. Changes in the Court's position have reflected changes in its membership. The one constant factor has been the Court's collective interest in addressing civil liberties issues.

Activism in the Warren Court. The Court was most supportive of civil liberties during the 1960s, the latter part of the period in which Earl Warren was chief justice (1953–1969). The policies of the Court during that period are often identified with Warren, but other liberal justices played roles of at least equal importance. Especially important were Hugo Black and William Douglas, Roosevelt appointees who served throughout Warren's tenure, and William Brennan, an Eisenhower appointee.

The best-known decision of the Warren era was *Brown v. Board of Education* (1954), in which the Court ordered the desegregation of southern school systems and began the long process of desegregation that continues today. The Court also supported the rights of black Americans in several other policy areas. During the 1960s, the

Court expanded the rights of criminal defendants in state trials, most notably in landmark decisions concerning the right to counsel (*Gideon v. Wainwright,* 1963), police search and seizure practices (*Mapp v. Ohio,* 1961), and the questioning of suspects (*Miranda v. Arizona,* 1966). The Court supported freedom of expression by expanding First Amendment rights in several areas, particularly obscenity and libel. In a series of cases beginning with *Baker v. Carr* (1962), the Court required that legislative districts be equal in population.

Partial Retrenchment in the Burger and Rehnquist Courts. When Earl Warren retired in 1969, he was succeeded as chief justice by Warren Burger, President Nixon's first appointee to the Court. Nixon made three more appointments in 1970 and 1971. The Court's membership changed much more slowly after that, but each new justice chosen in the next twenty years was selected by a conservative Republican president—one by Gerald Ford, three by Ronald Reagan, and two by George Bush. In 1986 Reagan named Nixon appointee William Rehnquist, the most conservative member of the Court, to succeed Warren Burger as chief justice. The string of Republican appointments was broken with Bill Clinton's two appointments in 1993 and 1994.

The Republican appointments gradually moved the Court's civil liberties policies in a conservative direction, though not uniformly. For example, there was only a limited shift in the Court's positions on freedom of expression. Perhaps the most decisive shift came on issues of criminal procedure, though the Court did not directly overturn any of the Warren Court's landmark expansions of defendants' rights. Indeed, in *Dickerson v. United States* (2000), the Court reaffirmed *Miranda* by a 7–2 vote. The Rehnquist Court's interpretations of federal anti-discrimination statutes tended to narrow their impact, with exceptions on some issues such as sexual harassment.

The Court's positions on non–civil liberties issues changed as well. Its interpretations of environmental and labor laws became increasingly conservative. In the late 1990s it began to narrow congressional power to regulate activities in the private sector and especially in state governments,[50] and a continuation of this trend might result in substantial limits on the federal government's controls over business practices and protections of civil liberties.

The Supreme Court's policies continue to evolve in complex ways; recent history has underlined the difficulty of predicting where the Court is going. The Court's history has also taught us that its direction is largely a reflection of its membership, so the selection of justices is a crucial process. I examine that process in the next chapter.

NOTES

1. Richard L. Berke, "Who Will Name the Next Supreme Court Justice?" *New York Times,* May 21, 2000, sec. 4, 3. The justice was not identified.
2. See *Colorado Republican Federal Campaign Committee v. Federal Election Commission* (1996). Full legal citations for the cases mentioned in this book are provided in the Case Index.
3. Donald Grier Stephenson Jr., *Campaigns and the Court: The U.S. Supreme Court in Presidential Elections* (New York: Columbia University Press, 1999).
4. Examples include *Maryland v. Dyson* (1999); *Florida v. White* (1999); and *Wyoming v. Houghton* (1999).
5. Alexis de Tocqueville, *Democracy in America,* trans. Henry Reeve, rev. Francis Bowen (New York: Knopf, 1945), 1:280.
6. Bradley C. Canon, "A Framework for the Analysis of Judicial Activism," in *Supreme Court Activism and Restraint,* ed. Stephen C. Halpern and Charles M. Lamb (Lexington, Mass.: Lexington Books, 1982), 385–419.
7. *Mora v. McNamara* (1967); *Massachusetts v. Laird* (1970); *Sarnoff v. Shultz* (1972).
8. See Vincent L. McKusick, "Discretionary Gatekeeping: The Supreme Court's Management of Its Original Jurisdiction Docket Since 1961," *Maine Law Review* 45 (1993): 185–242.
9. *Thompson v. City of Louisville* (1960).
10. Kim Eisler, "Supreme Court's High Honor But Low Pay Could Send Justice Scalia Job Hunting," *The Washingtonian,* March 2000, 11.
11. Paul Leavitt and Dave Moniz, "High Court Justices Disclose Their Assets," *USA Today,* June 28, 2000, 5A.
12. Tony Mauro, "Slow Pace for Protest Cases," *Legal Times,* February 1, 1999, 8–9. The case was *California Public Employees' Retirement System v. Felzen* (1999).
13. Linda Greenhouse, "Justices Skeptically Review Law on Cable System Access," *New York Times,* October 8, 1996, A10. The case was *United States v. Hatter* (1996).
14. David N. Atkinson, *Leaving the Bench: Supreme Court Justices at the End* (Lawrence: University Press of Kansas, 1999), chap. 2.
15. John Schwartz and Saundra Torry, "Thomas Tells Tobacco Firms to Divulge Internal Papers," *Washington Post,* April 3, 1998, A2; "Plaintiffs Gain Tobacco Industry Documents," *New York Times,* April 7, 1998, A21. The case was *Philip Morris, Inc. v. Minnesota* (1998).
16. John C. Jeffries, Jr., *Justice Lewis F. Powell, Jr.* (New York: Scribner's, 1994), 445. See Edward Lazarus, *Closed Chambers* (New York: Times Books, 1998), 119–123, 157–165.
17. See, for example, Linda Greenhouse, "Chief Justice's Annual Report Notes Progress in the Judiciary," *New York Times,* January 1, 2000, A20.

18. See Joan Biskupic, "Emerging From Margins, Rehnquist Adapts to Role," *Washington Post,* January 23, 1999, A13.
19. See Bernard Schwartz, *Decision: How the Supreme Court Decides Cases* (New York: Oxford University Press, 1996), 73–74.
20. This discussion is based in part on research by Corey Ditslear and Lawrence Baum. The information on clerks' backgrounds in this paragraph is drawn from that research.
21. David Savage, *Turning Right: The Making of the Rehnquist Supreme Court* (New York: Wiley, 1992), 306.
22. Zerline A. Hughes, "Civil Rights Advocates Arrested in Protest of Law Clerk Hirings," *Los Angeles Times,* October 6, 1998, A16.
23. Joan Biskupic, "Clerks Gain Status, Clout in the Temple of Justice," *Washington Post,* January 2, 1994, A23.
24. See Richard A. Posner, *The Federal Courts: Challenge and Reform* (Cambridge: Harvard University Press, 1996), 139–159; Mark Tushnet, "Thurgood Marshall and the Brethren," *Georgetown Law Journal* 80 (August 1992): 2110–2119; and Lazarus, *Closed Chambers.*
25. Sean Donahue, "Behind the Pillars of Justice: Remarks on Law Clerks," *The Long Term View* 3 (Spring 1995): 81–82.
26. "Justices Can Trot the Globe without Footing the Bills," *Columbus Dispatch,* June 28, 2000, A8.
27. Benjamin Pimentel, "Lizzie Acquitted Again," *San Francisco Chronicle,* September 17, 1997, A16.
28. Ron Shaffer, "From Here to Infiniti, the Chief Justice Has the Answer," *Washington Post,* July 12, 1999, B1.
29. "If It Pleases the Pit," *National Law Journal,* February 22, 1999, A28.
30. Joan Biskupic, "Shedding Silence, Justice Thomas Takes on Critics," *Washington Post,* September 23, 1998, A1, A16, A17; Thomas B. Edsall, "Justice Thomas Urged to Cancel Appearance at Conservative Event," *Washington Post,* February 2, 1999, A2.
31. James Rowen, "FBI Files Show Justice Violated Court Secrecy," *Milwaukee Journal,* January 21, 1990, 1A, 20A. On Marshall, see Juan Williams, *Thurgood Marshall: American Revolutionary* (New York: Times Books, 1998), 340–344.
32. Seymour M. Hersh, "Nixon's Last Cover-Up: The Tapes He Wants the Archives to Suppress," *New Yorker,* December 14, 1992, 81.
33. Joan Biskupic, "Has the Court Lost Its Appeal?" *Washington Post,* October 12, 1995, A23.
34. American Bar Association, *Perceptions of the U.S. Justice System* (1998), 13. (Published at ABA website: www.abanet.org/media/perception/perception.html)
35. Savage, *Turning Right,* 236.
36. Kim Isaac Eisler, *A Justice for All: William J. Brennan, Jr., and the Decisions That Transformed America* (New York: Simon & Schuster, 1993), 247.
37. Ronald Goldfarb, "The Invisible Supreme Court," *New York Times,* May 4, 1996, 15.
38. Annie Groer and Joan Biskupic, "Toni House, Washington's Supreme Spokeswoman," *Washington Post,* September 30, 1998, D10.
39. Barbara A. Perry, *The Priestly Tribe: The Supreme Court's Image in the American Mind* (Westport, Conn.: Praeger, 1999).
40. Robert Schmidt, "May It Please the Court," *Brill's Content,* October 1999, 73. On coverage of the Court, see Elliot E. Slotnick and Jennifer A. Segal,

Television News and the Supreme Court: All the News That's Fit to Air? (New York: Cambridge University Press, 1998).

41. American Bar Association, *Perceptions of the U.S. Justice System,* 32. See Perry, *The Priestly Tribe,* 5.
42. Joan Biskupic, "In June, Rulings Move With Supreme Speed," *Washington Post,* May 26, 1998, A15.
43. Joan Biskupic, "The Art of 'Holding Five' in Peak Season," *Washington Post,* June 7, 1999, A17.
44. See William R. Casto, *The Supreme Court in the Early Republic: The Chief Justiceships of John Jay and Oliver Ellsworth* (Columbia: University of South Carolina Press, 1995). For another perspective, see Scott Douglas Gerber, ed., *Seriatim: The Supreme Court Before John Marshall* (New York: New York University Press, 1998).
45. Robert G. McCloskey, rev. by Sanford Levinson, *The American Supreme Court,* rev. ed. (Chicago: University of Chicago Press, 1994), 64–66.
46. This figure was calculated from data in Congressional Research Service, *The Constitution of the United States of America: Analysis and Interpretation* (Washington, D.C.: Government Printing Office, 1987), 1885–2113.
47. The cases included *Carter v. Carter Coal Co.* (1936), *United States v. Butler* (1936), and *Schechter Poultry Corp. v. United States* (1935).
48. The cases included *National Labor Relations Board v. Jones & Laughlin Steel Corp.* (1937), *Steward Machine Co. v. Davis* (1937), and *West Coast Hotel Co. v. Parrish* (1937).
49. See Barry Cushman, *Rethinking the New Deal Court: The Structure of a Constitutional Revolution* (New York: Oxford University Press, 1998).
50. The decisions included *United States v. Lopez* (1995) and *Alden v. Maine* (1999).

Chapter 2

The Justices

M ost of the time, the Supreme Court attracts little attention
from the American public. But all this changes when a justice
leaves the Court. The news media speculate about whom the president will nominate, and the actual nominee receives intense
scrutiny. This scrutiny reaches its zenith when the nominee is called
to testify before the Senate Judiciary Committee. The dramatic
hearings on Clarence Thomas's nomination still fascinate people a
decade after they occurred, but even the more mundane testimony
of most other nominees receives a level of interest that is most unusual for the Court.

This interest is appropriate. The course that the Supreme Court
takes is a product of many influences, but the dominant influence
is its membership. The Court's frequent 6–3 and 5–4 votes are a reminder that different people would make different choices as justices. Thus the identity of the people who become justices is a matter of fundamental importance for the Court.

As of mid-2000 there have been 148 nominations to the
Supreme Court, and 108 justices have sat on the Court. Four candidates were nominated and confirmed twice, 8 declined appointments or died before beginning service on the Court, and 28 did
not secure Senate confirmation.[1] This chapter focuses on the past
several decades. (Table 2-1 lists the 50 nominations to the Court
since 1920 and the 41 justices chosen since that time.) The chapter's three sections discuss the selection of justices, the characteristics of the people who are selected, and how and why they leave
the Court.

TABLE 2-1

Nominations to the Supreme Court since 1920

Name	Nominated by	Replaced	Years served
William Howard Taft (CJ)	Harding	White	1921–30
George Sutherland	Harding	Clarke	1922–38
Pierce Butler	Harding	Day	1923–39
Edward Sanford	Harding	Pitney	1923–30
Harlan Fiske Stone	Coolidge	McKenna	1925–46
Charles Evans Hughes (CJ)	Hoover	Taft	1930–41
John Parker	Hoover	(Sanford)	Defeated for confirmation, 1930
Owen Roberts	Hoover	Sanford	1930–45
Benjamin Cardozo	Hoover	Holmes	1932–38
Hugo Black	F. Roosevelt	Van Devanter	1937–71
Stanley Reed	F. Roosevelt	Sutherland	1938–57
Felix Frankfurter	F. Roosevelt	Cardozo	1939–62
William Douglas	F. Roosevelt	Brandeis	1939–75
Frank Murphy	F. Roosevelt	Butler	1940–49
James Byrnes	F. Roosevelt	McReynolds	1941–42
Harlan Fiske Stone (CJ)[a]	F. Roosevelt	Hughes	1941–46
Robert Jackson	F. Roosevelt	Stone	1941–54
Wiley Rutledge	F. Roosevelt	Byrnes	1943–49
Harold Burton	Truman	Roberts	1945–58
Fred Vinson (CJ)	Truman	Stone	1946–53
Tom Clark	Truman	Murphy	1949–67
Sherman Minton	Truman	Rutledge	1949–56
Earl Warren (CJ)	Eisenhower	Vinson	1953–69
John Harlan	Eisenhower	Jackson	1955–71

Name	President	Replacing	Term
William Brennan	Eisenhower	Minton	1956–90
Charles Whittaker	Eisenhower	Reed	1957–62
Potter Stewart	Eisenhower	Burton	1958–81
Byron White	Kennedy	Whittaker	1962–93
Arthur Goldberg	Kennedy	Frankfurter	1962–65
Abe Fortas	Johnson	Goldberg	1965–69
Thurgood Marshall	Johnson	Clark	1967–91
Abe Fortas (CJ)[a]	Johnson	(Warren)	Nomination withdrawn, 1968
Homer Thornberry	Johnson	(Fortas)	Nomination became moot, 1968[b]
Warren Burger (CJ)	Nixon	Warren	1969–86
Clement Haynsworth	Nixon	(Fortas)	Defeated for confirmation, 1969
G. Harrold Carswell	Nixon	(Fortas)	Defeated for confirmation, 1970
Harry Blackmun	Nixon	Fortas	1970–94
Lewis Powell	Nixon	Black	1971–87
William Rehnquist	Nixon	Harlan	1971–
John Paul Stevens	Ford	Douglas	1975–
Sandra Day O'Connor	Reagan	Stewart	1981–
William Rehnquist (CJ)[a]	Reagan	Burger	1986–
Antonin Scalia	Reagan	Rehnquist	1986–
Robert Bork	Reagan	(Powell)	Defeated for confirmation, 1987
Douglas Ginsburg	Reagan	(Powell)	Withdrew before formal nomination, 1987
Anthony Kennedy	Reagan	Powell	1988–
David Souter	Bush	Brennan	1990–
Clarence Thomas	Bush	Marshall	1991–
Ruth Bader Ginsburg	Clinton	White	1993–
Stephen Breyer	Clinton	Blackmun	1994–

[a] Nominated as chief justice while serving as associate justice.

[b] When Fortas's nomination for chief justice was withdrawn, no vacancy for his seat as associate justice existed.

The Selection of Justices

Selection of a Supreme Court justice begins with the creation of a vacancy, when a member of the Court dies or steps down from the Court. Inevitably, vacancies occur at an irregular rate. Bill Clinton was able to select two new justices in his first eighteen months in office, but none during the rest of his eight-year tenure.

The formal process for selection of justices is simple. When a vacancy occurs, the president makes a nomination, which must be confirmed by a majority of those voting in the Senate. When the chief justice's position is vacant, the president has two options: to nominate a sitting justice to that position and also nominate a new associate justice, or to nominate a person as chief justice from outside the Court. Presidents usually have taken the latter course, chiefly to have a wider field from which to select the chief. But President Ronald Reagan elevated Justice William Rehnquist to the position of chief justice after Warren Burger retired in 1986.

The actual process of selection is more complicated than the simple formal process suggests. The president and the Senate make their decisions surrounded by individuals and groups who are deeply interested in these decisions, and the process of reaching decisions can be quite complex. In examining this process it will be useful first to discuss the roles of unofficial participants and then to consider how the president and Senate reach their decisions.

Unofficial Participants

Since Supreme Court appointments are so important, a variety of individuals and groups seek to influence the president and Senate. Apart from members of the president's administration, the most important of these participants fall into three categories: the legal community, other interest groups, and potential justices.

The Legal Community. Because the Supreme Court is a court, lawyers have a particular interest in its membership. Because they are lawyers, their views about potential justices may carry particular weight. Occupying a special position is the American Bar Association (ABA), the largest organization of lawyers and the most prominent voice of the legal profession. The ABA seeks to influence the appointments of federal judges through evaluations of the candidates by its fifteen-member "Committee on Federal Judiciary."

The primary function of the ABA committee is to investigate and evaluate presidential nominees who await confirmation. In each instance, it rates a nominee as "well qualified," "qualified," or "not qualified." The committee has never rated a nominee as "not qualified." But the extent of its enthusiasm for a nominee can affect the confirmation process. A unanimous rating of "well qualified," one awarded to both Ruth Bader Ginsburg and Stephen Breyer, helps to smooth the path to Senate approval. By the same token, when four committee members rated Robert Bork as "not qualified" in 1987 and two did so for Clarence Thomas in 1991, the prospects for confirmation were weakened.

The ABA committee was once perceived as ideologically conservative, but—in part because of the votes against Bork, a prestigious legal scholar—many conservatives now see it as unduly liberal. For that reason, some Republican senators give little weight to its judgments, and its power over appointments has declined somewhat.

Other legal groups and individual lawyers also participate in the selection process. Law professors and other prominent attorneys often announce their evaluations of nominees the Senate is considering. Such evaluations may have considerable impact. The criticism of Richard Nixon's nominees Clement Haynsworth and G. Harrold Carswell by prominent attorneys countered the ABA's official judgment that the two nominees were qualified and thus contributed to their rejection by the Senate.

The lawyers involved in the selection of justices sometimes include sitting members of the Supreme Court. Even though they have a direct interest in who their colleagues will be, justices usually stay out of the selection process. When they do participate, most often it is by recommending a potential nominee.

The most active Supreme Court lobbyist in the past half century was Chief Justice Warren Burger. He lobbied in the Senate for Haynsworth and Carswell and, a year after his retirement, testified on behalf of Bork. He also sought to influence nominations, suggesting the name of his longtime friend Harry Blackmun to the Nixon administration and recommending Sandra Day O'Connor to the Reagan administration.

Judicial intervention sometimes has a decisive effect. If Burger had not suggested his name, Blackmun might not have been considered for nomination. But justices cannot exert strong pressure on presidents, and their recommendations can be ignored or rejected. The same, of course, is true of intervention by lower court judges. In 1994, about one hundred federal judges wrote to President Clinton to endorse Richard Arnold of the Eighth Circuit Court of Appeals. Clinton was hardly hostile to Judge Arnold, a longtime friend from Arkansas, and he came close to nominating Arnold. But ultimately Clinton decided to nominate Stephen Breyer instead.[2]

Other Interest Groups. Because they have a stake in Supreme Court decisions, many interest groups seek to influence the selection of justices. At the nomination stage, groups that are politically important to the president are in a good position to exert influence. A Democratic president, for instance, generally gives some weight to the views of labor and civil rights groups. Such groups usually can communicate directly with the president or with top presidential advisers, the best way to affect the president's views. They can also make their wishes known publicly. When President Clinton was considering his choice of a nominee to succeed Byron White in 1993, leaders of several women's groups made statements emphasizing their desire to have a woman appointed to the Court. Groups that are opposed to the president ideologically can also try to influence the nomination decision by threatening to fight the confirmation of any nominee whose views they consider too "extreme." After White's retirement, the leader of one conservative group announced that "if Clinton makes this nomination an ideological battleground, it will turn into a judicial Armageddon."[3]

Once a nomination has been announced, groups often work for or against Senate confirmation. Group opposition to a nominee is more common than support, because groups that favor a nominee may perceive confirmation as assured even if they do nothing.

Significant interest group activity at the confirmation stage can be traced back as far as 1881, but it was fairly limited and sporadic until the late 1960s.[4] In 1968 conservative groups opposed the confirmation of Abe Fortas, President Lyndon Johnson's nominee for chief justice, while liberal groups worked in support of Fortas. This activity, and Fortas's defeat, initiated an era of more frequent and more intensive interest group involvement in confirmation decisions. Labor and civil rights groups opposed President Nixon's nominations of Clement Haynsworth and G. Harrold Carswell; their efforts made possible the defeats of both nominees. Several liberal groups worked against the elevation of William Rehnquist to chief justice in 1986, helping to build significant opposition, but ultimately Rehnquist was confirmed with about a two-thirds majority.

President Reagan's nomination of Robert Bork in 1987 gave rise to an unprecedented level of group activity.[5] Liberal groups feared that the strongly conservative Bork would move an ideologically divided Court substantially to the right. Accordingly, they devoted considerable effort, and an estimated $12 million to $15 million, to achieving his defeat.[6] Their activities ranged from newspaper advertisements to direct lobbying of senators. Groups favorable to Bork's nomination took action as well. The pro-Bork groups did not mobilize as quickly or as fully as the opposition groups, and the higher level of activity against Bork helped to bring about his defeat.[7]

The nomination of Clarence Thomas in 1991 also provoked considerable group activity. Among Thomas's supporters were the United States Chamber of Commerce and Young Americans for Freedom. Opponents included the Leadership Conference on Civil Rights, a coalition of 185 groups concerned with civil rights and civil liberties, and a smaller coalition called the Alliance for Justice; both had played central roles in the opposition to Bork as well. Individual groups such as the AFL-CIO and the National Abortion Rights Action League were also involved. The opposition groups were unable to achieve the same kind of massive campaign against Thomas that they had launched against Bork. But their opposition helped to create concern about Thomas among liberal senators and thereby contributed to the decisions by most Democratic senators to vote against Thomas's confirmation.

Interest groups played a more limited role in the confirmations of Ruth Bader Ginsburg in 1993 and Stephen Breyer in 1994; the numbers of group representatives testifying before the Senate Judiciary Committee hearings on Ginsburg and Breyer were the lowest since the nomination of John Paul Stevens in 1975.[8] In the current era as a whole, however, the level of group involvement in the confirmation process is higher than ever. That change reflects the increased number of interest groups and the increased intensity of group activity, greater awareness that nominations to the Court are important, and group leaders' learning from past episodes how to participate effectively in the confirmation process.[9] Ideological groups have also found that opposition to controversial nominees is a good way to generate interest in their causes and monetary contributions from their supporters.

Candidates for the Court. One difference between the Supreme Court and the lower federal courts is that people often become members of the Court without taking any actions to obtain their appointments. Because presidents consider Court appointments so important, they look for candidates who best serve presidential goals rather than restricting their choices to candidates who seek the job openly. For this reason most potential justices believe it is counterproductive to conduct campaigns on their own behalf.

Some people do work to obtain appointments, and some of them are successful. Hard work secured a nomination for William Howard Taft, a somewhat reluctant president who really wanted to be chief justice. As president he worked toward his eventual selection by appointing an older chief justice, Edward White, to increase the likelihood of a vacancy in that position in the foreseeable future. White returned the favor by refusing to retire or die, despite his extreme disability, until a Republican replaced President Woodrow Wilson. When White died early in President Warren Harding's term, Taft was appointed to replace him; the appointment came after an intensive campaign by Taft that had begun even before Harding's election. One commentator appropriately described Taft as "virtually appointing himself" chief justice.[10]

In the case of Ruth Bader Ginsburg, it was her husband who did the campaigning. Apparently without his wife's knowledge, Martin Ginsburg mobilized support for her candidacy among legal scholars and members of the women's movement.[11] His activity on her behalf may have been decisive in making Ginsburg a leading candidate and ultimately the successful nominee.

An alternative approach for an aspiring judge is to take public positions that would appeal to an appointing president. In a 1992 decision by a federal court of appeals, judge Emilio Garza wrote a concurring opinion in which he implied that he would vote to overturn *Roe v. Wade* if given the opportunity. President George Bush had seriously considered nominating Garza to the Supreme Court in 1991. A caustic newspaper editorial charged that Garza had used this opinion "shamelessly" to show his agreement with the Bush administration's position on an issue that had been critical in the selection of nominees to the Court.[12]

Despite the success stories, campaigning for the Court is a chancy matter. There are far more aspiring justices than there are vacancies on the Court, and presidents make their choices for their own reasons. As one observer remarked in 1990, "Trying to get yourself appointed to the court by George Bush is likely to be as successful as trying to kill yourself by getting hit by lightning." [13] And someone who wants to get on the Court cannot control who becomes president. If Judge Garza was trying to appeal to President Bush, his effort became irrelevant when Bush lost his bid for reelection six weeks later.

While some people actively seek appointments to the Court, others are reluctant to accept them. A number of candidates have declined nominations or taken themselves out of the running when they appeared likely to be nominated. In 1993 and 1994 at least four candidates for nominations to the Court withdrew from consideration. One, Senate Majority Leader George Mitchell, was even offered a nomination. [14]

Among those who accept nominations, some are ambivalent about doing so. After accepting an invitation to interview for a position on the Court, David Souter called Senator Warren Rudman—who had brought about Souter's candidacy for the position—to ask "what have you done to me now?" [15] Byron White in 1962, Abe Fortas in 1965, and Lewis Powell in 1971 were all reluctant to take the nominations that they ultimately accepted.

Such cases are exceptions, however. Whether or not they actively sought a position on the Supreme Court, most of those who are offered a nomination have little difficulty in accepting it. Speaking of William Brennan's appointment in 1956, President Dwight Eisenhower's press secretary reported, "I never saw a man say 'yes' so fast when the President asked him to take the job." [16] That may have been a wise choice. President Nixon offered a nomination to Senator Howard Baker in 1971 but nominated William Rehnquist instead while Baker contemplated the offer. [17]

In past eras, nominees typically played little part in the confirmation process. Today, they participate actively in that process. Nominees visit with senators (Clarence Thomas, setting a record, paid "courtesy calls" on more than half of the senators) and testify before the Senate Judiciary Committee.

That testimony presents a challenge to nominees. When there is already substantial opposition to confirmation, nominees try to use their testimony to win the support of wavering senators. When confirmation seems assured, nominees seek to avoid saying something that raises doubts about them.

Nominees face their greatest challenge in responding to questions about their views on legal issues. Senators try to determine where a nominee stands on important issues such as abortion and the death penalty. For their part, nominees prefer not to make their positions clear, so that they do not "prejudge" issues that might come before the Court or arouse opposition from senators who disagree with their positions. Yet nominees also know that refusal to respond to questions about their views may anger senators.

Nominees' typical response to this dilemma is to offer some information about their views but to speak only vaguely about matters that might create trouble for them. Clarence Thomas was asked repeatedly and in various ways where he stood on abortion as a constitutional issue, and he adamantly refused to indicate his views. In response to questions from Senator Patrick Leahy of Vermont, Thomas said that he had never "debated the contents" of *Roe v. Wade* and that "I have not made, Senator, a decision one way or the other" about whether the case was properly decided.[18]

Both the specifics of nominees' testimony and the general impression they give can make a difference when confirmation is not assured. Robert Bork's appearance before the committee in 1987 left no doubt about his impressive legal skills, but many liberal and moderate senators remained convinced that he was too conservative—and some felt that he had not been candid about his views. Thomas's answers to questions about abortion and other issues also raised doubts in some senators' minds about his candor. Their testimony thereby contributed to Bork's Senate defeat and to the narrowness of Thomas's victory. In contrast, David Souter's testimony avoided raising concerns about his views and reassured many senators that he was not strongly conservative; as a result, his confirmation was assured.

The President's Decision

For the president, a Supreme Court vacancy provides a valuable opportunity to influence the Court's direction, and presidents seek to make the most of these opportunities. But the individuals and groups for whom nominations are important can subject the president to heavy and conflicting pressures, and increasingly so in recent years. As a result, according to Mark Silverstein, for the Clinton White House the nominations of two justices "emerged as an unexpected burden rather than a cause for celebration." [19]

Presidents differ in their decision-making styles, and these differences are reflected in the nomination process. In his examination of presidents since Harry Truman, David Yalof has described two kinds of differences.[20] One concerns what Yalof calls the "decisional framework." In some instances, major decisions about priorities and criteria for a nomination are made only after a vacancy arises. This approach, predominant in the Truman administration, has been rare since then. At the other extreme, some nominees effectively are chosen even before a vacancy arises. This was true of each of Johnson's nominees. But most common, especially among recent presidents, is an intermediate approach: general criteria for selection of nominees are developed prior to a vacancy, but those criteria are not used to select a nominee until the vacancy arises.

The second kind of difference is the extent to which presidents delegate work on nominations to other officials in the executive branch. Reagan and Bush gave considerable responsibility to officials in the White House and Justice Department, while Clinton exerted far more direct control over the selection process even in its early stages. Delegation can save presidents time and increase the options and information available to them, but if advisers have narrow perspectives or get into conflicts with each other, the decision-making process may suffer. Some of Reagan's nominations encountered this difficulty. In any case, no president delegates the final decision to subordinates, because Supreme Court nominations are perceived as too important to leave to other people.

The criteria that are used to select nominees fall into several categories: the "objective" qualifications of potential nominees, their policy preferences, rewards to political and personal associates, and the building of political support. Cutting across these criteria and helping to determine their use is the inescapable reality that the Senate must confirm a nominee. Presidents prefer to avoid a tough confirmation battle that would require them to expend valuable political resources, and Senate defeat of a nominee is a defeat for the president as well. The relative importance of these criteria, including concern with confirmation, is another characteristic that varies among presidents.

"Objective" Qualifications. Presidents have strong incentives to select Supreme Court nominees who have demonstrated high levels of legal competence and adherence to ethical standards. A candidate who falls short on either of these criteria is vulnerable to opposition and potential defeat in the Senate. Further, most presidents have considerable respect for the Supreme Court and thus want to uphold high standards in selection.

In general, presidents' choices reflect a concern for competence. This does not mean that all nominees are highly skilled in the law, but in only a few cases has a nominee's capacity to serve on the Court been questionable. One of those few cases was that of G. Harrold Carswell (chosen by Nixon in 1970), whose legal ability was doubted strongly and widely; Carswell was denied confirmation.

The ethical behavior of most nominees has been unexceptionable, at least so far as that behavior was known, but there are some exceptions. Abe Fortas (when nominated to be chief justice), Clement Haynsworth, and Stephen Breyer were attacked for alleged financial conflicts of interest; Fortas was also criticized for continuing to consult with President Johnson while serving as an associate justice. The charges against Fortas and Haynsworth helped bring about their defeats in the Senate. After Douglas Ginsburg was announced as a Reagan nominee, disclosures were made about a possible financial conflict of interest when he was in the Justice Department and about his past use of marijuana. The latter disclosure was especially damaging, and Ginsburg withdrew his name from consideration. An allegation that Clarence Thomas had sexually harassed an assistant while he was a federal administrator resulted in a special set of Senate hearings on the charge and put his confirmation in jeopardy.

To minimize the possibility of such embarrassments, administrations today give close scrutiny to potential nominees. After its difficulty with Douglas Ginsburg, the Reagan administration wanted to ensure that Anthony Kennedy, its choice as the next nominee, had no problems in his personal life. White House counsel A. B. Culvahouse came to Kennedy with a twenty-one-page list of questions. The FBI, itself embarrassed by its failure to discover Ginsburg's drug use, undertook a massive investigation of its own. Culvahouse stopped Kennedy during a visit to the White House to tell him that the investigation had uncovered a problem: Kennedy's daughter had an unpaid parking ticket. When nothing else turned up, Kennedy was nominated.[21]

Competence and ethics can be considered screening criteria for potential nominees. These criteria may eliminate some people from consideration, but enough candidates survive the screening process to give presidents a wide range of choices for a nomination.

Policy Preferences. By policy preferences, I mean a person's attitudes toward policy issues. These criteria have always been a major consideration in the selection of Supreme Court justices, because the Court's role in policy making is well understood. Presidents recognize that the ability of their appointees to influence the Court's policies is among their major legacies. On leaving the presidency, William Howard Taft reported that he had told his six appointees, "If any of you die, I'll disown you."[22] Thus all presidents seek to put on the Court individuals who share their views on important policy questions.

Presidents differ in the weights they give to the policy preferences of potential nominees. Presidents who seek to usher in a new political era are especially concerned with bringing the Supreme Court more in line with their own positions.[23] This was true of Richard Nixon and Ronald Reagan, who sought to move the country and the Court in a more conservative direction. Presidents with less ambitious policy agendas, such as Harry Truman, have put less emphasis on policy preferences as a basis for their choices. In periods when the Court plays an especially prominent role in policy making, as it does today, presidents give more weight to the policy positions of potential nominees. In any period, some specific issues may be especially important to presidents and their political allies, as abortion has been in recent years. Bill Clinton indicated that he would not have nominated Ruth Bader Ginsburg if he had not concluded that she took a pro-choice position on abortion, and several candidates for the Republican presidential nomination in 2000 said that they would choose only pro-life candidates.[24]

It is in relation to this criterion that the Senate's role creates the greatest complications. Most Democratic presidents are distinctly liberal, most Republicans distinctly conservative. If a strongly liberal president chose a nominee whose preferences were also strongly liberal, that nominee's views would be somewhat distant from the views of Senate moderates and very distant from the views of many

Bill Clinton's nomination of Stephen Breyer in 1994 reflected his interest in choosing nominees who were unlikely to arouse strong opposition from senators.

Republican senators. Of course, a strongly conservative president is in a similar situation. Thus most presidents face a dilemma: choose a nominee whose views mirror their own and risk difficulty with confirmation, or choose a more moderate nominee and reduce their ability to reshape the Court.

Presidents react to this dilemma in different ways, giving varying weights to the collective views of the Senate. When President Reagan nominated Robert Bork and President Bush chose Clarence Thomas even though the Senate had a Democratic majority, they risked a Senate battle and defeat of their nominee in the interest of putting a strong conservative on the Court. Bill Clinton was more cautious, declining to nominate people whose reputations for strong liberalism might arouse opposition in the Senate. Indeed, Clinton gave greater weight than most presidents to the goal of avoiding confirmation battles.[25]

It is not always easy for presidents to ascertain the policy preferences of a potential nominee and to determine how those preferences would be reflected in votes and opinions on the Supreme Court. This is the primary reason that every nominee since 1986 has come from a federal court of appeals. As Reagan's attorney general Edwin Meese said, "You know the judicial philosophy of those judges because they've had experience and they've written opinions you can look at."[26] Administrations usually examine a judge's record with some care. According to one reporter, the Reagan administration ruled out federal judge Patrick Higginbotham of Texas because a footnote in one of his opinions "could be read as endorsing the *Roe v. Wade* ruling."[27] On the whole, sitting judges appointed to the Court have been less likely to disappoint their nominators with their votes and opinions than have other justices.[28]

Whether or not candidates are judges, their views about legal issues can be gauged from their public expressions or from their interactions with people whom the president trusts. Sometimes presidents or their representatives question prospective nominees directly about their views. Sandra Day O'Connor was questioned by two sets of administration officials and then by President Reagan himself, with whom she discussed abortion and other issues.

Here, too, the need for confirmation comes into play. Presidents sometimes choose nominees whose views on major issues are not very clear to give potential opponents less of a target. In doing so, however, they run the risk of guessing wrong themselves about a nominee's views. President Bush chose David Souter in 1990 partly because Souter had a very short record of statements and positions on controversial judicial issues, but people who knew Souter assured Bush that he was suitably conservative. Souter indeed was confirmed easily, but his record as a justice suggests that he was not nearly as conservative as Bush thought.

Souter is not the only justice whose positions on the Court have surprised the appointing president. Dwight Eisenhower was unhappy about the liberalism of two of his appointees, Earl Warren and William Brennan. Indeed, according to a story that is widely circulated but of uncertain accuracy, when Eisenhower was asked if he had made any mistakes as president, he replied, "Yes, two, and they are both sitting on the Supreme Court."[29]

Such disappointments are not rare, but most justices turn out to be ideologically compatible with the presidents who appoint them. And presidents who were especially careful to select compatible justices have suffered relatively few disappointments. Both Franklin Roosevelt and Richard Nixon did rather well in getting what they wanted from the justices they selected. Presidents who emphasized other criteria or chose with less care, such as Truman and Eisenhower, often did less well.

When careful presidents suffer disappointments, it is often because a justice shifts position after reaching the Court. Nixon's one "failure" in this respect was Harry Blackmun, who had a distinctly conservative record in his early years on the Court but gradually adopted more liberal positions. To a lesser degree, Anthony Kennedy also may have shifted in a liberal direction after reaching the Court—most notably, on abortion. When President Reagan was considering Kennedy, according to one aide, the administration "knew it for a fact" that Kennedy would vote to overturn *Roe v. Wade*. "His clerks had talked to him about it. He is Catholic, too. I can be emphatic about it because we were certain."[30] Indeed, Kennedy joined a 1989 opinion by William Rehnquist that seemed to support the overturning of *Roe* in an appropriate case. But three years later, Kennedy collaborated with two colleagues in an opinion that reaffirmed *Roe* in most respects.[31] (In the Court's next major abortion decision, *Stenberg v. Carhart,* 2000, Kennedy did dissent strongly from the Court's ruling that struck down a Nebraska prohibition of certain abortion methods.) In 1996 a conservative publication referred to Kennedy as "surely Reagan's biggest disappointment."[32]

Presidents cannot be assured of their appointees' support even on cases that affect the president directly. President Clinton's two appointees, Ruth Bader Ginsburg and Stephen Breyer, supported Clinton when they alone voted to hear two cases involving the investigation of possible wrongdoing by Clinton.[33] But Ginsburg and Breyer joined in the unanimous decision in *Clinton v. Jones* (1997) that allowed a lawsuit against him for sexual harassment to go forward, and President Nixon's three appointees joined in the unanimous decision in *United States v. Nixon* (1974) that required him to yield tape recordings of his conversations as president. After learning of the decision, Nixon reportedly "exploded, cursing the man he had named chief justice, reserving a few choice expletives for Blackmun and Powell, his other appointees." [34]

Political and Personal Reward. Abe Fortas was one of Lyndon Johnson's closest associates. In 1948 Fortas's legal skills had helped preserve Johnson's victory in a disputed Senate election. As Fortas became an increasingly eminent lawyer, he continued to advise Johnson, who came to rely heavily on his counsel. Not surprisingly, when Johnson had his first opportunity to choose a Supreme Court justice, he chose Fortas. The nomination rewarded someone who had done much for Johnson, even if Fortas was quite reluctant to accept the reward. It also put on the Court someone whose ability and policy views Johnson knew well from personal experience. Three years later, Johnson nominated Fortas for elevation to chief justice. To replace Fortas as associate justice, Johnson selected Homer Thornberry, a federal judge from Texas who was also a close friend of the president.

In choosing Fortas and Thornberry, Johnson was taking a common approach. About 60 percent of the nominees to the Court had known the nominating president personally.[35] Most of Johnson's recent predecessors—Franklin Roosevelt, Truman, and John F. Kennedy—had selected primarily personal acquaintances. For Truman, reward for political associates seemed to be the main criterion for selection.

Some appointments to the Court were direct rewards for political help. Eisenhower selected Earl Warren to serve as chief justice in part because of Warren's crucial support of Eisenhower at the 1952 Republican convention. As governor of California and leader of that state's delegation, Warren had provided needed votes on a preliminary issue, and Eisenhower's success on that issue helped to secure his nomination.

Since the 1968 nominations of Fortas and Thornberry (both of which failed when Fortas's confirmation was blocked), no president has chosen a close associate or political ally to serve on the Supreme Court. Only William Rehnquist, an official in the Nixon Justice Department, might qualify as an associate. And Nixon, three months before nominating Rehnquist, recalled his name as "Renchburg." [36]

Some other appointees knew the president who selected them, but the relationships were not close.

Perhaps the main reason for the decline in the selection of personal acquaintances is that such nominees are vulnerable, as Fortas was, to charges of "cronyism." In any case, one element of political reward continues to be important: about 90 percent of all nominees to the Court—and all those chosen since 1975—have been members of the president's party. One reason is that lawyers who share the president's policy views are more likely to come from the same party, but there is also a widespread feeling that such an attractive prize should go to one of the party faithful.

Building Political Support. If nominations can reward those who helped the president politically in the past, they can also be used to seek political benefits in the future. Most often, presidents select justices with certain characteristics in order to appeal to leaders and voters who share those characteristics.

For most of the Court's history, the most important characteristic was geography. Presidents sought to provide each region with representation on the Court. In part, this reflected a high level of regional consciousness among voters. And until 1891 the justices "rode circuit," helping to staff lower federal courts in designated regions of the country, and it made sense to choose justices from the circuits they would represent. But with the end of circuit-riding and a perceived decline in sectional consciousness, geography has become less important to presidents; Nixon's effort to choose a southerner was unusual for the current era.

Religious affiliations were of some importance during much of the twentieth century, as presidents sought to maintain Catholic and Jewish representation on the Court. But the relevance of religion has also declined. When Clarence Thomas rejoined the Catholic Church in 1996 and gave the Court its first non-Protestant majority, that landmark was noticed but not viewed as highly significant.[37]

In contrast, representation by race and gender has become quite important. President Bush's nomination of Clarence Thomas to succeed Thurgood Marshall reflected the pressure he felt to maintain black representation on the Court. According to one scholar, "gender was the primary and decisive factor" in President Reagan's nomination of Sandra Day O'Connor, at a time when there was a widespread feeling that a woman should be appointed.[38] By nominating

Ruth Bader Ginsburg, Clinton reaffirmed his support for groups that seek greater representation of women in government—support reflected as well in his appointing a higher proportion of women to lower court judgeships than any prior president.

Important though they are, it is doubtful that Supreme Court nominations have much direct impact on people's votes in presidential elections. It is more likely that nominations help presidents gain support from political leaders and activists, which can improve their electoral prospects indirectly. And in nominating a woman (to take one example), a president may act not just for political advantage but in the belief that the country benefits from female representation on the Court.

Summary. Nominations to the Supreme Court depend on a variety of criteria, and most appointments serve multiple goals. All the considerations discussed here have been important to some nominations, but their importance has changed over time and varies from one nomination to another.

The Court's importance has at least two effects on the criteria for selection of justices. First, it makes presidents and their representatives weigh all the criteria more carefully than they generally do in making lower court nominations. Second, it leads to an emphasis on the criteria of competence and policy preferences rather than on the "political" considerations of reward and support building. If Supreme Court justices are better jurists than lower court judges, and if their policy preferences are more accurate reflections of their nominators' views, it is largely because presidents have a strong incentive to achieve those results.

Senate Confirmation

Once the president has made a nomination it goes to the Senate for confirmation. The nomination is referred to the Judiciary Committee, which gathers extensive information on the nominee, holds hearings at which the nominee and other witnesses testify, and then votes its recommendation for Senate action. After this vote the nomination is referred to the floor, where it is debated and a confirmation vote taken. The length of this process depends primarily on the degree of controversy concerning the nomination, though the general trend in recent years has been toward lengthier consideration of nominees.

The Senate's Role. When the president nominates someone to any position in the executive branch or the judiciary, the presumption typically is in favor of confirming that nominee. That presumption applies to the Supreme Court. But the Senate gives Supreme Court nominations a collective scrutiny that district court nominations seldom receive, and the occasional defeats of nominees are reminders that confirmation is not automatic. Thus the president has good reason to take the Senate's likely reaction into account in making a nomination.

The Senate's Record. As of mid-2000 the Senate had failed to confirm twenty-six nominations to the Supreme Court, either through an adverse vote or through a refusal to act. These twenty-six cases constituted about one-sixth of the nominations that the Senate considered. This proportion of defeats is higher than for any other position to which the president makes appointments. For instance, presidents have made far more nominations of cabinet members, but only nine were defeated.

Presidents in the twentieth century were more successful with Supreme Court nominations than were presidents in the nineteenth. Since 1900, only five of the sixty nominations considered by the Senate have failed: Herbert Hoover's nomination of John Parker in 1930, Johnson's elevation of Abe Fortas to chief justice in 1968 (withdrawn after Fortas's supporters failed to end an anticonfirmation filibuster), Nixon's nominations of Clement Haynsworth in 1969 and G. Harrold Carswell in 1970 (both for the same vacancy), and Reagan's nomination of Robert Bork in 1987. And only two successful nominees were confirmed by less than a two-thirds margin in the Senate.

To a degree, however, this record of success is misleading. The Senate has continued to scrutinize nominations carefully. This has been especially true since the late 1940s. Of the twenty-eight nominees considered by the Senate from 1949 through mid-2000, four were defeated, seven received more than ten negative votes, and others faced serious opposition. The Senate votes in this period are shown in Table 2-2. As the table suggests, nominees have faced especially close scrutiny since 1968.

Of course, nominees vary a great deal in the number of votes for confirmation that they win. This variation reflects characteristics of nominees and of the situations in which the Senate considers them.[39]

TABLE 2-2

Senate Votes on Supreme Court Nominations, 1949–1994

Nominee	Year	Vote
Tom Clark	1949	73–8
Sherman Minton	1949	48–16
Earl Warren	1954	NRV[a]
John Harlan	1955	71–11
William Brennan	1957	NRV
Charles Whittaker	1957	NRV
Potter Stewart	1959	70–17
Byron White	1962	NRV
Arthur Goldberg	1962	NRV
Abe Fortas	1965	NRV
Thurgood Marshall	1967	69–11
Abe Fortas[b]	1968	withdrawn[c]
Homer Thornberry	(1968)	no action
Warren Burger	1969	74–3
Clement Haynsworth	1969	45–55
G. Harrold Carswell	1970	45–51
Harry Blackmun	1970	94–0
Lewis Powell	1971	89–1
William Rehnquist	1971	68–26
John Paul Stevens	1975	98–0
Sandra Day O'Connor	1981	99–0
William Rehnquist[b]	1986	65–33
Antonin Scalia	1986	98–0
Robert Bork	1987	42–58
Douglas Ginsburg	(1987)	no action
Anthony Kennedy	1988	97–0
David Souter	1990	90–9
Clarence Thomas	1991	52–48
Ruth Bader Ginsburg	1993	96–3
Stephen Breyer	1994	87–9

Source: Joan Biskupic and Elder Witt, *Guide to the U.S. Supreme Court,* 3d ed. (Washington, D.C.: Congressional Quarterly, 1997), 1099.

[a] No recorded vote.

[b] Elevation to chief justice.

[c] Nomination withdrawn after Senate vote failed to end filibuster against nomination; vote was 45–43 to end filibuster, and two-thirds majority was required.

Nominees and Situations. As suggested already, the most important characteristics of nominees in the confirmation process are their perceived ideological positions and qualifications. Nominees who are thought to be highly liberal or highly conservative have greater difficulty than those who seem to be moderate, simply because extremists are more distant ideologically from the average senator. Nominees who seem less qualified also may arouse opposition. Of course, a perceived absence of excellence in legal skills or ethical standards might cause senators who are otherwise favorable to oppose a nominee. More important, senators who are ideologically distant from a nominee often use questions about a nominee's qualifications as an "objective" justification for opposing the nominee.

Whatever a nominee's personal characteristics, the outcome of the confirmation process is also influenced by several aspects of the situation that exists at the time. One is the president's political strength in the Senate. According to one count, presidents whose party holds a Senate majority have had 90 percent of their nominees confirmed, as against 61 percent for presidents who faced an opposition majority.[40] One reason for this difference is that senators of the majority party chair the Judiciary Committee and schedule votes on the floor. Another reason is that a Senate controlled by the opposition has more senators who are politically opposed to the president and who are ideologically distant from a nominee.

Other factors affect the president's strength. Presidents with high public approval have an advantage, because strong public support deters opposition to their nominees. And nominations made late in a president's term are more vulnerable because the president's popularity tends to decline, some presidents are "lame ducks" who will leave office shortly, and partisanship often increases. Nearly half of the nominees selected in the last year of a presidential term were defeated in the Senate.[41]

A second aspect of the situation is the mobilization of activity for and against the nominee. Substantial interest group activity against a nomination can overcome the assumption that a nominee will be confirmed and thus cause senators to consider voting against confirmation. It is also important whether some senators decide to play an active role in mustering votes against a nominee and whether the administration mounts a strong effort to secure confirmation.[42]

Finally, the perceived impact of a nomination helps to determine whether senators feel that efforts to defeat the nominee are worth-

while. Probably the key explanation for the intense scrutiny given
to recent nominations is the increased prominence of the Supreme
Court in the resolution of controversial policy issues. And if a nominee has the potential to change the Court's policies substantially,
senators will attach particular importance to that nomination.

Among recent nominees, David Souter and Clarence Thomas illustrate the importance of personal characteristics. The two were
chosen by President Bush a year apart, with the Democrats holding
majorities in the Senate. Each would replace a strongly liberal justice and thus change the Court's ideological balance considerably.
But Souter won confirmation with only moderate difficulty while
Thomas's margin was only four votes. The difference can be explained primarily by two widespread perceptions: that Souter was a
moderate conservative and Thomas a strong conservative, and that
Souter was well qualified while Thomas's qualifications might be
questioned.

Another pair of nominees illustrates the importance of the situation. President Reagan selected Antonin Scalia in 1986 and Robert
Bork in 1987. Both were viewed as highly conservative, and both
were former legal scholars who were thought to be well qualified for
service on the Court. But Scalia was confirmed unanimously while
Bork was defeated. One difference was that the Senate in 1986 had
a Republican majority, but Bork the next year faced a Democratic
majority. Another was that Scalia would replace another strong conservative, while Bork would replace a moderate conservative on a
Court with a close ideological balance. Finally, in 1986 liberal senators and interest groups focused their efforts on defeating William
Rehnquist, nominated for elevation to chief justice, and largely ignored Scalia. In 1987, in contrast, Senator Edward Kennedy took
the lead in opposing Bork and liberal interest groups mounted a
massive campaign against him, while the Reagan administration
did relatively little to mobilize support for him.

These generalizations can be applied to the Senate's treatment
of nominations since 1968. The Senate's actions in this period fall
into three categories: confirmations that involved little difficulty,
confirmations that were achieved with more difficulty, and defeats
of nominees.

The Easy Confirmations. Of the seventeen nominees who were considered by the Senate between 1968 and 1994, nine achieved rela-

tively easy confirmation: Warren Burger, Harry Blackmun, Lewis Powell, John Paul Stevens, Sandra Day O'Connor, Antonin Scalia, Anthony Kennedy, Ruth Bader Ginsburg, and Stephen Breyer. Five of these nominees received no negative votes, Powell received one negative vote, and Burger and Ginsburg each received three. Breyer also fits in this category, even though nine senators voted against his confirmation.

This does not mean that these nominees aroused universal enthusiasm. Certainly liberal Democrats would have preferred nominees less conservative than Burger and Scalia. Antiabortion groups opposed O'Connor and Ginsburg. But these nominees escaped strong challenges because their objective qualifications seemed unassailable and because there was only limited concern about their ideological positions.

Circumstances favored other nominees besides Scalia. Blackmun probably would have won confirmation easily in any case, but that result was ensured by the Senate's collective desire to avoid a third consecutive battle over a Nixon nomination. Observers disagreed about how liberal Ginsburg was, but her presence on the Court could do no more than moderate its conservative tendencies.

Breyer received negative votes from nine Republican senators. Some argued that his investment in Lloyd's of London, an insurance syndicate, showed a lack of prudence in making a risky investment and that it had created conflicts of interest in some cases in which he had participated. Other opponents said that he was too liberal. But most senators saw Breyer as only moderately liberal, so that his replacement of the moderate liberal Harry Blackmun would have little impact on the Court. His abilities as lawyer and judge were clear, and he had won the respect of both Democrats and Republicans while serving on the staff of the Senate Judiciary Committee. Thus his confirmation was never in real jeopardy.

The Difficult Confirmations. Some of the successful nominees have been confirmed with difficulty. They include William Rehnquist, when nominated as associate justice in 1971 and as chief justice in 1986; Clarence Thomas in 1991; and—with somewhat less difficulty—David Souter in 1990. In each instance, the nominee's apparent conservatism aroused opposition from liberal senators and interest groups.

When Rehnquist was first nominated in 1971, the Leadership Conference on Civil Rights led the opposition. Rehnquist's opponents argued that his conservatism on civil liberties was so extreme as to be unacceptable in a Supreme Court justice. But the case against him was weakened by the general perception that he was a highly competent lawyer. The opposition thus had to be based almost entirely on ideological grounds, and even for some liberals those grounds were insufficient to justify a negative vote. Rehnquist was confirmed by a 68–26 vote.

Rehnquist's record as an associate justice was as conservative as had been expected, so his prospective elevation to chief justice in 1986 also aroused strong opposition from liberal interest groups and senators. These opponents sought to gain support by raising questions about Rehnquist's ethical standards. They made several charges, of which the most important was that Rehnquist had sought to intimidate black and Hispanic voters in Arizona during the 1960s. These charges attracted attention but ultimately had little impact. Rehnquist was confirmed by a 65–33 vote; with few exceptions, Northern Democrats voted against him and other senators voted for him.

When David Souter was nominated in 1990, the prospective replacement of liberal William Brennan by a conservative on a closely divided Court helped to arouse the opposition of some liberal senators and interest groups. But Souter's objective qualifications were generally considered quite good. Moreover, his record gave few clues about his views on policy issues. One commentator wrote, "The chief qualification for confirmation was not being Robert Bork."[43] Once Souter had given indications that he was more moderate in views and personal style than Bork, his confirmation was assured; the Senate vote was 90–9.

A year later, Clarence Thomas won confirmation by the smallest margin in the twentieth century. His very conservative record aroused opposition from several liberal interest groups, but initially they had little impact. Thomas benefited from effective support by the Bush administration, and many Democrats favored the continuation of black representation on the Court.

Opposition grew after Thomas testified before the Judiciary Committee. His testimony raised doubts about his candor and abilities, and the committee split 7–7 on whether to recommend his confirmation. Still, as senators announced their positions, Thomas seemed assured of success. The disclosure of Anita Hill's sexual harassment charge against Thomas threatened his confirmation. But after committee hearings on that charge few senators changed their position, and Thomas was confirmed by a 52–48 vote. The vote was primarily along party lines. But Thomas won crucial support from eleven southern Democrats, responding in part to their perception of support for Thomas by black constituents.[44] This response underlines the public visibility of controversial confirmation decisions in the current era.

The Defeats. Of the four confirmation defeats since 1968, three came in a two-year period, 1968–1970. The first was that of Abe Fortas, a sitting justice nominated to be chief justice by President Johnson in 1968. Fortas's strong liberalism on the liberal Warren Court aroused early opposition by conservative senators, and some Republicans wanted to prevent Fortas's confirmation in order to reserve the vacancy for a new president—expected to be Republican—in 1969. These opponents pointed to two activities that raised doubts about Fortas's ethical fitness: his continued consultation with the president about policy matters while a member of the Court, and an arrangement by which he gave nine lectures at American University, in Washington, D.C., for a fee of $15,000 raised from businesses. The Judiciary Committee approved the nomination by a divided vote, but it ran into a filibuster on the Senate floor. A vote to end the filibuster fell fourteen votes short of the two-thirds majority then required; the opposition came almost entirely from Republicans and southern Democrats. At Fortas's request, his nomination was then withdrawn.

In 1969, Fortas resigned from the Court. President Nixon selected Clement Haynsworth, chief judge of a federal court of appeals, to replace him. Haynsworth was opposed by labor groups and the National Association for the Advancement of Colored People (NAACP), both of which disliked his judicial record. Liberal senators, concerned about this record, sought revenge for Fortas's defeat as well. Haynsworth was also charged with unethical conduct: he had sat in two cases involving subsidiaries of companies in which he owned stock, and in another case he had bought the stock of a corporation in the interval between his court's decision in its favor and the announcement of the decision. These charges aroused additional opposition by Senate moderates. Haynsworth ultimately was defeated by a 45–55 vote, with a large minority of Republicans voting against confirmation.

President Nixon then nominated another court of appeals judge, G. Harrold Carswell. After the fight over Haynsworth, most senators were inclined to support the next nominee. One senator predicted that any new Nixon nominee "will have no trouble getting confirmed unless he has committed murder—recently."[45] But Carswell drew almost immediate opposition from civil rights groups for what they perceived as his hostility to their interests, and their cause gained strength from a series of revelations about Carswell that suggested an active opposition to black civil rights. Carswell was also criticized for his alleged lack of judicial competence. Legal scholars attested to his limited abilities, and data indicated that an unusually high proportion of his decisions had been reversed on appeal. Carswell's supporters were not successful in countering this attack. The nomination was defeated by a 45–51 vote; the lineup was similar to that in the vote on Haynsworth.

Robert Bork's 1987 defeat differed from the three that preceded it in that no serious charges were made about his competence or his ethical standards. But liberals were concerned about his strong conservatism on civil liberties issues and his potential to shift the Court's ideological balance. As noted earlier, Senator Kennedy and liberal interest groups worked hard to secure votes against Bork. Concern about Bork's views was intensified by his testimony before the Senate Judiciary Committee, in which he discussed in detail his positions on issues such as the right to privacy.

This growing concern, combined with the unprecedented level of interest group activity against Bork, made his defeat possible. Also important was President Reagan's political weakness: not only did the Democrats control the Senate, but Reagan's popularity both inside and outside Congress had declined. Even so, a more effective campaign for Bork by the administration might have secured his confirmation. In any event, confirmation was denied by a 42–58 vote. All but eight senators voted along party lines; the overwhelming and unexpected opposition of southern Democrats made the difference in the outcome.

Summary. Since 1968, the Senate has taken a more active role in scrutinizing nominees to the Supreme Court. One spur prompting it to take this active role has been the increasing efforts of interest groups to defeat some nominees. Another spur has been the growing awareness that a single Court appointment can have considerable impact on national policy. In both respects one issue—abortion—has been especially important. As a result of these developments, the confirmation battles over Robert Bork and Clarence Thomas became national spectacles. And even relatively uncontroversial nominations, such as those of David Souter and Ruth Bader Ginsburg, received a good deal of scrutiny.

Even so, the great majority of nominees from 1968 to 1994 still were confirmed—most with little difficulty. One reason for this success is that presidents often sought nominees whom they expected the Senate to accept. More fundamentally, the Senate as a whole still typically began with a presumption in favor of confirming nominees. Because of this presumption, presidents continued to hold most of the power to determine who would sit on the Supreme Court.

This situation is not necessarily permanent. After they gained majority status in 1995, Senate Republicans took an assertive stance in slowing the confirmation of Bill Clinton's lower court nominees and blocked some nominees on ideological grounds. They would have been more assertive in opposing any Supreme Court nominees who seemed unduly liberal or who were subject to attack on other grounds. In turn, Clinton almost surely would have exhibited even more caution in choosing a nominee than he did when the Senate was under Democratic control. In response to Republican assertiveness under Clinton, Democratic senators may be less willing to acquiesce in nominations by future Republican presidents. The roles of the president and Senate in selecting Supreme Court justices should be viewed as dynamic, especially in a period of strong partisan contention.

The Impact of the Selection Process

The process of selecting people to hold a particular office is likely to affect the office itself. Certainly this is true of the Supreme Court. Most important, the process helps to determine what kinds of people become justices. In the current era, for instance, the eagerness of many senators to oppose nominees whose views they dislike gives presidents an incentive to choose people who seem ideologically moderate and who have avoided controversial positions on policy issues.

Further, the intense scrutiny that nominees now undergo may affect people's willingness to be considered as candidates for nomination. David Souter told his friend and Senate sponsor Warren

Rudman that "if I had known how vicious this process is, I wouldn't have let you propose my nomination."[46] Prospective nominees may take themselves out of the running because they want to spare themselves and their families what has become a considerable ordeal.[47]

Among those who win confirmation, the experience may shape their behavior as justices. Hugo Black's 1937 confirmation was difficult, largely because of charges that he had been a member of the Ku Klux Klan—charges that he admitted to be true after his confirmation. One commentator concluded that Black "came on the Court determined to prove that he was not a racist member of the Klan,"[48] and he did establish himself as one of the strongest civil libertarians in the Court's history. Years after the hard-fought battle over his confirmation, Clarence Thomas remained bitter about what he called "a plain whipping,"[49] and observers have suggested that this experience strengthened his resolve to take strongly conservative positions on the Court.[50] Whatever may be true of Black and Thomas, undoubtedly some justices are changed by what they go through to achieve their positions.

Who Is Selected

A recent children's book about Justice O'Connor concludes with a set of suggestions "if you want to be a Supreme Court justice."[51] While other observers might add or delete specific suggestions, the list underlines an important reality: because of the workings of the selection process, certain kinds of people are more likely to reach the Supreme Court than others.

The kinds of people who become justices can be understood in terms of the paths that they take to the Court. These paths have changed over time. In this section I give particular attention to the period extending from the presidency of Franklin Roosevelt to the present. In that period thirty-three justices were selected. Some characteristics of these justices are listed in Table 2-3. The box on pages 62–63 summarizes the careers of the justices who sat on the Court in 2000.

Career Paths

The Legal Profession. The Constitution does not require that Supreme Court justices be attorneys. In practice, however, this restriction has been absolute. Most of those involved in the selection

TABLE 2-3

Selected Characteristics of Justices Appointed since 1937

Justice	Age[a]	State of residence[b]	Law school	Position at appointment[c]	Years as judge	Elective office[d]	Administrative position[e]
Black	51	Ala.	Alabama	Senator	1	Senate	—
Reed	53	Ky.	Columbia	Solicitor general	0	State leg.	Solicitor general
Frankfurter	56	Mass.	Harvard	Law professor	0	—	Subcabinet
Douglas	40	Wash.	Columbia	Chair, Sec. & Exchange Comm.	0	—	Sec. & Exchange Comm.
Murphy	49	Mich.	Michigan	Attorney general	7	Governor	Attorney general
Byrnes	62	S.C.	None	Senator	0	Senate	—
Jackson	49	N.Y.	Albany	Attorney general	0	—	Attorney general
Rutledge	48	Iowa	Colorado	U.S. Ct. App.	4	—	—
Burton	57	Ohio	Harvard	Senator	0	Senate	—
Vinson	56	Ky.	Centre (Ky.)	Sec. of Treasury	5	House of Rep.	Sec. of Treasury
Clark	49	Texas	Texas	Attorney general	0	—	Attorney general
Minton	58	Ind.	Indiana	U.S. Ct. App.	8	Senate	Asst. to president
Warren	62	Calif.	Calif.	Governor	0	Governor	—
Harlan	55	N.Y.	New York	U.S. Ct. App.	1	—	Asst. U.S. Attorney
Brennan	50	N.J.	Harvard	State Sup. Ct.	7	—	—
Whittaker	56	Mo.	Kansas City	U.S. Ct. App.	3	—	—
Stewart	43	Ohio	Yale	U.S. Ct. App.	4	City council	—
White	44	Colo.	Yale	Dep. atty general	0	—	Dep. atty general
Goldberg	54	Ill.	Northwestern	Sec. of labor	0	—	Sec. of labor

Justice	Age[a]	State[b]	Law school	[c]	[d]		[e]
Fortas	55	D.C.	Yale	Private practice	—	0	Subcabinet
Marshall	59	N.Y.	Howard	Solicitor general	—	4	Solicitor general
Burger	61	Minn.	St. Paul	U.S. Ct. App.	—	13	Asst. atty general
Blackmun	61	Minn.	Harvard	U.S. Ct. App.	—	11	—
Powell	64	Va.	Wash. & Lee	Private practice	—	0	State Bd. of Education
Rehnquist	47	Ariz.	Stanford	Asst. atty general	—	0	Asst. atty general
Stevens	55	Ill.	Northwestern	U.S. Ct. App.	—	5	—
O'Connor	51	Ariz.	Stanford	State Ct. App.	State leg.	6	State asst. atty general
Scalia	50	D.C.	Harvard	U.S. Ct. App.	—	4	Asst. atty general
Kennedy	51	Calif.	Harvard	U.S. Ct. App.	—	11	—
Souter	51	N.H.	Harvard	U.S. Ct. App.	—	12	State atty general
Thomas	43	D.C.	Yale	U.S. Ct. App.	—	1	Equal Empl. Opp. Comm.
Ginsburg	60	D.C.	Harvard, Columbia	U.S. Ct. App.	—	13	—
Breyer	56	Mass.	Harvard	U.S. Ct. App.	—	13	—

Sources: Leon Friedman and Fred L. Israel, *The Justices of the United States Supreme Court, 1789–1969: Their Lives and Major Opinions* (New York: R. R. Bowker Co., 1969; 1978 supplement); Harold W. Chase and Craig R. Ducat, *Constitutional Interpretation*, 2d ed. (St. Paul: West, 1979), 1361–1376; Joan Biskupic and Elder Witt, *Guide to the U.S. Supreme Court*, 3d ed. (Washington, D.C.: Congressional Quarterly, 1997), 930–962.

a Age at time of appointment.

b Primary state of residence before selection.

c In this and following columns, positions are federal except where noted otherwise.

d Highest office.

e Highest appointive administrative position. Minor position omitted.

Careers of the Supreme Court . . .

William H. Rehnquist (born 1924)

Law degree, Stanford University, 1952
Supreme Court law clerk, 1952–1953
Private law practice, 1953–1969
U.S. Justice Department, 1969–1971
Appointed to Supreme Court, 1971
Appointed chief justice, 1986

John Paul Stevens (born 1920)

Law degree, Northwestern University, 1947
Supreme Court law clerk, 1947–1948
Private law practice, 1949–1970
Judge, U.S. Court of Appeals, 1970–1975
Appointed to Supreme Court, 1975

Sandra Day O'Connor (born 1930)

Law degree, Stanford University, 1952
Deputy county attorney, 1952–1953
Civilian attorney, U.S. Army, 1954–1957
Private law practice, volunteer work, family
  responsibilities, 1957–1965
Assistant state attorney general, 1965–1969
Arizona legislator, 1969–1975
Arizona trial judge, 1975–1979
Judge, Arizona Court of Appeals, 1979–1981
Appointed to Supreme Court, 1981

Antonin Scalia (born 1936)

Law degree, Harvard University, 1960
Private law practice, 1960–1967
Law school teaching, 1967–1971
Legal positions in federal government, 1971–1977
Law school teaching, 1977–1982
Judge, U.S. Court of Appeals, 1982–1986
Appointed to Supreme Court, 1986

Anthony M. Kennedy (born 1936)

Law degree, Harvard University, 1961
Private law practice, 1961–1975
Judge, U.S. Court of Appeals, 1975–1988
Appointed to Supreme Court, 1988

David H. Souter (born 1939)

Law degree, Harvard University, 1966
Private law practice, 1966–1968

David H. Souter (continued)

New Hampshire attorney general's office,
1968–1978
Attorney General, New Hampshire, 1976–1978
Judge, New Hampshire trial court, 1978–1983
Justice, New Hampshire Supreme Court,
1983–1990
Judge, U.S. Court of Appeals, 1990
Appointed to Supreme Court, 1990

Clarence Thomas (born 1948)

Law degree, Yale University, 1974
Missouri attorney general's office, 1974–1977
Attorney for Monsanto Company, 1977–1979
Legislative assistant to a U.S. senator, 1979–1981
Assistant U.S. secretary of education, 1981–1982
Chair, U.S. Equal Employment Opportunity Commission,
1982–1990
Judge, U.S. Court of Appeals, 1990–1991
Appointed to Supreme Court, 1991

Ruth Bader Ginsburg (born 1933)

Law degree, Columbia University, 1959
Federal district court law clerk, 1959–1961
Law school research position, 1961–1963
Law school teaching, 1963–1980
Judge, U.S. Court of Appeals, 1980–1993
Appointed to Supreme Court, 1993

Stephen G. Breyer (born 1938)

Law degree, Harvard University, 1964
Supreme Court law clerk, 1964–1965
U.S. Justice Department, 1965–1967
Law school teaching, 1967–1980
Staff, U.S. Senate Judiciary Committee,
1974–1975, 1979–1980
Judge, U.S. Court of Appeals, 1980–1994
Appointed to Supreme Court, 1994

Source: Based chiefly on information in Kenneth Jost, *The Supreme Court Yearbook,
1998–1999* (Washington, D.C.: CQ Press, 2000), 321–339.

Note: With the exception of Justice Breyer's Senate staff service, only the primary position held by a future justice during each career stage is listed.

process assume that only a person with legal training can serve effectively on the Court. If a president nominated a non-lawyer to the Court, this assumption—and the large number of lawyers in the Senate—probably would prevent confirmation.

Thus the willingness and ability to obtain a law degree constitute the first and least flexible requirement for recruitment to the Court. Most of the justices who served during the first century of the Court's history had followed what was then the standard practice, apprenticing under a practicing attorney. In several instances, the practicing attorney was a leading member of the bar.[52] James Byrnes (chosen in 1941) was the last justice to study law through apprenticeship; all his successors have taken what is now the conventional route of law school training. A high proportion of justices have graduated from the more prestigious schools. Of the nine justices sitting in 2000, seven received their law degrees from Harvard, Yale, or Stanford.

High Positions. If legal education is a necessary first step in the paths to the Court, almost equally important as a last step is attaining a high position in government or the legal profession. Obscure private practitioners or state trial judges might be superbly qualified for the Court, but their qualifications would be questioned because of their lowly positions. A high position in government or the legal profession also makes a person more visible to the president and to others involved in the nomination process.

At the time they were selected, the thirty-three justices appointed since 1937 held positions of four types. Ten justices served in the federal executive branch, seven in the Justice Department. The other three justices served as chair of the Securities and Exchange Commission (Douglas), secretary of the Treasury (Vinson), and secretary of labor (Goldberg).

Sixteen of the justices appointed in this period were appellate judges at the time of selection. Fourteen of them served on the federal courts of appeals; the other two (Brennan and O'Connor) served on state courts. Five of the fourteen federal judges (Rutledge, Burger, Scalia, Thomas, and Ginsburg) came from the District of Columbia circuit, which is particularly visible to the president and to other officials in Washington.

Of the other seven justices appointed since 1937, four held high elective office; three were senators (Black, Byrnes, and Burton) and the fourth was governor of California (Warren). The other three held positions outside government. Each had attained extraordinary success and respect—as a legal scholar (Frankfurter), a Washington lawyer (Fortas), and a leader of the legal profession (Powell). Frankfurter and Fortas had also been informal presidential advisers.

The Steps Between. The people who have become Supreme Court justices took a variety of routes from legal education to the high positions that made them credible candidates for the Court. Frankfurter, Fortas, and Powell illustrate one simple route: entry into legal practice or academia, followed by a gradual rise to high standing in the legal profession. Some justices took a similar route through public office. Earl Warren held a series of appointive and elective offices, leading to his California governorship. Clarence Thomas held a series of nonelected positions in government, culminating in positions as chair of the federal Equal Employment Opportunity Commission and then as judge on a federal court of appeals.

Since 1975, the most common route to the Court has been through private practice or law teaching, often combined with some time in government, before appointment to a federal court of appeals. Antonin Scalia, Stephen Breyer, and Ruth Bader Ginsburg were law professors. John Paul Stevens and Anthony Kennedy went directly from private practice to a court of appeals. During their careers, all five had held government positions or participated informally in the governmental process.

The path that Sandra Day O'Connor took was unusual. She spent time in private practice and government legal positions, with some career interruptions for family reasons, before becoming an Arizona state senator and majority leader of the senate. O'Connor left the legislature for a trial judgeship. Her promotion to the state court of appeals through a gubernatorial appointment put her in a position to be considered for the Supreme Court.

O'Connor's career underlines the multiplicity of paths to the Court. Justices have brought to the Court a broad range of career experiences. What they have shared is their credential as lawyers and their success in reaching the higher levels of the legal profession or government that make them candidates for nomination to the Court.

Implications of the Career Paths

The paths to the Supreme Court help to explain some significant characteristics of the justices. They also underline the role of chance in determining who becomes a justice.

Age. Young people are not appointed to the Supreme Court. Most of the justices selected in the twentieth century were in their fifties when they joined the Court; of the remainder, most were over the age of sixty. William Douglas was the youngest appointee, at age forty; only three other appointees—Potter Stewart, Byron White, and Clarence Thomas—were under forty-five.

In one sense, this pattern is surprising. We might expect presidents to select relatively young candidates in order to maximize the length of time "their" justices would serve. The main reason they do not do so is the time required to achieve the high positions that most justices hold when they are selected and to attain the eminence that makes one a serious candidate for selection.

Within this constraint, most recent presidents have sought to select justices who are relatively young. Thomas was forty-three when selected; the other four Reagan and Bush appointees were all aged fifty or fifty-one. This pattern reflects strong presidential interest in the Court's future direction. In this respect Clinton's selection of sixty-year-old Ruth Bader Ginsburg—the oldest appointee in more than twenty years—stands out.

Class, Race, and Gender. The Supreme Court's membership has been quite unrepresentative of the general population in terms of social class; most justices grew up in families that were relatively well off. One study found that one-third of the justices were from the upper class and one-quarter were from the upper middle class. Only one-quarter were from the lower middle class or below.[53]

Since the 1930s, an unusually high percentage of appointees to the Court have had lower-status backgrounds; this is especially true of Democrats. Still, the recent justices as a group grew up in better than average circumstances. The 2000 Court included one justice from the upper class (John Paul Stevens), four from the upper middle class, three from the middle class, and one (Clarence Thomas) whose family was impoverished.

The predominance of higher-status backgrounds can be explained by the career paths that most justices take. First and most important, a justice must obtain a legal education. To do so is easiest for individuals of high status, because of the cost of legal training and the education that necessarily precedes it. Second, individuals of high status have a variety of advantages in their post-educational careers. Those who can afford to attend elite law schools, for instance, have the easiest time obtaining positions in successful law firms.

The partial deviation from this pattern since the 1930s reflects the increasing availability of legal education. In addition, the increase in size of the legal profession, the judiciary, and the federal government has made high positions in these sectors more accessible to individuals with lower-status backgrounds who previously might have been excluded. If these explanations have some validity, then we should expect that the proportion of justices with lower-status backgrounds will remain relatively large and may increase in the future.

Until 1967 all the justices were white men. This pattern is not difficult to understand. Women and members of racial minority groups had extreme difficulty pursuing a legal education because of legal and other restrictions. As a result, the number of potential justices from these groups who passed the first barrier to selection was quite small. Moreover, prejudice against women and members of racial minorities limited their ability to advance in the legal profession and in politics. As a result, very few individuals who were not white men could achieve the high positions that people generally must obtain to be considered for nomination to the Court.

Since 1967, two women (O'Connor and Ginsburg) and two African Americans (Marshall and Thomas) have won appointments to the Court. These appointments reflect changes in society that made it at least somewhat less difficult for people other than white men to achieve high positions. They also reflect the growing willingness of presidents to consider women and members of racial minority groups as prospective nominees. Still, because of the various advantages they enjoy, white men are likely to enjoy disproportionate representation on the Court for some time.

If the Court has been composed primarily of white men with higher-status backgrounds, what has been the effect on its policies? It seems likely that the legal claims of racial minority groups and of women would have been taken seriously at an earlier time if members of these groups had sat on the Court, because these justices would have influenced their colleagues' perceptions of discrimination. Of course, it is impossible to do more than speculate about this possibility.

Political and social attitudes differ somewhat between people of higher and lower socioeconomic status, so justices' class origins might affect the Court's decisions. But the justices typically are people who have achieved high status themselves even if their origins were humble. The sympathies of people who have "climbed" upward from a low socioeconomic level may differ little from those of people who started out with social and economic advantages. Notably, the justices with humble backgrounds have included solid conservatives such as Warren Burger and Clarence Thomas as well as liberals such as Earl Warren and Thurgood Marshall. Some commentators argue that the Court's decisions generally reflect the values and interests of people who are well off.[54] If so, this may result from the status that the justices achieve in their own lives more than from their origins.

Prior Judicial Service. Recent presidents have preferred to nominate lower court judges to the Supreme Court because these candidates' judicial records provide information about their policy views. As a result, the current Supreme Court is unusual in having eight justices who served on lower courts (all but William Rehnquist). But historically a majority of the justices had judicial experience before reaching the Court. Many commentators think that such service is desirable, even a prerequisite to superior work on the Supreme Court. On a different level, some conservatives have argued that a lack of lower court service encourages judicial activism.

Yet a comparison of justices with and without lower court experience indicates that the two groups do not behave very differently. To take one example, the leaders of the activist Warren Court were Earl Warren, with no lower court experience, and former state judge William Brennan. Their strongest opponents were John Marshall Harlan, who came to the Court from a federal court of appeals, and Felix Frankfurter, who came from Harvard Law School. And all four of these justices have been viewed as outstanding.

This apparent lack of difference is easy to explain. Of the twenty justices appointed since 1937 who had lower court experience, the justice with the most experience had served for thirteen years; ten justices had been lower court judges for five years or less. Undoubtedly even a short period on a lower court shapes a justice's perspective, but a stint of three or five years—or even of thirteen years—is not likely to have as much impact on a person's thinking and approach to judicial policy issues as the much longer period of education and professional development that preceded it.

Partisan Political Activity. One characteristic shared by most current justices, like their predecessors, is a degree of involvement in partisan politics. Antonin Scalia, for instance, held several positions in the Nixon and Ford administrations. Anthony Kennedy drafted a state ballot proposition for California governor Ronald Reagan. William Rehnquist was active in the Arizona Republican Party. Clarence Thomas worked with John Danforth when Danforth was the Missouri attorney general and a U.S. senator, and Thomas later served in the Reagan and Bush administrations.

This pattern reflects the ways that justices are chosen. Even if nominations to the Court are not used as political rewards, presidents look more favorably on those who have contributed to their party's success. Partisan activity is also a way to come to the attention of presidents, their staff members, and others who influence nomination decisions. Perhaps more important, it enables people to win the high offices and appointive positions that make them credible candidates for the Court. To take the most important current example, lawyers who avoid any involvement in politics are unlikely to win federal judgeships.

Historically, many justices were career politicians who achieved high elective office. Of the current justices, only O'Connor comes close to fitting that pattern. She became majority leader of the Arizona Senate, though she left the legislature after only six years to run for (and win) a trial court judgeship. In filling two Court vacancies in his first term, Bill Clinton seriously considered three people who had won high elective office. But Clinton ultimately followed the example of Gerald Ford, Reagan, and Bush in choosing lower court judges who had never run for office.

Changes in Career Paths. Even in the period since 1937, there have been changes in paths to the Supreme Court and in the characteristics of people who become justices. The numerical dominance of people from privileged backgrounds and of white men has declined, a decline reflecting social and political changes in the United States. That trend is unlikely to be reversed.

As noted already, justices' career patterns have also changed. Among the twelve justices appointed since 1969, only one (O'Connor) ever held elective office, only one (Rehnquist) came to the Court directly from the executive branch, and all but two (Rehnquist and Powell) were appellate judges when they received their Court appointments. In a sense, there is less politics and more law in the backgrounds of justices than there used to be. This change may be a transitory phenomenon, the result of a series of specific appointment decisions. But it might represent a long-term shift. If the backgrounds of justices *are* becoming more legal and less political, this represents a noteworthy change in the ways that people reach the Supreme Court.

The Role of Chance. A person does not become a Supreme Court justice through an inevitable process. Rather, advancement from membership in the bar to a seat on the Court is a result of luck as much as anything else. This luck comes in two stages. First, good fortune is often necessary to achieve the high positions in government or law that make individuals possible candidates for the Court; it is not necessarily the "fittest" who become cabinet members or federal appellate judges. Second, once they achieve such positions, whether candidates are seriously considered for the Court and actually win an appointment depends largely on the existence of several favorable circumstances.

For one thing, a potential justice gains enormously by belonging to a particular political party at the appropriate time. Every appointment to the Court between 1969 and 1992 was made by a Republican president. As a result, potential justices who were liberal Democrats had to watch their chances slip away. Further, someone whose friend or associate achieves a powerful position becomes a far stronger candidate for a seat on the Court. David Souter was fortunate that someone who described Souter as "my closest friend" (Warren Rudman) became a U.S. senator and that a person who knew and admired him (John Sununu) became the president's chief of staff.[55]

More generally, everyone appointed to the Court has benefited from a favorable series of circumstances. Eisenhower's attorney general became aware of William Brennan because Brennan gave a conference address in place of a colleague on the New Jersey Supreme Court who was ill. John Paul Stevens has reported that his *pro bono* volunteer services for a client led to favorable publicity that later helped him win a judicial appointment.[56]

This does not mean that the Court's direction, as shaped by presidential appointments, is random. No matter which individuals they choose, Democratic presidents generally nominate people with liberal views and Republicans tend to select conservatives. But it does mean that specific individuals achieve membership on the Court in large part through good fortune. "You have to be lucky," said Sandra Day O'Connor about her appointment,[57] a statement that reflects realism as well as modesty.

Leaving the Court

Congress has not changed the size of the Supreme Court for more than a century, and it is not likely to do so in the near future. Thus new members can come to the Court only when a sitting justice leaves that institution.

Voluntary Departures

In the nineteenth century, most justices left the Supreme Court through death. In contrast, most recent departures have come as the result of a justice's voluntary decision to leave.[58] Indeed, the last justice to die in office was Robert Jackson in 1954. Table 2-4 illustrates this and other patterns in departures from the Court since 1965.

Early in the Court's history, several justices left the Court to take more attractive opportunities, but only a handful of justices did so in the twentieth century. The most recent was Arthur Goldberg, who resigned in 1965 to become U.S. ambassador to the United Nations. The main reason for this change is simple: the Court's prestige and influence on American life have made it more and more attractive to its members.

Because the Court is so attractive, justices may be reluctant to leave. William Brennan said that he had regretted retiring in 1990 "every minute since I did. God, when I see some of the decisions . . . I think, 'Jeez, if only I were there.'"[59] The prospect of such regrets may weigh heavily on justices.

TABLE 2-4
Reasons for Leaving the Court, 1965–1994

Year	Justice	Age	Primary reasons for leaving	Length of time from leaving until death
1965	Goldberg	56	Appointment as ambassador to U.N.	24 years
1967	Clark	67	Son's appointment as attorney general	10 years
1969	Fortas	58	Pressures based on possible ethical violations	13 years
1969[a]	Warren	78[a]	Age	5 years
1971	Black	85	Age and ill health	1 month
1971	Harlan	72	Age and ill health	3 months
1975	Douglas	77	Age and ill health	4 years
1981	Stewart	66	Age	4 years
1986	Burger	78	Responsibilities for Commission on the Bicentennial of the Constitution, possibly age	9 years
1987	Powell	79	Age and health concerns	11 years
1990	Brennan	84	Age and ill health	7 years
1991	Marshall	83[b]	Age and ill health	2 years
1993	White	76[b]	Desire to allow another person to serve, possibly age	—
1994	Blackmun	85	Age	5 years

Sources: Joan Biskupic and Elder Witt, *Guide to the U.S. Supreme Court,* 3d ed. (Washington, D.C.: Congressional Quarterly, 1997), 931–954; other biographical sources, newspaper stories.

[a] Warren originally announced intent to leave the Court in 1968 at age 77.

[b] Marshall announced intent to leave the Court at 82, White at 75.

Yet age and its accompanying infirmities may give the justices little choice. When Harry Blackmun retired from the Court in 1994, he explained that "it's not easy to step aside, but I know what the numbers are, and it's time."[60] The "numbers" referred to his age. Later, Blackmun said, "Eighty-five is pretty old. I don't want to reach a point where my senility level reaches unacceptable proportions."[61]

Justice Byron White in March 1993, one week before announcing his retirement from the Court while he was still in good health.

Some justices do stay on the Court past the time at which they can function effectively as justices. William Douglas's health problems had become so great by 1975 that his colleagues took the extraordinary step of agreeing to set aside for later rehearing any case in which Douglas was part of a 5–4 majority. (Such action was never taken because Douglas retired a few weeks later, before there were any decisions that met this criterion.)[62]

On the whole, however, justices have become more willing to

leave the Court when ill health makes it difficult to do their jobs well. One reason is the establishment of a pension system that removes financial incentives to remain on the Court. Congress first established a judicial pension in 1869. Today justices who are at least seventy years old and who have served on the federal courts for at least ten years, or who are at least sixty-five and have served for fifteen years, can retire and continue to receive the salaries they earned at the time of their retirements. Justices who meet these criteria can retire and receive any salary increases granted sitting justices, so long as they perform a certain amount of service for the federal courts—generally equal to one-quarter of full-time work. (Disabled justices are exempt from this requirement.)

With financial considerations irrelevant for most justices, the decision whether to leave the Court involves primarily a weighing of the satisfactions of the job against the effects of health problems. Political considerations may come into play, in that a justice will be happier about giving up the position when the president holds views similar to the justice. The Court's liberals were reluctant to retire when Ronald Reagan or George Bush would select their successors. William Brennan and Thurgood Marshall left the Court during the Bush administration only when they felt that their health left them no choice; Marshall explained his 1991 retirement by saying that "I'm getting old and falling apart."[63] Harry Blackmun held out longer, saying in 1990 that he would stay on the Court "until the third day of November 1992"—the day on which the voters would choose between President George Bush and Bill Clinton.[64] After Clinton won, Blackmun retired at the end of the 1992 Court term. By the same token, the continued service of William Rehnquist on the Court despite his age and health problems may reflect the reluctance of a conservative Republican to allow Clinton to choose his successor.

One current justice has given very early notice of his retirement. In 1993, two years after he joined the Court, Clarence Thomas told two of his clerks that he would remain on the Court until 2034. He explained, "The liberals made my life miserable for 43 years, and I'm going to make their lives miserable for 43 years."[65]

External Pressure

Though justices make their own decisions to resign or retire, Congress and the president can try to influence those decisions. Of course, legislation creating attractive pension rights has had considerable impact. The other branches can also try to induce specific justices to leave the Court. Presidents have good reason to do so, in order to create vacancies they can fill. Occasionally they try to induce retirements. John Kennedy reportedly persuaded Felix Frankfurter to retire after ill health had decreased his effectiveness,[66] but Thurgood Marshall bitterly resisted efforts by the Carter administration to convince him to retire.[67]

Presidents can also try to lure justices away from the Court by offering them other positions. Lyndon Johnson offered Arthur Goldberg the position of ambassador to the United Nations and then exerted intense personal pressure to induce him to accept that position. But Byron White rejected the idea of becoming FBI director when the Reagan administration sounded him out about it. James Byrnes's resignation in 1942 was somewhat different; Byrnes was quite unhappy on the Court and wanted to return to the executive branch, but Franklin Roosevelt still had to offer him a central position in the war effort to secure his resignation and his services.[68]

Very different is the use, or threat, of impeachment. Under the Constitution, justices, like other federal officials, can be removed through impeachment proceedings for "treason, bribery, or other high crimes and misdemeanors."[69] President Thomas Jefferson actually sought to gain control of the largely Federalist (and thus anti-Jefferson) judiciary through the use of impeachment, and Congress did impeach and convict a federal district judge in 1803. Justice Samuel Chase made himself vulnerable to impeachment by participating in President John Adams's campaign for reelection in 1800 and by making some injudicious and partisan remarks to a Maryland grand jury in 1803. Chase was impeached, an action justified chiefly by his handling of political trials, but the Senate acquitted him in 1805. His acquittal effectively ended Jefferson's plans to seek the impeachment of other justices.

No justice has been impeached since then. But more recently there was serious discussion about the possible impeachment of two justices. Several efforts were made to remove William Douglas (most seriously in 1969 and 1970), motivated by opposition to his strong liberalism. The reasons stated publicly by opponents were his financial connections with a foundation and his outside writings; the impeachment effort was encouraged privately by

President Nixon.[70] A special House committee failed to approve a resolution to impeach Douglas, however, and the resolution died in 1970.

Had Abe Fortas not resigned from the Court in 1969, he actually might have been removed through impeachment proceedings.[71] Fortas had been criticized for his financial dealings at the time he was nominated unsuccessfully to be chief justice in 1968. A year later, it was disclosed that he had a lifetime contract as a consultant to the Wolfson Foundation and had received money from that foundation at a time when the person who directed it was being prosecuted by the federal government. The Nixon administration orchestrated a campaign of pressure on Fortas through the mass media and through the Court itself. Fortas's explanation of his conduct proved unconvincing, and he soon resigned. The resignation came too early to determine how successful an impeachment effort would have been, but it almost certainly would have been serious.

The Fortas incident seems unlikely to be repeated, in part because it reminds justices of the need to avoid questionable financial conduct. The removals of three federal judges through impeachment proceedings between 1987 and 1989 make it clear that impeachment is a real option. But it is used only in cases with strong evidence of serious misdeeds, often involving allegations of corrupt behavior.

Thus the timing of a justice's leaving the Court reflects primarily the justice's own inclinations, health, and longevity. Those who want to affect the Court's membership may have their say when a vacancy occurs, but they have little control over the creation of vacancies.

Conclusion

The recruitment of Supreme Court justices is a complex process. People do not "rise" to the Court in an orderly fashion. Rather, whether they become credible candidates for the Court and whether they actually win appointments depend on a wide range of circumstances. Indeed, something close to pure luck plays a powerful role in determining who becomes a justice.

The recruitment process has changed over time. To take one example, the balance of power between president and Senate in selecting justices has shifted a good deal. Even more important, justices today are drawn from a larger portion of American society than they were during most of the Court's history.

Recruitment to the Court is shaped by the power and prestige of the Court. Because of those characteristics, presidents have a wide range of prospective nominees to choose from. The Court's standing also makes justices reluctant to leave it.

Also consequential, especially in the current era, is the belief that there is a strong link between the Court's membership and its decisions. That belief leads presidents to accord heavy weight to the policy preferences of candidates when they choose a nominee. For the same reason, the Senate gives Court nominees greater scrutiny than it does nominees to any other positions. Interest groups regularly seek to influence president and Senate, and they sometimes engage in massive campaigns over nominees.

This belief is well founded. In later chapters I will examine the ways that the identities of the justices shape the positions that the Court takes on legal and policy issues.

NOTES

1. The four who were nominated and confirmed twice include three individuals elevated from associate justice to chief justice (Edward White, Harlan Stone, and William Rehnquist) and one (Charles Evans Hughes) who resigned from the Court and was later appointed chief justice. Douglas Ginsburg is counted as a nominee even though he withdrew from consideration in 1987, before he was officially nominated.
2. "Excerpts From Clinton's Remarks Announcing His Selection for Top Court," *New York Times,* May 14, 1994, 10.
3. Joan Biskupic, "Promises, Pressure in Court Search," *Washington Post,* March 21, 1993, A13.
4. This discussion is based in part on John Anthony Maltese, *The Selling of Supreme Court Nominees* (Baltimore: Johns Hopkins University Press, 1995); and Gregory A. Caldeira and John R. Wright, "Lobbying for Justice: The Rise of Organized Conflict in the Politics of Federal Judgeships," in *Contemplating Courts,* ed. Lee Epstein (Washington, D.C.: CQ Press, 1995), 44–71.
5. Michael Pertschuk and Wendy Schaetzel, *The People Rising: The Campaign against the Bork Nomination* (New York: Thunder's Mouth Press, 1989); Patrick B. McGuigan and Dawn M. Weyrich, *Ninth Justice: The Fight for Bork* (Washington, D.C.: Free Congress Research and Education Foundation, 1990); Mark Gitenstein, *Matters of Principle: An Insider's Account of America's Rejection of Robert Bork's Nomination to the Supreme Court* (New York: Simon & Schuster, 1992).
6. Richard Hodder-Williams, "The Strange Story of Judge Robert Bork and a Vacancy on the United States Supreme Court," *Political Studies* 36 (December 1988): 628.
7. Gregory A. Caldeira and John R. Wright, "Lobbying for Justice: Organized Interests and the Bork Nomination in the United States Senate" (Paper presented at the annual meeting of the American Political Science Association, Chicago, September 1992).

8. Maltese, *Selling of Supreme Court Nominees,* 90–91.
9. Caldeira and Wright, "Lobbying for Justice: The Rise of Organized Conflict," 59–69.
10. Henry J. Abraham, *Justices, Presidents, and Senators: A History of the U.S. Supreme Court Appointments from Washington to Clinton,* rev. ed. (Lanham, Md.: Rowman & Littlefield, 1999), 140.
11. Eleanor Randolph, "Husband Triggered Letters Supporting Ginsburg for Court," *Washington Post,* June 17, 1993, A25.
12. "No Litmus Test Needed Here," *New York Times,* September 25, 1992, A12. The case was *Sojourner T. v. Edwards* (5th Cir. 1992).
13. David A. Kaplan, "Campaigning for the High Court," *Newsweek,* July 2, 1990, 61.
14. Naftali Bendavid, "Just Saying No to Chance for Supreme Court," *Legal Times,* April 18, 1994, 1, 22, 23.
15. David Garrow, "Justice Souter Emerges," *New York Times Magazine,* September 25, 1994, 52.
16. Abraham, *Justices, Presidents, and Senators,* 200.
17. George Lardner Jr., "Rehnquist Got Call That Baker Missed for Nixon Court Nomination," *Washington Post,* December 18, 1998, A6, A7.
18. U.S. Congress, *Nomination of Judge Clarence Thomas to Be Associate Justice of the Supreme Court of the United States,* Committee on the Judiciary, U.S. Senate, 102d Congress, 1st session (Washington, D.C.: Government Printing Office, 1993), 222–223.
19. Mark Silverstein, "Bill Clinton's Excellent Adventure: Political Development and the Modern Confirmation Process," in *The Supreme Court in American Politics: New Institutionalist Interpretations,* ed. by Howard Gillman and Cornell Clayton (Lawrence: University Press of Kansas, 1999), 136.
20. David Alistair Yalof, *Pursuit of Justices: Presidential Politics and the Selection of Supreme Court Justices* (Chicago: University of Chicago Press, 1999), esp. 6–7.
21. David G. Savage, *Turning Right: The Making of the Rehnquist Supreme Court* (New York: Wiley, 1992), 180–181.
22. Henry F. Pringle, *The Life and Times of William Howard Taft* (New York: Farrar & Rinehart, 1939), 854.
23. This formulation is adapted from one presented in Sheldon Goldman, "Judicial Appointments and the Presidential Agenda," in *The Presidency in American Politics,* ed. Paul Brace, Christine B. Harrington, and Gary King (New York: New York University Press, 1989), 19–47.
24. "Ginsburg, Economy, Budget Encourage Upbeat Clinton," *Congressional Quarterly Weekly Report,* June 19, 1993, 1602; Nat Hentoff, "To Get a Supreme Court Seat," *Washington Post,* August 14, 1999, A17.
25. See George Stephanopoulos, *All Too Human: A Political Education* (Boston: Little, Brown, 1999), 168.
26. Fred Barnes, "Reagan's Full Court Press," *New Republic,* June 10, 1985, 18.
27. Savage, *Turning Right,* 169.
28. Data supporting this conclusion are presented in David W. Rohde and Harold J. Spaeth, *Supreme Court Decision Making* (San Francisco: W. H. Freeman, 1976), 107–109.
29. Alyssa Sepinwall, "The Making of a Presidential Myth" (letter), *Wall Street Journal,* September 4, 1990, A11; Tony Mauro, "Leak of Souter Keeps McGuigan in Plan," *Legal Times,* September 10, 1990, 11.
30. Savage, *Turning Right,* 177.

31. *Webster v. Reproductive Health Services* (1989); *Planned Parenthood v. Casey* (1992).

32. "Justice Anthony Kennedy: Surely Reagan's Biggest Disappointment," *Human Events,* May 31–June 7, 1996, 3.

33. *Office of the President v. Office of Independent Counsel* (1998); *Rubin v. United States* (1998).

34. J. Anthony Lukas, *Nightmare: The Underside of the Nixon Years* (New York: Viking Press, 1976), 569. (William Rehnquist, also a Nixon appointee, did not participate in the decision because of his prior position in the Justice Department during the Nixon administration.)

35. Robert Scigliano, *The Supreme Court and the Presidency* (New York: Free Press, 1971), 95, updated by the author.

36. Abraham, *Justices, Presidents, and Senators,* 268.

37. Tony Mauro, "The Court's Religious Conversion," *Legal Times,* July 1, 1996, 8.

38. Barbara A. Perry, *A "Representative" Supreme Court? The Impact of Race, Religion, and Gender on Appointments* (New York: Greenwood Press, 1991), 122.

39. See George L. Watson and John A. Stookey, *Shaping America: The Politics of Supreme Court Appointments* (New York: HarperCollins, 1995), chaps. 2–3; and Jeffrey A. Segal, Charles M. Cameron, and Albert D. Cover, "A Spatial Model of Roll Call Voting: Senators, Constituents, Presidents, and Interest Groups in Supreme Court Confirmations," *American Journal of Political Science* 36 (February 1992): 96–121.

40. These percentages are based on figures in Jeffrey Segal, "Senate Confirmation of Supreme Court Justices: Partisan and Institutional Politics," *Journal of Politics* 49 (November 1987): 1008, updated by the author. Percentages differ among sources, chiefly because of differences in assignment of partisan affiliation to some presidents.

41. Based on ibid., updated by the author. Nominations made during a president's fourth year but after the president's reelection are not included.

42. See Maltese, *Selling of Supreme Court Nominees.*

43. Calvin Trillin, "How to Become a Supreme Court Justice," *San Francisco Chronicle,* October 7, 1990, This World section, 5.

44. L. Marvin Overby, Beth M. Henschen, Michael H. Walsh, and Julie Strauss, "Courting Constituents? An Analysis of the Senate Confirmation Vote on Justice Clarence Thomas," *American Political Science Review* 86 (December 1992): 997–1003.

45. "Here Comes the Judge," *Newsweek,* February 2, 1970, 19. Quoted in John Massaro, *Supremely Political: The Role of Ideology and Presidential Management in Unsuccessful Supreme Court Nominations* (Albany: State University of New York Press, 1990), 105.

46. Warren B. Rudman, *Combat: Twelve Years in the U.S. Senate* (New York: Random House, 1996), 181.

47. Bendavid, "Just Saying No to Chance for Supreme Court," 23.

48. Kim Isaac Eisler, "Black Bio Lacks Shades of Gray," *Legal Times,* November 25, 1996, 78. See Roger K. Newman, *Hugo Black: A Biography* (New York: Pantheon, 1994), 233–268.

49. Jeff Franks, "Justice Thomas Still Healing From 'Whipping' on Hill," *Washington Post,* February 13, 1998, A9.

50. On Thomas's reaction to the confirmation battle, see John C. Danforth, *Resurrection: The Confirmation of Clarence Thomas* (New York: Viking Press,

1994); and Jeffrey Toobin, "The Burden of Clarence Thomas," *The New Yorker,* September 27, 1993, 38–51.

51. Lisa Tucker McElroy, *Meet My Grandmother: She's a Supreme Court Justice* (Brookfield, Conn.: Millbrook Press, 1999), 32.
52. For this observation and for much of the information on which the analysis in this section is based, I am indebted to John R. Schmidhauser, *Judges and Justices: The Federal Appellate Judiciary* (Boston: Little, Brown, 1979), 41–100.
53. Lee Epstein, Jeffrey A. Segal, Harold J. Spaeth, and Thomas G. Walker, *The Supreme Court Compendium,* 2d ed. (Washington, D.C.: Congressional Quarterly, 1996), 227–238. This source was also used to classify the justices sitting in 2000.
54. See William J. Daniels, "Justice Thurgood Marshall: The Race for Equal Justice," in *The Burger Court: Political and Judicial Profiles,* ed. Charles M. Lamb and Stephen C. Halpern (Urbana: University of Illinois Press, 1991), 235.
55. See Rudman, *Combat,* 152–194. The quotation is on p. 153.
56. Richard C. Reuben, "Justice Stevens: I Benefited from Pro Bono Work," *Los Angeles Daily Journal,* August 11, 1992, 11.
57. Laurence Bodine, "Sandra Day O'Connor," *American Bar Association Journal* 69 (October 1983): 1394.
58. This discussion of resignation and retirement draws on David N. Atkinson, *Leaving the Bench: Supreme Court Justices at the End* (Lawrence: University Press of Kansas, 1999).
59. From an interview with NBC News, quoted in Tony Mauro, "High Court Highs and Lows," *Legal Times,* December 18–25, 1995, 20.
60. "Departing Justice Blackmun Garners Clinton's Praise," *Congressional Quarterly Weekly Report,* April 9, 1994, 859.
61. Douglas Jehl, "Mitchell Viewed as Top Candidate for High Court," *New York Times,* April 7, 1994, A1.
62. Dennis J. Hutchinson, *The Man Who Once Was Whizzer White: A Portrait of Justice Byron R. White* (New York: Free Press, 1998), 434–436, 463–465.
63. Neil A. Lewis, "Marshall Urges Bush to Pick 'the Best,'" *New York Times,* June 29, 1991, 7.
64. Tony Mauro, "Court 'Name Game' Enters New Inning," *Legal Times,* November 9, 1992, 10.
65. Neil A. Lewis, "2 Years After His Bruising Hearing, Justice Thomas Still Shows the Hurt," *New York Times,* November 27, 1993, 6.
66. Juan Williams, "Marshall's Law," *Washington Post Magazine,* January 7, 1990, 29.
67. From an interview with Marshall conducted by Carl Rowan, quoted in "The Justice and the President," *Washington Post,* September 11, 1987, A23.
68. David Robertson, *Sly and Able: A Political Biography of James F. Byrnes* (New York: W. W. Norton, 1994), 301–319.
69. U.S. Constitution, art. 2, sec. 4.
70. John Ehrlichman, *Witness to Power: The Nixon Years* (New York: Simon & Schuster, 1982), 122.
71. Laura Kalman, *Abe Fortas: A Biography* (New Haven: Yale University Press, 1990), 359–376; Bruce Allen Murphy, *Fortas: The Rise and Ruin of a Supreme Court Justice* (New York: Morrow, 1988).

Chapter 3

The Cases

E very year, millions of people in the United States suffer injuries
in accidents; businesses make millions of contracts with individuals or other businesses; police officers stop millions of cars.

Supreme Court decisions have their origins in these incidents
and in similar kinds of incidents in other areas of life. But the
Court currently decides fewer than one hundred cases a year. Of
the events and interactions that might lead to legal cases, only a
very small percentage are filed in court. Of the cases that do get
filed in court, whether civil or criminal, the great majority are settled by the parties before they reach a judge or jury. Of the cases in
which trial courts do rule, few move up the court system to a point
at which one party could petition the Supreme Court for a hearing, and most parties who could file a petition choose not to do so.
And when someone does petition the Court to hear a case, the
odds are very heavily against the Court's granting the petition. A
case that the Court hears and decides is something like a one-in-a-
million event.

This chapter examines agenda setting in the Supreme Court, the
process by which an enormous number of potential Supreme Court
cases are narrowed to the few dozen that the Court fully considers
and decides each year. Several kinds of people and institutions play
a role in the process. Congress determines the Court's jurisdiction
and writes the statutes on which many cases are based. The Court
cannot reach out and decide issues that the justices find important;
rather, it depends on individual parties to file cases and bring them
through the legal system to the Court. Whether a case reaches the
Court and whether the Court finds it worthwhile to hear often de-

pend to a considerable degree on the assistance that lawyers provide to their clients. Interest groups frequently help people get their cases to the Court and try to convince the Court to accept cases. Finally, the Supreme Court itself has the ultimate power to determine whether it will hear a case. As I will discuss, this power helps to give the Court a degree of control over its agenda that is far greater than that of most other courts.

In the chapter's first section I examine how and why cases are brought to the Court. The next section considers the Court's selection of cases from those that come to it. The chapter's final section discusses growth in the Court's caseload and its impact on the Court.

Reaching the Court:
Litigants, Attorneys, and Interest Groups

In the 1998 term, just over 7,100 cases were filed in the Supreme Court.[1] In this section I consider how and why these cases came to the Court, examining the activities of litigants, their attorneys, and interest groups. I consider separately the litigation activities of the federal government, the most frequent and most distinctive participant in Supreme Court cases.

Litigants

Every case that comes to the Supreme Court has at least two formal parties, or litigants—at least one on each side. For a case to reach the Court, of course, one or more of the parties must have taken action to initiate the litigation and to move it upward through the court system.

As we would expect, litigants in the Supreme Court are a diverse lot.[2] Of those who petition the Court to hear cases, the great majority are individuals; most of these individuals are criminal defendants. Of the litigants (generally called respondents) that are brought to the Court by petitioners, governments and government agencies from the federal level to the local level constitute the largest category. Individuals are also respondents in many cases. Corporations frequently appear as petitioners or respondents. Other kinds of litigants, such as nonprofit groups and labor unions, also participate in many Court cases.

Cynthia Herdrich talks with reporters in February 2000 after the Supreme Court heard oral arguments in her case, *Pegram v. Herdrich*. She suffered complications after her health maintenance organization delayed in providing diagnostic tests. Of all the situations like hers that might involve people in the law, only a very small percentage lead to Supreme Court decisions.

The Motivations of Litigants. Perhaps the most important questions concerning litigants are why they become involved in court cases and why they carry them to the Supreme Court. The motives of litigants can be thought of as taking two general forms, resulting in two "ideal types" of Supreme Court litigation; there are also some cases in which litigants have mixed motives.

The first type of case may be called "ordinary" litigation because of its relative frequency. Ordinarily, parties bring cases to court or appeal adverse judgments because of a direct personal or organizational interest that they seek to advance. Plaintiffs file personal injury suits in court because they think they will probably obtain a monetary advantage from litigation. Similarly, litigants appeal court decisions because they believe that their potential gain from a successful appeal and the likelihood of success are sufficient to justify additional trouble and expense.

One example of ordinary litigation is *Lewis v. Brunswick Corporation* (1998).[3] Kathryn Lewis died in 1993 in a motorboat accident. Her parents believed that she might have survived if the boat's propeller had been equipped with a safety guard, so they sued the boat's manufacturer for damages in the Georgia courts. Brunswick Corporation, the manufacturer, argued that because federal law does not require safety guards on propellers, the Lewises had no basis for their lawsuit. Brunswick removed the case to federal court and won in both district court and the court of appeals, but the Supreme Court accepted the Lewises' petition for a hearing. After oral argument in the Court, Brunswick's lawyers feared an unfavorable ruling that would affect many other cases in which the company was involved. So they offered, and the Lewises accepted, a settlement that was estimated at about $700,000. The Lewises' acceptance of the settlement underlines the fact that they were not concerned with shaping legal policy. Rather, they pursued their lawsuit for their own individual reasons, including a desire to fix responsibility for what they saw as their daughter's avoidable death.

The second ideal type of case may be called "political" litigation. Here the motive of litigants is advancement not of their self-interest but of policies they favor. Most often, political litigation involves an effort to obtain a judicial decision that supports the litigant's policy goals. For instance, a group concerned with environmental protection might bring a suit to obtain a stringent interpretation of a statute that regulates air pollution. Someone who seeks to promote equality for disabled people may challenge a company practice on the ground that it violates protections of disabled workers stated in federal law.

Board of Regents v. Southworth (2000) is a good example of political litigation.[4] Scott Southworth and two other law students at the University of Wisconsin, conservative in their political views, objected to the use of part of their student fees to fund student organizations with which they strongly disagreed. Having failed to change the university's funding policies through other means, they contacted a sympathetic legal group that helped them to initiate a lawsuit challenging those policies on First Amendment grounds. Both a federal district court and the Seventh Circuit Court of Appeals ruled in favor of the students' challenge, and the Supreme Court accepted the university's petition to hear the case. Ultimately the Court ruled in favor of the university. Southworth and his fellow students had little to gain or lose directly from the Court's decision, and their interest from the start had been in the policies they were challenging.

Many cases have a large measure of both ordinary and political elements. For instance, individuals or companies may bring lawsuits to gain something directly, but along the way they may become concerned with the larger policy issues that arise from their cases. In cases brought by government agencies, ordinary and political elements may be difficult to separate: prosecutors file criminal cases to advance the specific mission of their agencies, but that mission is linked to the broader political goal of attacking crime.

The proportion of cases that can be classified as fully or partly political increases with each step upward in the judicial system, so political litigation is most common in the Supreme Court. This pattern is not accidental. Ordinary litigation is usually terminated at a relatively early stage because the parties find it more advantageous to settle their dispute or even to accept a defeat than to fight on. In contrast, political litigants often can obtain significant victories only by getting a case to the highest levels of the judicial system because a favorable verdict in a trial court may do little to advance their policy goals. And political litigation sometimes attracts the support of interest groups that help to shoulder the costs and other burdens of carrying a case through the judicial system.

Even so, the great majority of cases brought to the Supreme Court are best classified as ordinary litigation. A large proportion are criminal cases in which a convicted defendant who wants to get out of prison, or to stay out, seeks a hearing. Other cases come from business corporations that have a sufficient economic stake in the outcome to justify a petition to the Court. Still other cases concern a variety of individual grievances, big or small; in these cases the aggrieved party cannot resist going to the Supreme Court in one final effort to obtain redress.

Political litigation is more common in the cases that the Court agrees to hear, because those cases are more likely to concern the broad legal issues that interest the justices. Yet, as the *Lewis* case illustrates, ordinary litigation is by no means absent from the cases that the Court hears. Even in the biggest cases, the ones that attract the attention of large numbers of interest groups, the litigants are often motivated chiefly by their own direct interests.

Attorneys

Few Supreme Court decisions have had the impact of *Roe v. Wade,* the Court's 1973 decision requiring the legalization of abortion. Yet the lawyers who argued this case before the Court were not veterans of Supreme Court litigation. The Texas law prohibiting abortion was defended by Jay Floyd, an assistant state attorney general who had never argued a case before the Court. Sarah Weddington, the lawyer who challenged that law, was making her second argument in a contested case in *any* court; her first had been made in federal district court in the same case.[5]

National Collegiate Athletic Association v. Smith (1999) was a less consequential decision, one in which the Court rejected one argument for applying to the NCAA the federal prohibition of sex discrimination by schools. But the parties were represented by highly experienced attorneys. The attorney for the NCAA was John Roberts, who had argued more than two dozen cases in the Court for the federal government in the Office of the Solicitor General and later for private parties. His opponent was Carter Phillips, a former Supreme Court clerk and former member of the solicitor general's staff who had himself argued more than two dozen cases before the Court. The federal government also participated in oral argument, and its attorney, Edwin Kneedler, had substantially more experience than his two colleagues: over two decades of work in the Office of the Solicitor General he had presented more than sixty arguments to the Court.

These two cases illustrate the distinction between two kinds of lawyers who participate in Supreme Court litigation.[6] The first group consists of attorneys who come before the Court only on rare occasions; many of them come only once. Typically they become involved in a case at its inception, without any thought that it might go to the Supreme Court. When the Court does accept their case, they often resist entreaties to yield to a more experienced practitioner. Thus in *R.A.V. v. City of St. Paul* (1992) the lawyer who challenged a local "hate crime" law was the public defender who was on duty to represent juvenile defendants when the case first came to court. Later he rejected offers to have the case argued in the Supreme Court by a more experienced advocate. One reason was that "from a personal and professional standpoint I wanted the ultimate career challenge of arguing before the United States Supreme Court."[7]

The second group includes the lawyers who are frequent participants in cases at the Court. Most prominent are members of the solicitor general's staff; Supreme Court practice is their specialty. Some attorneys work for interest groups that frequently become involved in Supreme Court cases. Others have private practices in which Supreme Court advocacy is a major specialty. Many of these lawyers served in the solicitor general's office or as law clerks in the Court, gaining experience that attracted clients when they moved to the private sector.[8] The box on pages 88–89 presents profiles of three lawyers who are part of this "inner circle." Unlike other attorneys, those in this second group usually become involved in a case at the appellate level, often when it reaches the Supreme Court.

Of the two groups of lawyers who participate in Supreme Court cases, the first is by far the larger. As Table 3-1 shows, most attorneys who argued cases before the Court in its 1998 term were doing so for the first time. Of course, the lawyers who participate with some frequency are involved in a higher percentage of cases than their numbers suggest. Indeed, the federal government with its experienced advocates participates in a majority of the cases decided on the merits. As a result, the "inner circle" plays an important part in shaping the arguments that the Court hears in the cases it decides each term.[9]

Complaints about the quality of advocacy before the Court focus on inexperienced advocates. One example was the lawyer whom Chief Justice Rehnquist berated during one oral argument, saying that he had "made us gravely wonder . . . how well-prepared you are for this argument."[10] Indeed, Kevin McGuire found from his analysis of cases that the side whose lawyer had more experience before the Court enjoyed an advantage in winning a favorable decision.[11]

This advantage is not overwhelming. Inexperienced Supreme Court advocates sometimes do very good jobs. More important, the quality of lawyers' work is only one factor that helps to shape the Court's decisions, in part because the justices and their law clerks do their own close analysis of cases. It is hardly rare for a lawyer to secure a victory after arguing a case badly. One experienced advocate before the Court argued that "good lawyering can be a real plus" but "bad lawyering is not necessarily the death knell it is in other courts."[12]

In the legal system as a whole, a relationship exists between the wealth of an individual or institution and the quality of the legal ser-

Profiles of Three Lawyers Who Participate . . .

Carter G. Phillips. Phillips was a Supreme Court law clerk (for Chief Justice Warren Burger) and a member of the solicitor general's staff. He then joined the Washington office of Sidley & Austin, one of the largest law firms in the country. Phillips has represented many clients who are parties or amici in Supreme Court cases—primarily businesses, local governments, and professional groups (including, quite frequently, the American Medical Association). In the Court's 1998 term Phillips presented oral arguments in four cases, an unusual number for anyone who does not work in the solicitor general's office. Those cases involved interpretation of statutes in four distinct fields of law, involving subjects ranging from mineral rights to sex discrimination.

Laurence Gold. Gold has been a lawyer with the AFL-CIO since 1974, and he has served as its general counsel since 1984. The AFL-CIO and its member unions become involved in Supreme Court cases as parties or amici with some frequency, so Gold is also a regular participant in litigation before the Court. He has presented about three dozen oral arguments before the Court, and he helps to write briefs for parties or amici in many other cases. Because the interests of organized labor are broad, Gold participates in a wide

vices available to that party. To a considerable degree, this is true of the Supreme Court. The experienced Supreme Court advocates in private practice are most readily available to large corporations and other prosperous organizations that can afford their regular fees. Some "inner circle" lawyers charge clients between $300 and $400 an hour, and the total fee for handling a case in the Supreme Court can reach $500,000.[13]

On the other hand, parties without substantial resources often obtain excellent legal services. Many of the attorneys who regularly argue cases before the Court and who are most skilled in doing so represent segments of society that are relatively poor or powerless. And Supreme Court specialists in private practice sometimes take cases for clients who have limited resources. A poor person who lacks the support of an interest group may have to petition the Court for a hearing without a lawyer's help, and this certainly constitutes a disadvantage. If the Court accepts such a case, however, it will appoint an excellent attorney to represent the indigent litigant.

. . . *Frequently in Cases before the Supreme Court*

variety of cases. For instance, as attorney for state workers who wanted to sue their employer under a federal labor law, he argued in one of the Court's most important cases on federalism in recent years (*Alden v. Maine*, 1999).

Lawrence Wallace. No lawyer in the past century has appeared before the Supreme Court as often as Wallace, and no current lawyer is anywhere close. All his oral arguments—nearly 150—have been on behalf of one client, the federal government. Wallace joined the Office of the Solicitor General in 1968. Unlike most lawyers who work with the solicitor general, Wallace has made the office his career rather than moving into the private sector. On average, he argues before the Court four times each term, both in cases that involve the government as a party and those in which it participates as amicus curiae. The subject matter of his cases reflects the full range of issues in which the federal government is involved, and in the 1997 and 1998 terms his arguments dealt with such matters as antitrust, rules of evidence, and freedom of speech.

Sources: Kevin T. McGuire, *The Supreme Court Bar: Legal Elites in the Washington Community* (Charlottesville: University Press of Virginia, 1993); Supreme Court decisions; biographical sources.

Interest Groups

Leaders of interest groups are opportunists: they focus their efforts where they can make the most difference. For that reason, many groups give substantial attention to the Supreme Court. The Court's decisions establish important policies on issues as diverse as antitrust and obscenity. Groups that care about those issues understand that influencing the Court can be a way to advance their goals or to fight back against other groups with opposing goals. In the Supreme Court, as in the other branches of government, interest groups are major participants in the policy-making process.

The Forms of Group Activity. Groups that seek to influence congressional decisions try to make their case directly to members of Congress. In contrast, it is considered highly improper to lobby judges directly. Because of this norm, Supreme Court justices generally attempt to avoid contact with litigants and the groups that support them.

TABLE 3-1

Prior Oral Arguments (1988–1997 terms) by Lawyers Arguing One or More Cases in the 1998 Term

Prior oral arguments	Lawyers		
	Total	*Solicitor general's office*	*Other*
0	92	0	92
1	15	1	14
2	16	4	12
3	6	2	4
4	5	2	3
5–9	7	1	6
10–14	8	5	3
15–19	1	0	1
20–24	2	2	0
25–29	2	1	1
30 or more	3	3	0
	157	21	136

Note: Each lawyer who argued one or more cases in the 1998 term is counted only once. Because oral arguments before the 1988 term are not counted, the table underestimates slightly the overall level of experience.

But interest groups can attempt to influence the Court in other ways. As described in Chapter 2, some groups participate informally in the nomination and confirmation of justices. A group that helps to determine the Court's membership can affect its policies fundamentally.

Groups also can participate in litigation before the Court in two related ways. First, a group can help to get cases to the Court. Interest groups are allowed to bring suits in their own names only if they have legal standing because a case affects them directly. Organizations that exist primarily as interest groups generally lack standing. But other organizations that may be considered interest groups, especially businesses and governments, are often parties in Supreme Court cases.

A group that is not a party can "sponsor" a case on an issue that concerns it, providing attorneys' services and bearing the costs from the start. A very small proportion of all cases brought to the Court involve group sponsorship,[14] chiefly because of the considerable expense and practical difficulties of sponsorship. But cases that the Court actually hears, particularly cases of great significance, are far more likely to be sponsored. One study found that half of the most important decisions in the 1986–1991 terms were in cases sponsored by groups.[15] Alternatively, a group can become involved in cases that others have already initiated, helping to bear financial costs and supplying legal services and advice.

One example of group sponsorship was *Saenz v. Roe* (1999). Under a California statute, families who had resided in the state for less than a year were restricted to the level of welfare benefits that they would have received in the state they had left. The American Civil Liberties Union and the Legal Defense and Education Fund of the National Organization for Women challenged the law as soon as it went into effect, bringing a lawsuit on behalf of two anonymous welfare recipients "and all others similarly situated." A district judge issued an injunction against implementation of the statute, and the Ninth Circuit Court of Appeals affirmed that decision. The state brought the case to the Supreme Court, which granted a hearing and ruled that the statute was unconstitutional.

Second, by participating in oral argument or submitting briefs, a group can attempt to influence the Court's decisions whether to accept cases and how to decide those that are accepted. If a group effectively controls a case, its attorneys will submit a brief in support of (or in opposition to) the Supreme Court's acceptance of the case. If the case is accepted for decision on the merits, the group's attorneys will submit further briefs and participate in oral argument.

When a group does not control the case, it still may submit arguments to the Court in what are called *amicus curiae* (friend of the court) briefs. With the consent of the parties to a case or by permission of the Court, any person or organization may submit an amicus brief to supplement the arguments of the parties. (Legal representatives of government do not need to obtain permission.) Most of the time, the parties give their consent for the submission of amicus briefs. When the Court's consent is needed, it seldom is denied—only eight times in the 1994–98 terms. Amicus briefs can be submitted on the issue of whether a case should be heard or, after a case is accepted for hearing, directly on the merits of the case. An amicus can also participate in oral argument if allowed by the Court, and the federal government often does so. Occasionally, another amicus plays that role, as state governments did in two 1999 cases.[16]

Amicus briefs are by far the most common means by which groups other than parties participate in litigation before the Court. As might be expected, amicus briefs are especially common in cases that the Court has accepted for consideration on the merits. In the 1998 term, such briefs were submitted in more than 90 percent of the cases decided on the merits, and about half the cases had at least four briefs.[17] And, because groups or individuals can join in submitting briefs, the number of participants is considerably larger than the number of briefs. Some cases attract a large and diverse array of groups with an interest in the Court's decision. The box on page 93 lists some of the interest groups that submitted amicus briefs in two 1999 cases.

The popularity of amicus briefs reflects the relative ease of this route to the Court. An amicus brief is not inexpensive, typically costing several thousand dollars and often tens of thousands to prepare, but this is considerably cheaper than sponsoring a case. Similarly, the logistics of submitting an amicus brief are relatively simple. And, because of the widespread perception that amicus briefs influence the Court, groups consider the effort of filing or joining in a brief to be worthwhile. Amicus participation is useful in another way as well, as one group leader explained: "A group has to be able to show its members that their efforts are paying off, and filing amicus briefs is the easiest way to do that."[18]

Groups also lobby the Court outside the litigation process. In 1997 the attorney generals of twenty-four states issued a statement asking the Court to reverse its ruling in *Buckley v. Valeo* (1976), which had greatly restricted government power to regulate the financing of political campaigns. Groups on both sides of the abortion controversy conduct marches and demonstrations while the Court considers abortion cases, in part to put indirect pressure on the justices.

Finally, interest groups seek to influence media coverage of the Court's decisions.[19] After decisions are handed down, group representatives give interviews in which they try to put those decisions in the most favorable light. When the Supreme Court reporter for the *New York Times* returned to her office after the Court's major abor-

Selected Groups Participating in Amicus Curiae Briefs Submitted to the Supreme Court in Two Recent Cases

Department of Commerce v. U.S. House of Representatives (1999)

Issue: Is it illegal for the Census Bureau to use statistical sampling to calculate population for apportionment of House seats among the states?

Participating Groups

Commonwealth of Pennsylvania
National Urban League
National Republican Legislators Association
District of Columbia State Democratic Committee
American Conservative Union
Citizens for Judicial Reform
Americans for Tax Reform
English First Foundation
Small Business Survival Committee
National Council of La Raza
NAACP Legal Defense and Educational Fund
American Civil Liberties Union
NOW Legal Defense and Education Fund
Japanese American Citizens League

City of Monterey v. Del Monte Dunes (1999)

Issue: Was it proper for a jury to decide whether property had been effectively taken by a city through its regulation of the use of the property?

Participating Groups

United States
State of New Jersey
City and County of San Francisco
National League of Cities
Municipal Art Society of New York
Sierra Club
National Wildlife Federation
Chesapeake Bay Foundation
National Association of Home Builders
California Farm Bureau Federation
National Cattlemen's Beef Association
Defenders of Property Rights
Pacific Legal Foundation
International Council of Shopping Centers

tion decision in 1992, "there were two huge stacks of faxes on the floor by my desk, one pile generated by the right-to-life side and the other by the pro-choice side."[20] Group leaders understand that the impact of the Court's decisions depends in part on how those decisions are reported.

The Array of Groups in the Court. Interest group participation in Supreme Court litigation has increased dramatically in the past few decades. This change has several sources. Throughout government, the number of active interest groups and the level of their activity have increased considerably. The apparent success of some groups in shaping the Supreme Court's policies has encouraged attempts by other groups to exert a similar impact. And the Court's increased prominence as a policy maker reminds groups of its potential importance to their goals.

With this growth, hundreds of interest groups participate in Supreme Court cases in some way. Among them are nearly all the groups that are most active in Congress and the executive branch.

It is hardly surprising that so many groups focus their attention on the Court. In their efforts to influence government, interest groups go to the institutions that can affect them in significant ways. The Supreme Court decides issues that range from labor-management relations to freedom of expression to the powers of state governments. Thus it makes good sense for a wide range of interest groups to involve themselves in the work of the Court.

The groups that come to the Court can be placed in four broad categories. The largest category includes economic groups: individual businesses, trade associations, professional associations, labor unions, and farm groups. Economic groups predominate in the Court, as they do in the other branches, because they are numerous and relatively well funded. And the Court does a great deal that they care about. In particular, the business community is affected by most of the Court's decisions. Nearly all the subjects that the justices address—even those that seem unrelated to businesses—are of concern to them in some way. Cases on state-federal relations often arise from state taxation or regulation of businesses. Civil rights cases frequently concern the enforcement of antidiscrimination laws against employers.

In the second category are groups that represent segments of the population defined by something other than economics. The most prominent of these groups is the NAACP Legal Defense and Educational Fund (sometimes called the NAACP Legal Defense Fund or simply the Fund).[21] The Fund was created by the NAACP as a separate litigating group in 1939, and it is now fully independent of the parent organization. It initiates litigation through its staff of about thirty lawyers, most of whom are in New York City, and a large network of cooperating attorneys throughout the United States. The Fund initially focused its efforts on securing voting rights for black citizens and desegregating schools in the South. It has also worked to challenge capital punishment and to obtain effective enforcement of federal laws against employment discrimination. The Fund's successes in the Court have encouraged the development of similar organizations, such as the Mexican-American Legal Defense and Education Fund and several litigation groups representing women.

The groups in the third category represent broad ideological positions rather than the interests of a specific segment of society; an example is the American Civil Liberties Union.[22] Established in 1920 as an organization for the protection of civil liberties, the ACLU has always relied heavily on litigation as a means to that end. Although it has traditionally emphasized freedom of expression, the ACLU involves itself in virtually every area of civil liberties law. It acts primarily on complaints of civil liberties violations that people bring to local ACLU affiliates, which provide volunteer attorneys for cases they perceive as meritorious. If cases reach the Supreme Court, they are often handled by the national ACLU office. In the past few decades, the ACLU created special projects that have initiated concerted litigation campaigns in specific areas of concern, such as women's rights, capital punishment, prisons, and national security. The ACLU also submits amicus briefs in cases that it does not sponsor. Its amicus briefs in the Court's 1999 term dealt with such issues as government aid to religious schools, police "stop and frisk" searches of suspects, and limits on monetary contributions to political candidates.

The ACLU is one of many groups that work to achieve liberal policy goals. Two other such groups are the Sierra Club, which has a litigation arm devoted to environmental protection, and the Planned Parenthood Federation of America, for which abortion rights are a primary concern. In the 1960s Ralph Nader pioneered public interest law firms, which were established to handle cases that they perceived as serving the public interest from a liberal perspective. These firms have instituted litigation on such issues as consumer rights, civil liberties, and the environment. One of the firms, the Public Citizen Research Group, now gives some emphasis to litigation enforcing the separation of powers among the branches of the federal government.

Groups that favor conservative positions on legal issues were slower to involve themselves in litigation, but a number of such groups are now active.[23] Americans for Effective Law Enforcement supports narrow interpretations of the procedural rights of criminal defendants. Americans United for Life litigates on abortion and other issues. There are several conservative public interest law firms, such as the Washington Legal Foundation (WLF) and the Mountain States Legal Foundation, that are modeled in part after their liberal counterparts. The WLF helped to bring the challenge to *Miranda* that the Court rejected in *Dickerson v. United States* (2000).

There also are several litigating groups that represent conservative religious interests.[24] The first of these groups to participate actively in the Supreme Court was the American Center for Law and Justice (ACLJ), established by religious leader Pat Robertson in 1991.[25] The similarity between "ACLJ" and "ACLU" is no accident; the ACLJ was intended as a counterpart to the ACLU in supporting conservative Christian values. The organization gives some emphasis to assisting people who want to participate in religious activities in schools and other places. Chief counsel Jay Alan Sekulow has argued several cases in the Supreme Court.

Fourth, governments regularly appear as interest groups in the Court. The federal government is a special case and is examined later in this chapter. State and local governments often come to the Court as litigants, and they file many amicus briefs. It has become standard practice for several states, sometimes a majority, to join in a brief in order to emphasize their strong shared interest in a case.

Group Strategies and Tactics. In *Brown v. Board of Education* (1954), the Supreme Court ruled that public school students cannot be segregated by race. *Brown* and the four cases that accompanied it were sponsored by the NAACP Legal Defense Fund, and the Fund's victory was the culmination of a long campaign to achieve desegregation. Under the leadership of Thurgood Marshall, the Fund had begun with challenges to blatant discrimination against black students in graduate and professional schools; its successes in those cases helped move the Court toward the far more sweeping decision in *Brown*.

That litigation campaign was a landmark in American legal history. It has been the subject of a number of books and television movies. (In one movie Sidney Poitier played Marshall, who said that "Sidney was better than I was in the court, but he got paid more than I did."[26]) But the path to *Brown* was not as smooth as it appears in retrospect. The Fund's leaders struggled to garner the funds required to carry out their litigation campaign, and they had to worry about coordinating cases that they had not initiated. More important, the Fund's success in achieving school desegregation resulted not only from the skills and dedication of its lawyers but from favorable circumstances as well. When conditions are less favorable, interest groups—including the Fund itself—are likely to be less successful.

Only a minority of groups map out long-term litigation campaigns, but they all face strategic and tactical decisions.[27] At the strategic level, they must decide how much of their energy and resources to devote to litigation rather than other forms of political action, though groups that are set up specifically to litigate do not face this choice. They must also decide what kinds of issues to emphasize in their litigation work and how to coordinate their efforts with other groups that have similar interests. Groups concerned with racial discrimination have worked together a good deal. At the tactical level, a group's lawyers consider whether initiating a specific case or supporting a litigant in an existing case would serve their goals. They sometimes have a choice among different regions in which to initiate cases or between federal and state courts. And, like other lawyers, they have to choose which arguments to make in the cases in which they participate.

Many considerations affect these decisions, including the views of group members and the availability of resources. The great expense of litigation means that even relatively wealthy groups have to set priorities. Perhaps the most fundamental consideration is groups' perceptions of the courts in general and the Supreme Court in particular. It is not surprising that conservative groups have become more active in Supreme Court litigation since the 1970s as the Court has become more receptive to conservative arguments. Similarly, choices of specific cases and arguments reflect judgments about potential responses from the justices.

The Significance of Interest Groups. Interest groups can affect what the Supreme Court does in several ways; here, I focus on their effect in determining whether cases get to the Court. In this respect, cases may be placed in three categories.

The largest category includes the cases that come to the Court without any participation by interest groups. For the most part, these cases constitute what I have called ordinary litigation. The issues in these cases are too narrow to interest any group. They reach the Court because the parties and attorneys have sufficient motivation of their own to seek a Supreme Court hearing and sufficient resources to finance the litigation. These conditions exist in much of the litigation involving businesses, which often have substantial resources and a large financial stake in a case. They also exist when indigent criminal defendants face significant prison terms and do not have to pay lawyers' fees or most of the other expenses involved in getting a case to the Court.

The second category consists of cases that would have reached the Court without any interest group involvement, but in which one or more groups are involved in some way. An interest group may assist one of the parties by providing attorneys' services or financing to ensure that the case does reach the Supreme Court and to gain some control over the position that the party takes. Far more often, a group will submit an amicus brief supporting the petition for a hearing by the Court.

The third category includes cases that would not reach the Court without sponsorship by interest groups. There are many important legal questions in civil liberties that no individual litigant has the capability or sufficient incentive to take to the Supreme Court. For instance, one parent or even several parents could hardly arrange and finance a school desegregation suit on their own. And certainly challenges to practices that work against low-income people would be difficult to bring without group assistance. Only when the federal government set up the Legal Services Program in 1965 to represent indigent people in civil cases did the Court begin to hear substantial numbers of cases concerning the rights of the poor.[28]

It should be emphasized that only a small proportion of cases brought to the Court fall in this third category, because group sponsorship of cases in the Court is relatively rare. But groups are most likely to sponsor cases that have the potential to be heard by the Court and to produce major legal rulings. Indeed, much of the

Court's expansion of legal protections for civil liberties during the twentieth century was made possible by interest group action.[29] Of course, groups can do more than get cases to the Court; they can help to determine whether those cases are heard and how the Court rules. That influence is discussed later in this chapter and in Chapter 4.

The Federal Government as Litigant

Of all the litigants in the Supreme Court, the federal government appears most frequently. In the 1998 term it was a party in about one-third of the cases brought to the Court for consideration and in 39 of the 90 cases actually argued before the Court.[30] The federal government is also the most important interest group in the Court. In its own cases, the government takes a position on such major issues as the rights of criminal defendants and the scope of environmental protection. It frequently participates as an amicus in other cases, as it did in 37 cases that were argued in the 1998 term. Altogether, then, the government played an official role in 84 percent of the cases in which the Court heard arguments during that term.

Thus the group of lawyers that has the greatest impact on the Court is the set who work for the Office of the Solicitor General in the Justice Department. Fewer than two dozen lawyers work in that office, but they are primarily responsible for representing the federal government in the Supreme Court. They decide whether to bring federal government cases to the Court; only a few federal agencies can take cases to the Court without the solicitor general's approval. Lawyers in the solicitor general's office also do the bulk of the legal work in Supreme Court cases in which the federal government participates, including petitions for hearings, the writing of briefs, and oral arguments.

The solicitor general's office occupies a complicated position.[31] On the one hand, it represents the president and the executive branch, functioning as their law firm in individual cases. On the other hand, it has developed a strong relationship with the Supreme Court, a relationship that ultimately benefits the office and thus its clients as well. One central task of the solicitor general is to balance these two roles.

The solicitor general's unique relationship with the Court rests on the fact that it represents a unique litigant. The federal government participates in far more Supreme Court cases than any other party, thus creating a bond of familiarity between its lawyers and the justices. Partly for this reason, and partly because the federal government has a special status, the solicitor general and the Court can accommodate each other in important ways.

The solicitor general helps the Court by exercising self-restraint in requesting that the Court hear cases. In the cases acted on by the Court in the 1998 term, the federal government filed 21 petitions for certiorari while its opponents filed 2,682. Although the government has fewer losses in the courts of appeals than do its opponents, the primary reason for this difference is the solicitor general's willingness to forgo possible petitions for certiorari.

The solicitor general's office also tries to maintain credibility by taking a less partisan stance than other litigants. This stance is symbolized by the office's occasional practice of "confessing error" to the Supreme Court—stating in a brief that a lower court decision in favor of the federal government involved some kind of error. This relative evenhandedness and the office's expertise help to account for the Court's practice of "inviting" (in practice, ordering) the solicitor general to file amicus briefs in many cases that do not affect the federal government directly. In this role, the solicitor general is acting as the justices' "fifth clerk."[32]

The office's special relationship with the Court leads to a degree of independence from the president and attorney general. The solicitor general can argue that positions urged on the office by its formal superiors would weaken its credibility with the Court and thus its effectiveness in representing the executive branch. But the solicitor general usually is someone who shares the president's general point of view about legal policy, the office operates in a general climate created by the president and attorney general, and these superiors occasionally intervene in specific cases. These linkages between the solicitor general's office and the administration have strengthened in the last two decades, beginning with the Reagan presidency.

These linkages are reflected in the overall pattern of positions that the office takes in litigation. In cases in which the solicitor general has a choice about whether to participate and which side to take, the government's positions tend to reflect the president's policy positions and priorities.[33] Even where the solicitor general sees policy matters differently from the president, the president's perspective will have an effect. This was evident in the Clinton administration, in which solicitors general with liberal points of view took into account Clinton's less liberal views on most civil liberties issues and his desire to avoid being identified with unpopular positions. Paul Bender, the principal deputy to the solicitor general during the first Clinton term, said that the administration's

message was always "Don't get us in trouble.". . .Under the Republicans, they had their agenda items . . . where you had to toe the line. But with Clinton there was an even broader concern about politics, and on every issue you had to be afraid of looking too liberal.[34]

Direct intervention by the administration in the solicitor general's decisions is uncommon but not rare, occurring in perhaps 5 percent of all cases.[35] In the Clinton administration, one example of specific intervention occurred in a case involving interpretation of a federal statute prohibiting receipt and possession of child pornography. After solicitor general Drew Days initially argued for a narrow interpretation of the statute, thereby arousing heavy congressional criticism, attorney general Janet Reno personally signed a brief that argued for a broad interpretation of the statute.[36] Another case, *Romer v. Evans* (1996), involved the constitutionality of a Colorado voter initiative that prohibited laws against discrimination on the basis of sexual orientation. The administration chose to avoid a contentious issue by taking no position in the case, despite the contrary view of Solicitor General Walter Dellinger. "Nothing," he said, "makes me unhappier than the fact that we didn't file in Romer."[37]

In the past two decades the solicitor general's office has attracted considerable attention from members of Congress and others who disapprove of its positions. The lawyers who served as solicitor general in the Reagan and Bush administrations were criticized by liberals who charged them with pressing a conservative agenda on the Supreme Court and by conservatives for insufficient zeal in advocating that agenda. The Republican-controlled Senate Judiciary Committee called Days to testify in 1995 and questioned him sharply about several cases.[38] Two years later, while a Clinton nominee for a civil rights position awaited action by the Judiciary Committee, its chair, Orrin Hatch of Utah, suggested that the chances of getting the nomination through the committee would improve if the administration promised not to file an amicus brief in an affirmative action case that might come to the Supreme Court. Clinton refused to make that promise, and the nomination died.[39]

Although the Department of Justice is the primary legal representative of the federal government, Congress occasionally participates as a body in Supreme Court litigation when members believe that the solicitor general is not representing congressional interests adequately. More often, members of Congress submit amicus briefs to the Court as individuals or sets of individuals, seeking to influence the Court and—in some instances—to appeal to constituents by taking popular positions. Such submissions have become common only in recent years. During the years from 1900 through 1971, members of Congress submitted amicus briefs in only fourteen cases. In the eight terms from 1990 through 1997, they did so in forty-three cases.[40]

Deciding What to Hear: The Court's Role

It is routine practice for prosecutors to offer leniency to criminal defendants in exchange for their testimony against other defendants. But in 1998 a three-judge panel of the federal Tenth Circuit Court of Appeals in Denver ruled that this practice violates a federal statute that prohibits giving anything of value in exchange for testimony as a witness. The ruling threw panic into federal prosecutors and Justice Department officials. The panic abated when the full court of appeals reversed the panel's decision, but people throughout the criminal justice system waited eagerly to see whether the Supreme Court would side with the panel or with the full court. The Court did neither. Instead, it simply refused to hear *Singleton v. United States* (1999).

The Court treats most cases in the same way: it refuses to hear them. In its 1998 term, the Court granted certiorari and reached a decision on the merits in fewer than one in eighty cases brought to it.[41] This ratio is a reminder that the Court has enormous power to set its own agenda.

Newspapers and television often report a denial of certiorari as if the Supreme Court had affirmed the lower court decision.[42] In part for this reason, denials of certiorari sometimes have a substantial impact. After the Court in 1994 refused to hear a constitutional challenge to one city's curfew law for juveniles, "hundreds of American cities rushed to copy" that law.[43] The Court is more likely to

Larry Cockell, the Secret Service agent in charge of President Clinton's security detail, with Clinton in 1997. The question of whether Cockell and other agents could be required to testify about the president was important to Clinton and to the presidency, but the Supreme Court refused to hear a case on this question, *Rubin v. United States*, in 1998.

deny certiorari when most justices agree with the lower court decision in a case, so a denial may provide a clue to the justices' views. In all likelihood, the denial of certiorari in *Singleton* reflected the Court's collective agreement with the decision of the full Tenth Circuit. But the refusal to hear a case has no legal meaning in itself beyond its allowing the lower court decision in that case to become final.

Options

In screening petitions for hearings, the Court does not simply either accept or reject individual cases. Rather, its choices are broader and more complicated. To begin with, the Court does not consider petitions in isolation from one another; often, cases are linked. The justices may accept a case to clarify or expand on an earlier decision in the same policy area. They may accept several cases that raise the same issue in order to address that issue more fully than a single case would allow them to do. They may even reject a case because they are looking for a more suitable case on the same issue.

When the Court does accept a case, the justices can choose which issues they will consider. The Court often limits its grant of certiorari to one issue raised by the petitioner, and it sometimes asks the parties to address an issue that neither had raised. No matter what issues the parties address, the Court retains the freedom to determine the issues it actually resolves in its opinion. In a 1998 case, Justice Scalia's majority opinion and Justice Stevens's dissent disagreed about which issues in the case were appropriate for the Court to decide.[44] Regardless of who was right in this instance, in practice the Court can decide the issues it wants to decide. One striking example is *Mapp v. Ohio* (1961), in which the Court turned an obscenity case into a landmark decision on police searches and seizures.

When the Court accepts a case, it also determines the kind of consideration it will give that case. It may give the case full consideration, which means that the Court receives a new set of briefs on the merits from the parties and holds oral argument, then issues a decision on the merits with a full opinion explaining the decision. Alternatively, it may give the case summary consideration. This usually means that the case is decided without new briefs or oral argument; the Court relies on the materials that the parties already submitted. A large minority of the cases that the Court accepts receive summary consideration.

In most summary decisions, the Supreme Court issues a "GVR" order—Granting certiorari, Vacating the lower court decision, and Remanding the case to that court for reconsideration. Most of these orders are issued because some event since the lower court decision, usually a Supreme Court decision, is relevant to the case.

In other summary decisions, the Court actually reaches a decision on the merits and issues an opinion of several paragraphs or even several pages. This opinion typically is labeled *per curiam* (by the Court) rather than being signed by a justice, but it has the same legal force as a signed opinion.[45] When the Court takes this kind of action, justices sometimes complain that it should not have decided the case without getting full information from the parties through briefs that directly address the merits of the case and through oral argument. In *Maryland v. Dyson* (1999), the Court decided a case arising from an automobile search on the basis of the petition for certiorari and the accompanying brief. Dissenting, Justice Breyer argued that the Court should not have reached a decision on the merits without having at least a brief from the other side.

Even after accepting a case, the Court can avoid a decision by issuing what is called a "DIG" (for "Dismissed as Improvidently Granted"). A DIG occurs a few times each term, when the parties' briefs on the merits or the oral arguments suggest to the justices that the case is inappropriate for a decision. Occasionally it is the parties who avoid a decision by settling the case. One prominent example was a 1997 affirmative action case in which a major decision was expected. The case ended before the scheduled oral argument when civil rights groups that feared an unfavorable decision paid for a monetary settlement with the teacher who was challenging her school district's policy. The teacher's lawyer thereby lost his chance to argue before the Court, after he had spent $2,000 for a custom-made suit for the occasion.[46]

Screening Procedures

The Court uses a series of complex procedures to screen petitions for hearing, and these procedures are made more complex by two distinctions between types of cases. The first is between the certiorari cases, over which the Court's jurisdiction is discretionary, and the very small number of cases that the Court is required to decide, labeled appeals. Before 1988, the number of appeals was greater, and the Court used dismissals or summary affirmances to avoid granting full hearings in most of these cases. In 1988 Congress limited appeals to those cases decided by three-judge federal district courts. Few appeals now reach the Court—on average, about a dozen a term.[47] But the Court retains, and uses, the option of deciding them without holding oral argument or issuing full opinions. The second distinction, between paid cases and paupers' cases, requires more extensive discussion.

Paid Cases and Paupers' Cases. Less than one-third of the requests for hearings that arrive at the Supreme Court are "paid" cases, for which the Court's filing fee of $300 has been paid and all required copies of materials have been provided. The remaining cases are brought *in forma pauperis* by indigent people for whom the fee and the requirement of multiple copies are waived. The great majority of the "paupers' cases" are brought by prisoners in federal and state institutions. (A person responding to a petition may also be given pauper status.)

Criminal defendants who have had counsel provided to them in the lower federal courts because of their low incomes are automatically entitled to bring paupers' cases in the Supreme Court. Other litigants must submit an affidavit supporting their motion for leave to file as paupers. The Court has never developed precise rules specifying when a litigant can claim pauper status. But in recent years, it has denied a number of litigants the right to proceed as paupers in particular cases on the grounds that they were not truly paupers or that their petitions were frivolous or malicious. The Court has also gone further, issuing a general denial of pauper status to several litigants who had filed large numbers of paupers' petitions. In 1999, for instance, it ordered its Clerk of the Court not to accept any further paupers' petitions from a litigant who had filed fifty-seven petitions with the Court. According to the Court, this order would "allow this Court to devote its limited resources to the claims of petitioners who have not abused our processes."[48]

A very small proportion of paupers' petitions are accepted for full decisions on the merits—less than one-fifth of 1 percent in the 1998 term, compared with 3.5 percent of the paid cases in the same term.[49] The lack of inherent merit in many of these cases and the fact that many litigants have to draft petitions without a lawyer's assistance help to account for the low acceptance rate. It may also be that the Court looks less closely at paupers' petitions than at the paid petitions. One former law clerk said that after clerks have served for several months, "they flip through" the paupers' petitions "pretty fast. I wouldn't want my case to be in that pile."[50] But because there are so many paupers' petitions, even the small proportion that are accepted add up to a significant number of cases— an average of about a dozen a term in recent years—and they constitute an important part of the Court's work on issues of criminal procedure.

Prescreening: The Discuss List. Under its "rule of four," the Court grants a writ of certiorari and hears a case on the merits if at least four justices vote at conference to grant the writ. But petitions for hearings are considered and voted on at conference only if they are put on the Court's "discuss list."[51] The chief justice creates the discuss list, but other justices can and do add cases to it. Cases left off the discuss list are denied hearings automatically. This is the fate of most cases; Justice Ginsburg has estimated that, typically, only 10 to 13 percent of the petitions for hearing get on the discuss list.[52]

The discuss-list procedure serves to limit the Court's workload. But this procedure also reflects a belief that most petitions do not require collective consideration, because they are such poor candidates for acceptance. A great many petitions raise only very narrow issues, and many others make very weak legal claims, so it is easy to reject them.

Action in Conference. In conference, the chief justice or the justice who added a case to the discuss list opens discussion of the case. In order of seniority, from senior to junior, the justices then speak and usually announce their votes. If the discussion does not make the justices' positions clear, a formal vote is taken, also in order of seniority. Despite the prescreening of cases, a substantial majority of the petitions considered in conference are denied.

Most cases receive very brief discussion in conference, and ordinarily the justices simply state the positions they reached individually before the conference. In this sense, the conference usually serves only as a place for individual votes to be added together.

But some cases are given more extensive consideration, which sometimes extends beyond the initial discussion. In conference, any justice can ask that a case be "relisted" for a later conference. This might be done to obtain additional information, such as the full record of the case in the lower courts. A justice also might ask for relisting to circulate an opinion dissenting from the Court's tentative denial of a hearing and thereby try to change the Court's decision. As Justice Stevens once noted, such an opinion "sometimes persuades other Justices to change their votes and a petition is granted that would otherwise have been denied."[53]

When it accepts a case, the Court also decides whether to allow oral argument or to decide the case summarily on the basis of the available written materials. Four votes are required for oral argument. A case that is not given oral argument may be granted a hearing and decided on the merits at the same conference, so that the two stages of decision in effect become one.

The Court almost never issues an opinion to explain its acceptance or rejection of a case, though it offered brief explanations of its denials of certiorari in two related cases in 2000.[54] Nor are individual votes announced systematically. But justices occasionally record their dissents from denials of petitions for hearings, and these votes are usually accompanied by opinions. During the 1998 term there were ten cases in which one or more justices dissented. Justices who voted not to grant a hearing sometimes write an opinion to comment on the Court's decision. Twice during the 1998 term, Justice Stevens wrote such opinions—joined by Justice Souter and Justice Ginsburg—to emphasize that the Court was not affirming the lower court's decision on the merits of the case.[55]

The Clerks' Role. A key function of the justices' law clerks is to help in scrutinizing requests for hearings.[56] In 2000 eight of the nine justices—all but John Paul Stevens—were part of the "certiorari pool." Petitions and other materials on each case are divided among the clerks for these eight justices. The clerk who has responsibility for a case writes a memorandum of two to twenty-five pages. The memo typically includes a summary of the relevant facts and the parties' contentions and a recommendation for the Court's action on the petition. Some justices then have their own clerks examine and react to the memo for each case, thus providing a second point of view on the case.

Because of the press of time, the justices rely heavily on law clerks' analyses of cases. William Brennan, who retired in 1990, was the last of the justices who regularly read the petitions themselves. Some justices and other observers have expressed particular concern about the justices' collective reliance on the pool memo.[57] One recent law clerk has argued that this reliance is less problematic than it might appear: clerks typically write their pool memos with care, and justices frequently vote contrary to the memo's recommendation. "Still," he concluded, "any system that depends to a considerable degree on the views of a single novice lawyer is fairly subject to criticism."[58] Justice Stevens lessens this problem by staying out of the pool. But he delegates a good deal of responsibility to his own clerks, who write memoranda or refer petitions directly to him in only a minority of cases.

Substantial though it is, the impact of the law clerks on certiorari decisions should not be exaggerated. For one thing, the large majority of petitions would elicit the same reaction from any justice or clerk: an obvious denial. And justices involve themselves most fully in the screening process at the point where individual judgments make the most difference—in selecting cases to hear from those on the discuss list.

The Criteria for Decision

Supreme Court justices are free to choose cases to hear on any basis they wish, and they need not justify or explain their choices. When the Court decides a case, its opinion often includes a rationale for accepting the case, but the rationale is usually brief and not very illuminating. The Court seldom explains denials of petitions for hearing.

The Court's Rule 10 does provide general guidance by specifying some of the conditions under which the Court will hear a case. The rule emphasizes the Court's role in ensuring the certainty and consistency of the law. The criteria for accepting a case cited in Rule 10 include the existence of important legal issues that the Court has not yet decided, conflict among courts of appeals on a legal question, conflict between a lower court's decision and the Supreme Court's prior decisions, and departure "from the accepted and usual course of judicial proceedings" in the courts below.

These criteria make sense, but they suggest a conception of the Court's function and of its members' interests that is unrealistically narrow. Thus, it is necessary to take a broader view of the criteria for decision. The Court's pattern of screening decisions and evidence from other sources suggest the significance of several considerations.

The Technical Criteria. The Supreme Court will reject a petition for hearing if it fails to meet certain technical requirements. Some of these requirements are specific to the Court. For instance, paid petitions must comply with the Court's Rule 33, which establishes requirements on such matters as the size of print and margins used, type of paper, format and color of cover, and maximum length. In *Calderon v. Thompson* (1997), a litigant had to obtain special permission from the justices "to proceed with 8½- by-11-inch paper." These requirements are relaxed for the paupers' petitions, but even paupers' petitions may be rejected if their deviation from the rules is extreme.

The Court also imposes the same kinds of technical requirements for the hearing of cases that other courts apply. One specific requirement is that petitions for hearing be filed within ninety days of the entry of judgment in the lower court, unless the time has been extended in advance. In 1996 the Court refused to accept two certiorari petitions because they were one day late, apparently because the lawyers involved failed to take into account the extra day in February during a leap year.[59]

More fundamental are the requirements of jurisdiction and standing. If the Court receives a case that clearly falls outside its jurisdiction, it cannot accept that case for hearing. For instance, the Court could not hear a state case in which the petitioner raised no issues of federal law in state court.

The rule of standing holds that a court may not hear a case unless the party bringing the case is properly before it. The most important element of standing is the requirement that a party in a case have a real and direct legal stake in its outcome. This requirement precludes hypothetical cases, cases brought on behalf of another person, "friendly suits" between parties that are not really adversaries, and cases that have become "moot" (in effect, hypothetical) because the parties can no longer be affected by the outcome. In 2000 the Court dismissed a Florida prisoner's challenge to electrocution as a means of execution after the state enacted a new statute under which death sentences would be carried out by lethal injection unless the prisoner chose electrocution.[60] And the Court must dismiss a case if the parties have reached a settlement, as it did in 2000 in two important cases involving the federal statute that prohibits discrimination against disabled people.[61]

The technical requirements sometimes are easy to apply. But their application can be more ambiguous, arousing disagreement among the justices. Those disagreements often reflect views about the underlying merits of cases. For example, the justices who are most likely to grant standing to environmental groups are generally the ones most favorable to the policy positions of those groups. As this example indicates, the rules of jurisdiction and standing are not only requirements imposed on the Court but means by which the Court itself can regulate access to its judgments in accordance with its members' goals.

The technical criteria serve as preliminary screening devices by which some cases are eliminated. But most cases meet these criteria, and the Court must use others to choose among them.

Conflict between Courts. Early in 1999, Thomas Goldstein was a twenty-eight-year-old lawyer who had never appeared in court. But Goldstein had a striking achievement to his credit: he was scheduled to argue two cases before the Supreme Court.

Goldstein's achievement came through a novel strategy. He identified cases decided by the courts of appeals that he thought the Court might accept, and then he called the losing parties and offered to take their cases to the Court for free. In turn, his ability to identify promising cases rested heavily on his recognition that the justices are drawn to decide issues on which different courts of appeals have reached conflicting interpretations of the federal law.[62]

Research on the Court has underlined the importance of legal conflict among courts of appeals as a reason to accept cases, and it seems especially important in the Rehnquist Court.[63] Justice Ginsburg said in 1997 that "the overwhelming factor" in the granting of certiorari "is the division of opinions in the Circuits."[64]

This does not mean that the Court accepts all conflict cases. One scholar estimated that in its 1989 term, the Court refused to hear more than two hundred cases in which there were real conflicts in the interpretation of the law between courts of appeals.[65] That number indicates the primary reason that the Court does not hear every case involving such conflicts: there are simply too many.

Whether the Court accepts a conflict case depends in part on the extent of the conflict, and in part on the seriousness of its effects. The Court emphasized the latter criterion in 1995 when it revised its Rule 10 by inserting the word "important" in three places, indicating that it was inclined to hear cases involving conflicts only if they involved important matters or legal questions. But the Court occasionally accepts a case to resolve a conflict even though only two courts are in conflict on a seemingly minor issue. In contrast, the Court sometimes turns down cases involving fairly serious conflicts among several courts. Eventually, however, the Court is likely to resolve a conflict that is persistent and troublesome.[66]

Importance of the Issues. Whether or not a case involves conflict between lower courts, the importance of the issues has considerable influence on the Court's willingness to accept the case. Rule 10 also emphasizes this consideration, for good reason: the best way for the Court to maximize its impact is to decide those cases that affect the most people and that raise the most significant policy issues.

This consideration in itself eliminates most cases that come to the Court. The Court's rules require that a petition for hearing list the "questions presented" by the case on the first page, and a scanning of petitions makes the reason for this requirement clear: in a great many cases, the questions presented are almost certainly too narrow to merit the Court's attention. The Court occasionally hears cases that seem to be of minor importance, especially when several justices strongly disagree with a lower court decision, but such cases are clearly exceptions to the rule.

A case may seem important to members of the Court for various reasons. Cases typically are important not in themselves but because they raise broader legal or policy issues. It is not surprising when the Court hears cases on issues such as the power of presidents to veto individual items in spending bills or the power of states to set low monetary limits on campaign contributions. More broadly, justices may feel that certain policy areas merit continuing attention because of their importance. This feeling helps to explain the Court's long-standing interest in federalism cases and the prominence of civil liberties cases on its agenda in the current era.

Although a case raising an important issue has a relatively good chance to be accepted, the Court often rejects such cases. Justices may vote against hearing them for a variety of reasons, such as agreement with the lower court decision or a desire to delay before tackling a difficult issue. The press of conflict cases has also caused the Court to reject some relatively important cases that involve no conflicts.

Policy Preferences. Rule 10 does not mention justices' personal conceptions of good policy as a criterion for accepting or rejecting cases, but those conceptions are quite weighty in guiding the Court's choices. Because case selection is such an important part of the Court's policy making, members of the Court could scarcely resist use of the agenda-setting process as a way to advance their policy goals.

Justices could act on their policy goals primarily in two ways. First, they might vote to hear cases because they disagree with the lower court decision that they are reviewing; seeing what they think was an error by the lower court, they want to correct that error. Second, they might act strategically by voting to hear cases when they think that the policy they favor would gain a majority if the Court decided those cases on the merits.

In 1984, Justice Rehnquist attested to the justices' use of the first approach: "The most common reason members of our Court vote to grant certiorari is that they doubt the correctness of the decision of the lower court."[67] As the Court has reduced the number of cases it accepts, this may no longer be true. Justice Souter said in 1998 that it was "axiomatic that this Court cannot devote itself to error correction."[68] Still, a belief that the lower court has erred inclines the justices to accept cases. In the 1998 term, the Court affirmed lower courts in only 28 percent of the certiorari cases that it accepted and decided with full opinions,[69] a proportion far lower than the rate in appellate courts that must hear all the cases they receive. Of course, the justices' evaluations of lower court decisions reflect their ideological positions. If a lower court has reached a conservative decision, a liberal justice is more likely to view it as wrongly decided and vote to hear the case than is a conservative colleague.

The second, strategic, approach requires justices to predict how the Court would decide a case if it were accepted. Such predictions often can be made with some confidence, since the justices gain a good sense of each others' positions on legal issues. There is considerable evidence that justices do engage in this prediction process. One study demonstrated that justices are much more likely to vote to grant certiorari when the Court's decision could be expected to reflect their ideological leanings rather than to run contrary to those leanings.[70]

The practice of voting not to hear a case when a justice fears that the Court would make the "wrong" decision is so well established that justices and clerks routinely refer to "defensive denials" of certiorari.[71] Defensive denials are especially appealing to the members of the Court's ideological minority at any given time (such as liberals on the Rehnquist Court), since they have the most reason to fear the Court's prospective decisions. But any justice may engage in this practice. In a 1998 case, the conservative Justice Scalia complained that a lower court injunction against anti-abortion protests had made "a mockery of First Amendment law," but he concurred with the Court's denial of certiorari. One reason, he said, is that "experience suggests that seeking to bring the First Amendment to the assistance of abortion protesters is more likely to harm the former than help the latter."[72] In other words, he expected that the Court would uphold the injunction if it heard the case.

It is uncertain how these two ways of acting on policy preferences fit together. But research on this question indicates that both are important. Justices respond to both their evaluations of lower court decisions and their expectations about the Court's decision if a case is accepted.[73] And it is clear that justices' preferences, expressed in these ways, have considerable effect on their choices of cases.

Identity of the Petitioner. During its 1998 term, the Supreme Court considered twenty-one petitions for certiorari filed by the federal government. It granted eleven. The government also filed six amicus briefs supporting petitions for certiorari; the Court granted hearings in three of the six cases. Thus, the solicitor general's office secured hearings in fourteen cases—a success rate of 52 percent. The Court considered 7,697 other petitions for hearings, granting certiorari in 61—less than 1 percent.[74]

What accounts for this extraordinary rate of success? It can be ascribed chiefly to the advantages of what Marc Galanter calls a "repeat player"—a litigant engaged in many related cases over time.[75] This status provides the government with at least three advantages.

First, the solicitor general's staff chooses cases to bring to the Court from a large pool of cases that are eligible for Court consideration. Thus the staff can select those that are the most likely to be accepted. Almost any litigant who could be so selective would enjoy a fairly high rate of success in the Supreme Court.

Second, the solicitor general's selectivity earns some gratitude from the Court and builds credibility as well. If the federal government brought petitions at the high rates that other litigants bring them, the Court's caseload would be much heavier than it is. Thus the solicitor general plays an important role in easing pressures on the Court. In the last decade, the office of the solicitor general has brought even fewer cases to the Court than it did in the past; whether intentionally or not, the government has reduced its demands on the Court at a time when the justices have sought to reduce the number of cases they hear. The justices reciprocate for this restraint by viewing the government's petitions in a favorable light. Further, the justices know that the government takes to the Court only the cases that its lawyers deem most worthy, so they too are inclined to view those cases as worthy.

Third, the attorneys in the solicitor general's office handle a great many Supreme Court cases, so they develop an unusual degree of expertise in dealing with the Court. Few other lawyers learn as much about how to appeal to the Court's interests. As a result, the government can do more than most other litigants to make cases appear worthy of acceptance.

Of course, it helps that the solicitor general represents the federal government, a litigant with unique status. This status is reflected in the Court's treatment of the solicitor general's office as something of a partner. But it is primarily the advantage of the repeat player that accounts for the remarkable record of the solicitor general as a petitioner for certiorari.

Some other litigants and interest groups also enjoy advantages in securing hearings from the Court. As noted earlier, large corporations can hire experts in Supreme Court litigation, and lawyers who handle litigation for interest groups such as the AFL-CIO often develop that expertise. These expert lawyers—and certain interest groups themselves—may develop a degree of credibility with the Court. But no other litigant or group has anything like the full set of advantages that account for the solicitor general's success.

Avoiding Problematic Cases. Whatever their value in other respects, some cases are rejected by the Court because of characteristics that make their acceptance inconvenient, characteristics of two types.

First, the facts of some cases may be inappropriate. The facts may be too muddled to allow a clear decision, or they may require justices to reach a decision on grounds different from the ones they would like to use. In other cases, the circumstances of a dispute or the identity of the litigants may put the Court's likely decision in an unfavorable light.

Sometimes the justices select the "best" case on an issue after rejecting a large number of related cases because of their facts. In 1961 members of the Court had resolved that they would establish the right of indigents to a free attorney in felony cases. Then, with the assistance of their clerks, the justices searched for a case whose facts were appropriate for establishment of that principle. A large number of cases were rejected before Clarence Gideon's petition was accepted. His case was ideal for the Court's purposes, in part because it concerned the relatively minor felony of breaking and entering a poolroom with intent to commit a misdemeanor. A reversal of Gideon's conviction would provoke less public wrath than the reversal of a conviction for a violent offense.[76]

Second, justices may seek to avoid certain issues altogether because of their controversial nature, which can make them difficult to decide and—more important—can lead to attacks on the Court for the decisions it does reach. A good example is the Court's refusal to rule on the constitutionality of participation by the United States in the war in Vietnam. Few issues brought to the Court have been so important, but the Court refused to hear the cases that raised this question between 1967 and 1972. Undoubtedly, some justices wanted to avoid injecting the Court into the most important and most disputed issue of national policy.

The desire to avoid controversy may help to explain some denials of hearings in recent years. The Court declined to hear *Texas v. Hopwood* (1996), a case in which a federal court of appeals had implicitly challenged the Court's position on affirmative action in school admissions, despite the confusion that was thereby created on an important issue. It is likely that most justices preferred to avoid dealing with an issue that arouses strong emotions on both sides. In 2000 the Court refused to hear *Gonzàles v. Reno,* the case about whether six-year-old Eliàn Gonzàles would return to Cuba with his father. The justices may simply have concluded that the case did not contain a significant legal issue, but the desire to avoid involvement in a highly controversial dispute may have influenced them as well.

Often the Court refuses to address a difficult issue only temporarily, accepting a case later, after the issue has been allowed to "percolate" in the lower courts. And certainly the Court does accept a good many cases that are likely to embroil it in controversy. In a way, the Court's frequent willingness to take such cases is more noteworthy than is its avoidance of other difficult cases.

Summary. The Supreme Court's decisions about whether or not to hear cases are based on a complex set of considerations, reflecting the wide range of goals that the justices seek to advance through the selection of cases. Votes on the question of whether to hear cases are subjective decisions that depend on the values and perspectives of the justices. Justices differ in the priority they give to resolving conflicts between lower courts. They assess the importance of cases in various ways. And they work from quite different sets of policy preferences.

It follows that the Court's selection of cases to decide fully, like everything else it does, is affected by its membership at any given time. Most cases are unlikely to be accepted no matter who is on the Court. But the composition of the few dozen cases that the Supreme Court actually does accept in a term strongly reflects the identities of the justices who serve during that term.

Caseload Growth and the Court's Response

The Growth in Caseloads

The 7,109 cases that litigants brought to the Supreme Court during the 1998 term was a record number. That record symbolizes a massive increase in the number of filings in the past several decades. The Court never received even two thousand cases in a term until 1961, and 1979 was the first term in which it received as many as four thousand. The growth in the Court's caseload over the years is shown in Figure 3-1.

The long-term growth in caseload reflects two quite different processes in different periods. The first was a general growth that culminated in the 1960s. In part, that growth reflected broad developments in American society: increased population, an apparent increase in "rights consciousness" that led people to bring more legal claims, and the development of interest groups that assist litigants in carrying litigation through the courts. Another source was a massive growth in the activities of the federal government, growth that produced new laws and legal questions.

The Court itself contributed to the increase in cases by allowing indigent litigants to file paupers' petitions without meeting all the ordinary requirements for the filing of cases. Further, especially in the 1960s, the Court showed considerable sympathy for challenges to government action that were based on alleged violations of civil liberties. This sympathy encouraged those who felt their rights had been violated, whether they were criminal defendants or members of racial minority groups, to bring cases to the Court.

FIGURE 3-1

*Cases Filed in the Supreme Court per Term,
by Five-Year Averages, 1949–1998*

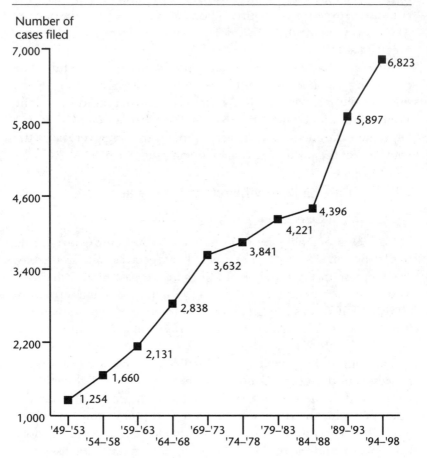

Number of
cases filed

7,000 ━

6,823

5,800 ━

5,897

4,600 ━

4,396

4,221

3,841

3,632

3,400 ━

2,838

2,200 ━

2,131

1,660

1,254

1,000 ━

'49–'53   '59–'63   '69–'73   '79–'83   '89–'93

'54–'58   '64–'68   '74–'78   '84–'88   '94–'98

Sources: Lee Epstein, Jeffrey A. Segal, Harold J. Spaeth, and Thomas G. Walker, *The Supreme Court Compendium: Data, Decisions, and Developments,* 2d ed. (Washington, D.C.: Congressional Quarterly, 1996), 74–76; "Statistical Recap of Supreme Court's Workload During Last Three Terms," *United States Law Week,* various years.

The caseload grew slowly in the 1970s and early 1980s, but since then a second period of rapid growth has taken place: the 7,109 cases filed in 1998 represented a two-thirds increase over the average of 4,200 in the 1982–1986 terms. This new rise in cases is entirely in the paupers' petitions. The numbers of paid petitions per term have remained remarkably stable, never falling below 1,800 and rising above 2,200 only twice since the 1975 term. In contrast, the numbers of paupers' petitions, which hovered around 2,000 per term from the early 1970s to the mid-1980s, grew to the point that there were more than 5,000 in the 1998 term.

The preponderance of paupers' petitions come from prisoners, and the number of inmates who were serving sentences of more than one year in prison tripled between 1982 and 1998.[77] This trend accounts for most if not all of the growth in paupers' cases. Indeed, this growth has occurred even though other factors that affect criminal petitions have worked in the opposite direction. The Court has become much less sympathetic to the claims brought by criminal defendants since the 1960s, and more recently both Court and Congress have limited the use of habeas corpus actions to challenge criminal convictions.

Responding to Caseload Growth

Growth as a Problem. Observers of the Court and the justices themselves have seen growth in the Court's caseload as a problem for the Court and for federal law. For the Court, the perceived problem is that its ability to do its job well is compromised. The growing caseload makes the justices busier. As a result, they may give less careful consideration to their work, particularly the cases they decide on the merits. Some observers think the justices write opinions with less care, fail to take the time needed to reach truly collective decisions, and delegate too much responsibility to law clerks.[78]

For the federal law, the perceived problem is that the Court does not resolve as many legal issues as it should. If the number of cases heard by the Court increased at the same rate as the number of petitions for hearing, the Court's workload would become impossible to handle. To avoid this outcome, over the years the justices have raised the standards for their acceptance of cases. As a result, seemingly meritorious cases were denied hearings. As Chief Justice Rehnquist said in 1987, "Today we decline to review cases involving important questions of federal law not previously decided by our Court, cases which the Court would have unquestionably heard and decided as little as thirty years ago."[79]

Jurisdictional Change as a Solution. The current period is not the first time that the Court's caseload has grown. During most eras the

Court has faced substantial increases in the numbers of cases brought to it. At least since the late nineteenth century, such increases have prompted complaints by the justices that they were overburdened and unable to handle their work effectively.

The primary solution that the justices sought and that Congress provided was to give the Court greater discretion in deciding whether to hear cases, primarily in two major steps. The first was the Court of Appeals Act of 1891, which created a new set of intermediate appellate courts and gave the Court discretionary jurisdiction over a large minority of cases for the first time. The second was the Judiciary Act of 1925, which expanded the discretionary jurisdiction by requiring that most cases come to the Court as requests for writs of certiorari, which the Court could reject without reaching any decision on the merits, rather than as appeals, which the Court could not.

The 1925 statute had an enormous impact. Its most obvious effect was to limit justices' workloads by allowing them to concentrate on only a portion of the cases brought to them. More subtly, it gave the Court more freedom to determine the scope of its activity, the kinds of issues it would address, and its role as a policy maker.

As the Court's caseload grew further, the justices sought to have the remaining categories of appeals eliminated. In 1988 Congress did eliminate most of those categories, but the number of appeals already was so low that they added little to the Court's workload—especially because the Court often gave them less than full consideration. For that reason, more radical changes in the Court's jurisdiction were proposed during the 1970s and 1980s.

The proposed changes would have involved creation of a new court between the courts of appeals and the Supreme Court. In some proposals, the new court would help the Supreme Court to screen petitions for hearings. Like increases in the Court's discretionary jurisdiction, these proposals were aimed at reducing the Court's burdens. In others, which received more serious consideration, the new court would actually decide some cases in place of the Supreme Court. These proposals were aimed at resolving more issues in federal law. While some justices supported these proposals, there was nothing approaching a consensus on the Court or elsewhere in government that a new court of a particular type was desirable. In the absence of such a consensus Congress is unlikely to make a major change in the structure of government, and it did not.

TABLE 3-2

*Size of the Court's Agenda for Decisions
on the Merits, 1984–1998 Terms*

Term	Petitions granted	Signed opinions
1984	185	139
1985	186	146
1986	167	145
1987	180	139
1988	147	133
1989	122	129
1990	141	112
1991	120	107
1992	97	107
1993	99	84
1994	93	82
1995	105	75
1996	87	80
1997	89	91
1998	81	75

Source: "Statistical Recap of Supreme Court's Workload During Last Three Terms," *United States Law Week,* various years.

Accepting Fewer Cases as a Solution. Beginning in the late 1980s, the justices have taken matters into their own hands by reducing the volume of cases they decide on the merits. As Table 3-2 shows, the number of cases that the Court accepts each term and the number that it decides with full, signed opinions have declined by about half.

A variety of explanations for this reduction have been put forward,[80] and the justices themselves have offered several explanations.[81] Some justices have said that there is no single overriding reason for the reduction, and one scholar's close analysis of the reduction supports this judgment.[82] But the central factor is that the justices collectively have raised their standards for granting of certiorari.

To a degree, this rise in standards reflects change in the Court's membership.[83] As measured by their dissents from denials of certiorari, during the 1980s Justices White, Brennan, and Marshall were the most eager to accept cases. Justice Blackmun was by far the most willing to cast "Join-3" votes, which indicated that he would provide the needed fourth vote for certiorari if three colleagues wished to hear a case. While the Court began to hear fewer cases before these four justices left the Court, almost surely their departures between 1990 and 1994 contributed to the continuing decline in the numbers of cases that the Court accepts.

Of the justices who commented on the case reduction, none said that the justices simply wanted to work less, and Justice Ginsburg said that "the cutback in opinions doesn't mean that the court is becoming a lazy lot." [84] The effect of the cutback, however, is a reduced workload. Thus, if the quality of the Court's decisions suffered from its heavy workload, the justices have solved that problem themselves.

Of course, accepting fewer cases might aggravate problems in the federal law. If the Court left too many important issues unresolved in 1987, as Chief Justice Rehnquist thought at the time, there would seem to be even more such issues now. This is not necessarily true. Some justices and commentators have suggested that new issues are arising at a slower rate than in the past, and the Court today seems to concentrate more on establishing general legal rules than on correcting misapplications of those rules by lower courts. Still, the Court almost surely bypasses more significant legal questions today than it did fifteen years ago. One former law clerk said that the Court "used to take too many cases, but, clearly, where they are now is too few." [85]

In any event, the difficulty of gaining a hearing in the Supreme Court has become even greater. In its 1985 term, the Court accepted about one in twelve of the paid petitions filed with it; in the 1998 term that rate had dropped to one in twenty-eight. For paupers' petitions the decline was even more precipitous, from an already low one in 108 in 1985 to a spectacularly low one in 548 in 1998. [86] As one disgruntled lawyer said when the Court rejected a seemingly promising case in 1998, "I don't think I'd ever advise anyone to file a pauper case again." [87]

Conclusion

A central theme of this chapter is the Supreme Court's ability to set its own agenda. Congress and litigants both play an important part in shaping that agenda, but what the Court hears is largely under its own control. From the wide variety of legal and policy questions brought to the Court, the justices can choose those few that they will address fully. They can also choose which issues in a case they will decide. And the Court affects the choices of lawyers and interest groups through its opinions by suggesting the kinds of legal claims that it will view favorably in future cases.

The Court has been criticized for the ways it uses its agenda-setting powers, but the justices employ these powers rather well to serve their purposes. They accept and reject cases on the basis of individual and collective goals such as avoiding troublesome issues, resolving legal conflicts, and establishing policies that the justices favor. Thus justices employ the process of selecting cases for full decisions to shape the Court's role as a policy maker. They also use that process to limit their workloads.

After the Court selects the cases to be decided, of course, it actually decides those cases. In the next chapter I examine the process by which the Court makes its decisions.

NOTES

1. "Statistical Recap of Supreme Court's Workload During Last Three Terms," *United States Law Week,* July 20, 1999, 3069.
2. This summary of the distribution of litigants across categories is based in part on Gregory A. Caldeira and John R. Wright, "Parties, Direct Representatives, and Agenda-Setting in the Supreme Court" (Paper presented at the annual conference of the Midwest Political Science Association, Chicago, April 1989).
3. Joan Biskupic, "Unusual Settlement Removes Third Case From Justices' Reach," *Washington Post,* May 26, 1998, A2.
4. See Marcia Coyle, "How the Christian Right Came to Fund a Free Speech Case," *National Law Journal,* November 1, 1999, A7.
5. Sarah Weddington, *A Question of Choice* (New York: Putnam, 1992), 64.
6. This discussion is based in part on Kevin T. McGuire, *The Supreme Court Bar: Legal Elites in the Washington Community* (Charlottesville: University Press of Virginia, 1993).
7. Edward J. Cleary, *Beyond the Burning Cross: The First Amendment and the Landmark R.A.V. Case* (New York: Random House, 1994), 112.
8. See Kevin T. McGuire, "Lobbyists, Revolving Doors, and the U.S. Supreme Court" (Paper presented at the annual meeting of the Midwest Political Science Association, Chicago, April 23–25, 1998).
9. Kevin T. McGuire, "The Supreme Court Bar and Institutional Relationships," in *The Supreme Court in American Politics: New Institutionalist Interpretations,* ed. Howard Gillman and Cornell Clayton (Lawrence: University Press of Kansas, 1999), 115–132.
10. Quoted in Barbara A. Perry, *The Priestly Tribe: The Supreme Court's Image in the American Mind* (Westport, Conn.: Praeger, 1999), 109. The case was *Shalala v. Whitecotten* (1995).
11. Kevin T. McGuire, "Repeat Players in the Supreme Court: The Role of Experienced Lawyers in Litigation Success," *Journal of Politics* 57 (February 1995): 187–196.

12. Marcia Coyle, "High Court Bar's 'Inner Circle,'" *National Law Journal,* March 3, 1997, A16.
13. Ibid.
14. Caldeira and Wright, "Parties, Direct Representatives, and Agenda-Setting," tables 1 and 2.
15. Lee Epstein, "Interest Group Litigation during the Rehnquist Court Era," *Journal of Law and Politics* 9 (Summer 1993): 715–717.
16. *City of West Covina v. Perkins* (1999); *Amoco Production Company v. Southern Ute Indian Tribe* (1999).
17. Information on amicus briefs is taken from files in the LEXIS database.
18. Karen O'Connor and Bryant Scott McFall, "Conservative Interest Group Litigation in the Reagan Era and Beyond," in *The Politics of Interests: Interest Groups Transformed,* ed. Mark P. Petracca (Boulder: Westview Press, 1992), 271.
19. This paragraph is based primarily on Richard Davis, *Decisions and Images: The Supreme Court and the Press* (Englewood Cliffs, N.J.: Prentice-Hall, 1994).
20. Linda Greenhouse, "Telling the Court's Story: Justice and Journalism at the Supreme Court," *Yale Law Journal* 105 (April 1996): 1554.
21. This paragraph is based in part on Stephen L. Wasby, *Race Relations Litigation in an Age of Complexity* (Charlottesville: University Press of Virginia, 1995), esp. 61–64.
22. See Samuel Walker, *In Defense of American Liberties: A History of the ACLU,* 2d ed. (Carbondale: Southern Illinois University Press, 1999).
23. See Lee Epstein, *Conservatives in Court* (Knoxville: University of Tennessee Press, 1985).
24. Hans J. Hacker, "Conservative Christian Litigating Interests and Determinants of Interest Group Behavior" (Ph.D. dissertation, Ohio State University, forthcoming).
25. James H. Andrews, "Religious Right Fights for Rights," *Christian Science Monitor,* February 7, 1994, 14; Tim Stafford, "Move Over ACLU," *Christianity Today* 37 (October 25, 1993): 20–24.
26. George Stevens, Jr., "His Life's Work: When Thurgood Marshall Saw the Movie," *Washington Post,* January 29, 1993, A23.
27. See Wasby, *Race Relations Litigation in an Age of Complexity.*
28. Susan E. Lawrence, *The Poor in Court: The Legal Services Program and Supreme Court Decision Making* (Princeton: Princeton University Press, 1990).
29. Charles R. Epp, *The Rights Revolution: Lawyers, Activists, and Supreme Courts in Comparative Perspective* (Chicago: University of Chicago Press, 1998), 44–70.
30. Data on the 1998 term discussed here and later in this section were provided by the Office of the Solicitor General.
31. This discussion is based in part on Richard L. Pacelle Jr., *Between Law and Politics: The Solicitor General and the Structuring of Civil Rights, Gender, and Reproductive Rights Policy* (manuscript); and Rebecca Mae Salokar, *The Solicitor General: The Politics of Law* (Philadelphia: Temple University Press, 1992).
32. Pacelle, *Between Law and Politics,* chap. 1.
33. Salokar, *The Solicitor General,* 159; Stephen S. Meinhold and Steven A. Shull, "Policy Congruence Between the President and the Solicitor General," *Political Research Quarterly* 51 (June 1998): 527–537.
34. Jeffrey Toobin, "Clinton's Left-Hand Man," *The New Yorker,* July 21, 1997, 30.

35. Pacelle, *Between Law and Politics*, chap. 1.
36. See Pierre Thomas, "Reno Reverses Child Pornography Stance," *Washington Post*, November 11, 1994, A4. The case was *Knox v. United States* (1993, 1995).
37. Toobin, "Clinton's Left-Hand Man," 30.
38. Eva M. Rodriguez, "Senators Train Sights on Solicitor General," *Legal Times*, November 20, 1995, 1, 20, 21.
39. Steven A. Holmes, "Senator Wants Deal to Support Rights Nominee," *New York Times*, November 1, 1997, A1, A8.
40. Lee Epstein, Jeffrey A. Segal, Harold J. Spaeth, and Thomas G. Walker, *The Supreme Court Compendium*, 2d ed. (Washington, D.C.: Congressional Quarterly, 1996), 612; Eric S. Heberlig and Rorie L. Spill, "Congress at Court: Members of Congress as Amicus Curiae," *Southeastern Political Review* 28 (2000): 1–24.
41. "Statistical Recap of Supreme Court's Workload during Last Three Terms."
42. Elliot E. Slotnick and Jennifer A. Segal, *Television News and the Supreme Court: All the News That's Fit to Air?* (New York: Cambridge University Press, 1998), chap. 6.
43. Cindy Loose, "Watching the Curfew," *Washington Post*, October 2, 1999, B1. The case was *Qutb v. Bartlett* (1994).
44. *American Telephone and Telegraph Company v. Central Office Telephone, Inc.* (1998).
45. On per curiam opinions in general, see Stephen L. Wasby, Steven Peterson, James Schubert, and Glendon Schubert, "The Per Curiam Opinion: Its Nature and Functions," *Judicature* 76 (June–July 1992): 29–38.
46. Lisa Brennan, "Lawyer Loses Big Day in Court," *National Law Journal*, December 8, 1997, A4. The case was *Piscataway Township Board of Education v. Taxman* (1997).
47. This figure is taken from data provided by the Office of the Solicitor General.
48. *Antonelli v. Caridine*, 145 L. Ed. 2d 4, 6 (1999).
49. "Statistical Recap of Supreme Court's Workload during Last Three Terms."
50. Tony Mauro, "'Pauper' Petitions a Long Shot," *USA Today*, December 23, 1998, 10A.
51. This examination of the discuss list and of the conference are based in part on H. W. Perry, Jr., *Deciding to Decide: Agenda Setting in the United States Supreme Court* (Cambridge: Harvard University Press, 1991), 43–51, 85–91.
52. Ruth Bader Ginsburg, "Remarks for American Law Institute Annual Dinner May 19, 1994," *Saint Louis University Law Journal* 38 (Summer 1994): 884.
53. *Singleton v. Commissioner of Internal Revenue*, 439 U.S. 940, 945–946 (1978).
54. *Sims v. Moore* (2000); *Provenzano v. Moore* (2000).
55. *Equality Foundation of Greater Cincinnati, Inc. v. City of Cincinnati* (1998); *Riggs v. California* (1999).
56. This discussion of the clerks' roles is drawn in part from Perry, *Deciding to Decide*, 51–84; Dan T. Coenen, review of Perry, *Deciding to Decide*, in *Constitutional Commentary* 10 (Winter 1993): 180–193; and Sean Donahue, "Behind the Pillars of Justice: Remarks on Law Clerks," *The Long Term View* 3 (Spring 1995): 79–80.
57. Tony Mauro, "Ginsburg Plunges into the Cert Pool," *Legal Times*, September 6, 1993, 8.
58. Donahue, "Behind the Pillars of Justice," 80.

59. Martha M. Hamilton, "A Leap Year Lapse Abruptly Ends an Appeal to the Supreme Court," *Washington Post,* March 12, 1996, C1, C4.
60. *Bryan v. Moore* (2000). See "Court Dismisses Challenge to Florida Executions," *New York Times,* January 25, 2000, A18. .
61. *Alsbrook v. Arkansas* (2000); *Florida v. Dickson* (2000). See Joan Biskupic and Al Kamen, "2 Appeals Involving Disabilities Act Voided," *Washington Post,* March 2, 2000, A10.
62. David Segal, "For One Associate, a Supreme Court," *Washington Post,* February 8, 1999 (Washington Business), 9.
63. Gregory A. Caldeira and John R. Wright, "Organized Interests and Agenda Setting in the U.S. Supreme Court," *American Political Science Review* 82 (December 1988): 1109–1127; Caldeira and Wright, "Nine Little Law Firms? Justices, Organized Interests, and Agenda-Setting in the Supreme Court" (Paper presented at the annual conference of the Midwest Political Science Association, Chicago, April 1994).
64. "Judicial Conference, Second Judicial Circuit of the United States," 178 *Federal Rules Decisions* 210, 282 (1997).
65. Arthur D. Hellman, "By Precedent Unbound: The Nature and Extent of Unresolved Intercircuit Conflicts," *University of Pittsburgh Law Review* 56 (Summer 1995): 720–724.
66. See Arthur D. Hellman, "Light on a Darkling Plain: Intercircuit Conflicts in the Perspective of Time and Experience," in *The Supreme Court Review 1998,* ed. Dennis J. Hutchinson, David A. Strauss, and Geoffrey R. Stone (Chicago: University of Chicago Press, 1999), 247–302.
67. William H. Rehnquist, "Oral Advocacy: A Disappearing Art," *Mercer Law Review* 35 (1984): 1027.
68. *Calderon v. Thompson,* 523 U.S. 538, 569 (1998).
69. "The Supreme Court, 1998 Term," *Harvard Law Review* 113 (November 1999): 407.
70. Gregory A. Caldeira, John R. Wright, and Christopher J. W. Zorn, "Sophisticated Voting and Gate-Keeping in the Supreme Court," *Journal of Law, Economics, and Organization* 15 (October 1999): 549–572.
71. Perry, *Deciding to Decide,* 198–207. The quotation is on p. 200.
72. *Lawson v. Murray,* 142 L. Ed. 2d 320, 321 (1998).
73. Saul Brenner and John F. Krol, "Strategies in Certiorari Voting on the United States Supreme Court," *Journal of Politics* 51 (November 1989): 828–840; Robert L. Boucher Jr. and Jeffrey A. Segal, "Supreme Court Justices as Strategic Decision Makers: Aggressive Grants and Defensive Denials on the Vinson Court," *Journal of Politics* 57 (August 1995): 824–837; Caldeira, Wright, and Zorn, "Sophisticated Voting and Gate-Keeping."
74. These data were provided by the Office of the Solicitor General.
75. Marc Galanter, "Why the 'Haves' Come Out Ahead: Speculations on the Limits of Legal Change," *Law and Society Review* 9 (Fall 1974): 97–125.
76. Nathan Lewin, "Helping the Court with Its Work," *New Republic,* March 3, 1973, 18. The case was *Gideon v. Wainwright* (1963).
77. U.S. Department of Justice, *Sourcebook of Criminal Justice Statistics 1998* (Washington, D.C.: Government Printing Office, 1999), 490.
78. See, for example, Paul M. Bator, "What Is Wrong with the Supreme Court?" *University of Pittsburgh Law Review* 51 (Spring 1990): 685–687.
79. "Chief Justice Urges National Appeals Court, Repeal of Court's Mandatory Jurisdiction," *The Third Branch,* July 1987, 1, 5.

80. Arthur D. Hellman, "The Shrunken Docket of the Rehnquist Court," in *The Supreme Court Review* 1996, ed. Dennis J. Hutchinson, David A. Strauss, and Geoffrey A. Stone (Chicago: University of Chicago Press, 1997), 403–438.
81. Joan Biskupic, "The Shrinking Docket," *Washington Post,* March 18, 1996, A15; Biskupic, "Female Justices Attest to Fraternity on Bench," *Washington Post,* August 21, 1994, A24; Richard Carelli, "Supreme Court's Decisions Dwindle," *Montgomery Advertiser,* January 24, 1996, 17A; David J. Garrow, "The Rehnquist Reins," *New York Times Magazine,* October 6, 1996, 71, 82.
82. Hellman, "Shrunken Docket."
83. David M. O'Brien, "Join-3 Votes, the Rule of Four, the *Cert.* Pool, and the Supreme Court's Shrinking Plenary Docket," *Journal of Law and Politics* 13 (Fall 1997): 779–808.
84. Biskupic, "Female Justices Attest to Fraternity on Bench."
85. Tony Mauro, "Court's Inaction Allows Confusion," *USA Today,* December 23, 1998, 2A.
86. These figures are based on data in "Statistical Recap of Supreme Court's Workload During Last Three Terms," *United States Law Week,* various years.
87. Mauro, "'Pauper' Petitions a Long Shot," 10A.

Chapter 4

Decision Making

A t the heart of the Supreme Court's work is its decision making.
The selection of justices is important because the selection
process determines who makes the Court's decisions, and the
Court's choices of cases to hear are important because those
choices set the agenda for decisions on the merits. It is these decisions that give the Court an impact on people in the United States
and on the nation as a whole. This chapter examines how and why
the Court makes its decisions on the merits.

Decisions and the Decisional Process

Components of the Court's Decision

A Supreme Court decision on the merits has two components: its
treatment of the parties to the case and a statement of general legal
rules. In cases that the Court fully considers, the two components
are nearly always presented in an opinion. Generally at least five justices subscribe to this opinion, so that it constitutes an authoritative
statement by the Court.

The Court's opinions vary in form, but they usually begin by describing the background of a case. The opinion then turns to the legal issues in the case, discussing the opposing views on those issues
and indicating the Court's conclusions about the issues. The
Court's resolution of the case as a whole is presented at the end of
the opinion.

The first component of the decision, the Court's treatment of the
parties, is summarized in the end-of-opinion description. Except in
the few original cases that it hears, the Court is reviewing a lower
court's treatment of the parties—a win for one side or the other or

perhaps a partial win for each side. The Court can affirm the lower court decision, leaving the lower court's judgment undisturbed. Alternatively, it can modify or reverse the lower court decision, overturning that court's judgment altogether or in part. The terms *modify* and *reverse* are imprecise. In general, a reversal overturns the lower court decision altogether or nearly so, while modification is a more limited, partial overturning. The Court may also vacate (make void) the lower court decision, an action whose effect is similar to that of reversal.

When the Court does disturb a lower court decision, it usually *remands,* or sends back, the case to the lower court for reconsideration, with the Court's opinion as a whole providing guidance to the lower court. For instance, in a tax case the opinion may say that a court of appeals adopted the wrong interpretation of the federal tax laws and that the court should reexamine the case on the basis of a different interpretation. The Court's opinion in a 1999 case used typical language: "We reverse the judgment of the Second Circuit and remand the case for further proceedings consistent with this opinion."[1]

In most cases the outcome for the parties has little impact beyond the parties themselves. Rather, what makes most decisions consequential is the statement of general legal rules that apply to the nation as a whole. When the Court's opinion resolves the legal issues in a case, it is not just providing guidance to a specific lower court in a specific case. It is also laying down rules that any court must follow in a case to which they apply and that can affect the behavior of people outside of court.

As a result, decisions that directly affect only two ordinary people may have a substantial indirect effect on thousands or even millions of other people. When the Court decides a criminal procedure case, it is laying down rules that apply to the handling of all similar cases; *Miranda v. Arizona* (1966) affected not only Ernesto Miranda but every suspect who was questioned by law enforcement officers. In the same way, decisions interpreting the federal laws against employment discrimination often have an impact on large numbers of individuals and employers who become involved in disputes about discrimination.

In each case, of course, the Court has a choice about its treatment of the parties—who wins and who loses. The Court also has choices about the general legal rules that it states in its opinion. A ruling for one of the parties often could be justified on any of several grounds, and the ground chosen by the Court helps to determine the long-term impact of its decision. If the Court overturns the death sentence for a particular defendant, it might base that decision on an unusual type of error in the defendant's trial. Such a decision has a narrow impact. Alternatively, the Court could declare that the death penalty is unconstitutional under all circumstances and thereby make a revolutionary change in policy.

The Decision-Making Process

Presentation of Cases to the Court. The written briefs that the Court receives when it considers whether to hear a case often touch on the merits of the case. Once a case has been accepted for oral argument and decision, attorneys for the parties submit new briefs that focus on the merits. In most cases that reach this stage, interest groups submit amicus curiae briefs stating their own arguments on the merits.

Most of the material in these briefs concerns legal issues. The parties muster evidence to support their interpretations of relevant constitutional provisions and statutes. In their briefs they frequently offer arguments about policy as well, seeking to convince the justices that support for their position constitutes not only good law but good public policy.

Material in the briefs is supplemented by attorneys' presentations in oral argument before the Court. Attorneys for the parties to a case sometimes share their time with the lawyer for an amicus, almost always the federal government. In most cases each side is provided half an hour for its argument. When time expires a red light goes on at the attorneys' lectern. In one case an attorney then asked, "May I finish my sentence?" "Yes," Chief Justice Rehnquist responded, "assuming it's a short one."[2] His response was in jest, but it reflected his general inclination to enforce the time limit vigorously.

Oral argument allows attorneys to supplement and highlight material in their briefs. More important, it allows the justices to probe issues that concern them by questioning the lawyers. Presentations by lawyers are interrupted with great frequency by questions and comments from members of the Court, and it is the justices who control the flow of argument.

Justices differ in how often they interrupt attorneys. Clarence Thomas seldom asks a question, but several of his colleagues play

The Supreme Court's conference room. Discussions of cases among the justices are briefer and have less influence on their positions than might be expected.

quite active roles. As a result, the current Court features more lively argument sessions than in some past eras. Justice Ginsburg reports that "there are many more questions than there were in the days when I was arguing before the Court" in the 1970s. "Then, you could get at least five or six sentences out consecutively. Now we tend to interrupt not only counsel, but each other."[3]

The justices differ in their styles of questioning.[4] Rehnquist sometimes takes a stern approach, rebuking lawyers who have misstepped. In a 1997 argument, a lawyer tried to make a point by noting that "a '54 Mustang is worth real money." Rehnquist retorted that "they didn't make Mustangs until '63."[5] In contrast, John Paul Stevens has a polite and self-effacing style. One of his questions began, "Maybe I'll reveal my ignorance. . . ."[6] David Souter, one of the most frequent questioners on the Court, has a similar style.

Antonin Scalia, another frequent questioner, is the most likely to try to control the direction of the argument. "Often," one observer noted, "if an attorney fails to make the argument Scalia favors, the Justice simply intervenes and takes over the argument."[7] One attorney reported that Scalia "'speaks' through expressions, as well as words. . . . A roll of the eyes and reddening of the face all but said, 'It pains me beyond words to even imagine what I'm going to hear from you next.'" [8]

Justices ask questions to clarify issues for themselves, but they also use questions to shape their colleagues' perceptions of a case. Justice Stevens has said that "you have a point in mind that you think may not have been brought out . . . but you want to be sure your colleagues don't overlook that so . . . you'll ask a question to bring it out." [9] This use of the argument time makes sense. As Rehnquist points out, this is the only time before the conference discussion of a case "when all of the judges are expected to sit on the bench and concentrate on one particular case." [10]

Observers often try to discern the justices' likely positions in a case from their questions and comments during oral argument. Their predictions are correct more often than not, but occasionally even astute observers can be led astray. According to one expert on the Court who watched a week of arguments in 1999, "justices seemed to tip their hands during oral arguments more than usual last week." He noted that the justices "put up a nearly united front" against a California welfare law, and indeed the Court struck down the law by a 7–2 vote. He also reported in a sexual harassment case that "it was hard to count more than two justices, if that many," who favored the plaintiff, but ultimately she garnered the five votes needed to win the case. [11]

Tentative Decisions. After oral argument the Court discusses each case in one of its conferences later the same week. The conference is a closed session attended only by the justices. The discussion is fairly structured. [12] The chief justice presides and begins by summarizing the case, then states personal views on the case and usually a vote on the decision. The associate justices, starting with the most senior member (in terms of service on the Court, not age) and ending with the most junior, then present their own views and votes. Because their colleagues have already voiced similar positions, the more junior justices generally speak quite briefly. Typically, little or no additional discussion follows this presentation of positions. According to Justice Scalia, "To call our discussion of a case a conference is really something of a misnomer, it's much more a statement of the views of each of the nine Justices, after which the totals are added and the case is assigned." [13]

We might expect a more freewheeling discussion of cases, with justices speaking at length and arguing back and forth. But the Court's workload creates time pressures that preclude extended discussions. Just as important, the justices usually bring to the conference fixed views on the cases. They have already read the written materials and listened to oral argument, and often they have discussed the case with their law clerks. Furthermore, their views on cases are influenced by their own, frequently strong, attitudes about policy. As a result, Chief Justice Rehnquist reported, "it is very much the exception" for justices' minds to be changed in conference. He added that extended discussion ordinarily would have little impact on the justices' positions.[14]

After each two-week sitting, the writing of the Court's opinion in each case is assigned to a justice. If the chief justice voted with the majority, the chief assigns the opinion. In other cases, the most senior justice in the majority makes the assignment. Because so many conference votes are lopsided, the chief justice is usually among the majority. If the Court is divided, the senior justice in the minority assigns the primary dissenting opinion.

Reaching Final Decisions. After conference, the justice who was assigned the Court's opinion writes an initial draft, guided by the views expressed in conference. Once this opinion is completed and circulated, justices in the original majority may sign on to it. But others in that majority may hold back, either because they have developed doubts about their original vote or because they disagree with some of the language in the draft opinion. Members of the original minority also see the draft opinion for the Court. Some might decide to sign on to the opinion because their view of the case has changed, or they might see a possibility of signing on if the opinion is modified.

Justices who do not immediately sign on often let the assigned justice know about their doubts, indicating that they would be willing to sign on if certain changes are made. Their memos initiate a process of explicit or implicit negotiation, in which the assigned justice tries to gain the support of as many colleagues as possible. At the least, that justice wants to maintain the original majority for the outcome supported by the opinion and to win a majority for the language of the opinion, so that it becomes the official statement of the Court.

TABLE 4-1
Selected Characteristics of Supreme Court Decisions, 1998 Term

Characteristic	Number	Percentage
Number of decisions	81	—
Vote for Court's decision[a]		
Unanimous	28	35
Nonunanimous	53	65
Support for Court's opinion		
Unanimous for whole opinion	23	28
Unanimous for part of opinion	10	12
Majority but not unanimous	42	52
Majority for only part of opinion	6	7
No majority for opinion	0	0
Cases with		
Dissenting opinions[b]	52	64
Concurring opinions[c]	31	38
Total number of		
Dissenting opinions	67	—
Concurring opinions	44	—

Note: The decisions included are decisions on the merits that are listed in the front section of *Supreme Court Reports, Lawyer's Edition.*

[a] "Decision" refers to outcome for the parties. Partial dissents are not counted as votes for the decision.

[b] Opinions labeled "concurring and dissenting" are treated as dissenting opinions.

[c] Some concurring opinions are in full agreement with the Court's opinion.

In this effort, the justice who was assigned the Court's opinion often competes with other justices who write alternative opinions supporting the opposite outcome or arguing for the same outcome with a different rationale. Most of the time, assigned justices succeed in winning a majority for their opinions, though sometimes with very substantial alterations. More often than not, however, they fail to win the unanimous support of their colleagues. Table 4-1, which lists several characteristics of the Court's decisions in the 1998 term, shows that such unanimity was achieved only 28 percent of the time. In an extreme instance, Justice Scalia's majority opinion in a 1998 case had complete support from no colleague; it was a majority opinion because one set of four justices agreed with one part of the opinion and the other four justices agreed with the other part.[15]

Occasionally no opinion gains the support of a majority. Table 4-1 shows that the 1998 term was unusual in that in every case one opinion had a majority for at least some of its sections. Even so, in six cases that opinion lacked full majority support. Without a majority opinion there is no authoritative statement of the Court's position on the legal issues in the case, though the opinion on the winning side with the greatest support—the "plurality opinion"—may specify the points for which majority support exists. Lower court judges and other observers can attempt to discern what positions are shared by the justices on the majority side, but this is not always an easy task.

Concurring and Dissenting Opinions. In most cases, an opinion gains a majority but lacks unanimous support. Disagreement with the majority opinion can take two forms. First, a justice may cast a dissenting vote, which expresses disagreement with the result reached by the Court as it affects the parties to a case. If a criminal conviction is reversed, for instance, a justice who believes it should have been affirmed will dissent. Second, a justice may concur with the Court's decision, agreeing with the result in the specific case but differing with the rationale expressed in the Court's opinion. Both kinds of disagreement are common. Dissenting opinions are especially common; as Table 4-1 shows, for the 1998 term most decisions include at least one dissenting opinion.

A justice who disagrees with the majority opinion generally writes or joins in a dissenting or concurring opinion. Because they are individual expressions rather than statements for the Court, both types of opinions can vary a great deal in form and tone. For the same reason, they usually reveal more about the author's views, and often express those views in more colorful language, than do majority opinions.

When a justice writes a dissenting opinion after conference, one aim often is to persuade colleagues to change their positions and thus to convert a minority into a majority. After the Court reaches its final decision this aim is no longer relevant, but issuing a dissenting opinion can serve several purposes.

For one thing, dissenting opinions give justices who disagree with the result in a case the satisfaction of expressing unhappiness with that result and justifying their disagreement. Justice Scalia has said that the right to dissent "makes the practice of one's profession as a judge more satisfying."[16]

Dissenting opinions can have more concrete purposes. Through their arguments, dissenters may try to set the stage for a later Court to adopt their view. This may be one reason why the majority opinion sometimes responds to the arguments made by a dissenter. In the short term, a dissenting opinion may be intended to subvert the Court's decision by pointing out how lower courts can interpret it narrowly or by urging Congress to overturn the Court's reading of a statute.

When more than one justice dissents, most of the time all the dissenters join in a single opinion—most likely, the opinion originally assigned by the senior dissenting justice. During the 1998 term, there were a dozen instances in which four dissenters agreed on a single opinion. But often there are multiple dissenting opinions, each expressing its own view though sometimes indicating agreement with another opinion. In *Stenberg v. Carhart,* a 2000 abortion decision, there were four dissenting opinions as well as three concurring opinions.

One type of concurring opinion disagrees with the majority opinion, taking the position expressed by Harry Blackmun in one case: "I concur in the result the Court reaches in this case, but I cannot follow the route the Court takes to reach that result."[17] Sometimes this disagreement on doctrine is virtually total. In *Minnesota v. Carter* (1998), the Court ruled against a claim by two criminal defendants that they had been subjected to an illegal search. Chief Justice Rehnquist's majority opinion rested this decision on the ground that as visitors to an apartment the two had no right to privacy under the Fourth Amendment. Justice Breyer's concurring opinion flatly disagreed with this conclusion but upheld the search on the ground that the police officer in question had a right to look into the apartment from where he stood. Sometimes the disagreement is more limited. In her concurring opinion in *Michael H. v. Gerald D.* (1989), Justice O'Connor agreed with the majority opinion except for one potentially significant footnote.

Another type of concurring opinion is written by justices who join the majority opinion, indicating that they agree with both the outcome for the litigants and the legal rules that the Court establishes. Under those circumstances, why would justices write separate opinions? Most often, they do so to influence reactions to the Court's decisions by interpreting the majority opinion. Concurrences frequently offer narrow interpretations of Court rulings.

Indeed, like dissenting opinions, they sometimes advise lower courts, states, or litigants what they might do to limit the impact of the Court's decision.

Announcing the Decision. The process of decision making in a case ends when all the opinions have been put in final form and all justices have determined which opinions they will join. The decision is then announced in open court.

Typically, the justice who wrote the majority opinion reads a portion of the opinion. Justices occasionally offer further commentary. The authors of dissenting opinions also may read their opinions, though Chief Justice Rehnquist reportedly has an informal rule allowing each justice to do so only once a term.[18] Sometimes a dissenter adopts a strong tone in disagreeing with the Court's ruling. On the last day of the 1998 term the Court announced three decisions that established new limits on lawsuits against states. Each decision was by a 5–4 vote, and in each case one of the dissenters spoke forcefully against the decision. In one case, Justice Stevens accused the majority of creating a new legal doctrine "much like a mindless dragon that indiscriminately chews gaping holes in Federal statutes."[19]

The length of time required for a case to go through all the stages from filing in the Court to the announcement of a decision can vary a good deal, depending primarily on the backlog of cases scheduled for oral argument and the time the justices take to settle on a decision and set of opinions. In June 1999 the Court decided cases that were filed as early as the first week of 1998 and as late as the last day of that year.

After the Court decides a case—or declines to hear it—the losing party may petition for a rehearing. Such petitions are rarely granted.[20]

Influences on Decisions: Introduction

Perhaps the most important thing to understand about the Supreme Court is why the Court reaches the decisions that it hands down. Cases present the justices with choices: which party to favor, what rules of law to establish. How can these choices be explained?

This is a very difficult question to answer. Like policy makers elsewhere in government, Supreme Court justices are influenced by a broad range of considerations that interact in a complex way. Thus it is not surprising that people who study the Court offer quite different explanations for the Court's decisions.

The rest of this chapter is devoted to this important and difficult question. Of course, no conclusive answer is possible. But some insight into the bases for the Court's decisions can be gained by looking at four broad forces that shape those decisions: the state of the legal rules the Court interprets, the justices' personal values, interaction among the justices, and the Court's political and social environment. The sections that follow consider each of these forces.

The State of the Law

Every case requires the Supreme Court to choose among alternative interpretations of the law, usually provisions of the Constitution or federal statutes. In this sense a justice's job is very different from that of a legislator: justices interpret existing law rather than write new law. Thus, the state of the existing law is a good starting point for explanation of the Court's decisions.

The Law's Significance in Decisions

To what extent does the state of the law explain the Court's decisions? One possible position is that the law is the *only* explanation of what the Court does: its decisions simply reflect the provisions of law that it is called upon to interpret. In 1999 Justice Thomas told a group that "I just follow the law, so it doesn't make any difference what my opinions are."[21] But that position does not accord with two realities about the Court.

One reality is that justices care about more than just the law. In particular, they often hold strong preferences about the policy issues involved in cases, and they want to see their preferences reflected in the Court's decisions. For that reason they could be expected not just to accept the freedom that results from the legal ambiguity of cases but to seize upon that freedom to make what they view as good policy. As Justice Breyer said, "If you see the result is going to make people's lives worse, you'd better go back and rethink it. The law is supposed to fit together in a way that makes the human life of people a little bit better."[22]

The second reality is what might be called the legal ambiguity of the cases that the Supreme Court decides. The Court ordinarily chooses to hear only cases that involve ambiguous applications of the Constitution or federal statutes—cases in which the proper interpretation of the law is far from clear. If justices consciously seek to make good policy, the law's ambiguity in these cases leaves them considerable room to do so because they can justify the decision they prefer in legal terms. But even if justices consciously seek only to interpret the law properly, their "rooting interests" may steer them to the interpretation that is most consistent with their policy preferences. Thus it is not surprising that in most cases the justices disagree about the outcome for the litigants, the appropriate legal rules, or both; in those cases, the law's ambiguity causes justices with different policy preferences to reach different conclusions.

But the state of the law still can affect the justices. Even if decisions on either side could be justified under the law, the law may weigh more heavily on one side than the other. If the justices care about making good law, they would be drawn toward the side that seems to have a stronger legal argument.

And there is excellent reason to think that justices do care about making good law. They are trained in a tradition that emphasizes the law as a basis for judicial decisions. They are judged by a legal audience that cares about their ability to reach well-founded interpretations of the law. Perhaps most important, they work in the language of the law. The arguments they receive in written briefs and oral arguments are primarily about the law. And the same is true of arguments they make to each other in draft opinions and memoranda.[23]

As a result, justices are affected by the state of the law they interpret. That effect is clearest when they reach judgments that seem to conflict with their conceptions of good policy. Concurring with a 1996 decision that upheld a state's taking of an automobile under its forfeiture power, Justice Thomas expressed his concern about such uses of power. But, he concluded, "this case is ultimately a reminder that the Federal Constitution does not prohibit everything that is intensely undesirable."[24] Sometimes, in fact, the justices are sufficiently unhappy with their interpretation of a statute that they ask Congress to consider rewriting the statute to override their decision—to establish a policy that they feel powerless to adopt themselves because of their reading of the law.[25]

Means of Interpretation

Judges can employ a complex array of techniques with which to interpret provisions of law, but most of these techniques fit into a few broad approaches. We can get a fuller sense of the role of law in the Court's decisions by looking at those approaches.

"Plain Meaning." The most basic approach is analysis of the literal meaning of the words in question. Nearly everyone agrees that interpretation should begin with a search for plain meaning, and many possible interpretations of the law are ruled out because they are inconsistent with the plain meaning of a provision. For instance, the Twenty-second Amendment to the Constitution states, "No person shall be elected to the office of the President more than twice." It is difficult to imagine how the Supreme Court could justify a ruling that a twice-elected person can be elected to a third term.

The Court, of course, seldom faces such easy issues. Most of the Court's decisions involve ambiguous provisions such as the Fourteenth Amendment's protection of "due process of law," which has no plain meaning. And even a provision that may seem to have a plain meaning can be susceptible to multiple interpretations. The First Amendment states that "Congress shall make no law . . . abridging the freedom of speech," but justices and commentators have disagreed about the meaning of "freedom of speech" and even of "speech." Legal scholar Cass Sunstein has written that "on so many of the central constitutional questions . . . the Constitution's words tell us much less than we need to know." [26]

Federal statutes typically are less vague, but even they often leave large gaps. One commentator complained that Congress "cannot or will not be specific." [27] And even specific language can be quite ambiguous. One statute requires at least five years' imprisonment for someone who "during and in relation to any crime of violence or drug trafficking crime . . . uses or carries a firearm." [28] But the meaning of both "uses" and "carries" can be uncertain. Has someone used a gun by offering to trade it for cocaine? Does keeping a gun in a car trunk constitute using or carrying the gun? The Court has wrestled with these questions as well as others involving the language of this statute, and more often than not the justices have disagreed about the answers. [29]

Intent of Framers or Legislators. Where the plain meaning of a legal provision is unclear, justices can seek to ascertain the intentions of those who wrote the provision. Evidence concerning legislative intent can be found in congressional committee reports and floor debates, which constitute what is called the "legislative history" of a statute. For provisions of the original Constitution, similar evidence is found in records of the Constitutional Convention of 1787.

Sometimes the intent of the Framers of the Constitution or of Congress is fairly clear. Frequently, however, it is not. The body that adopted a provision may not have spoken on an issue; the members of Congress who wrote the broad language of the Fourteenth Amendment could hardly indicate their intent concerning all the issues that have arisen under that amendment. And evidence about intent may be contradictory. When Congress adopts a statute, its members sometimes offer differing interpretations of language in the statute, trying in this way to influence the courts. This was the case with the Civil Rights Act of 1991, which changed the law's language on a number of civil rights issues. In speeches and statements, congressional liberals and conservatives put forward their own versions of what the new language meant. And some evidence of legislative intent comes from sources such as committee reports that may represent the views of congressional staff more than those of the members.

The use of intent has been the subject of considerable controversy in constitutional interpretation. Some people argue that the Court should adhere to the intent of the framers of each provision as closely as possible; others believe it is appropriate to interpret the Constitution in terms of the current meaning of its language and its underlying values. To a considerable extent this is an ideological debate, with liberals wanting the freedom to adopt broad interpretations of constitutional rights. For instance, some conservative justices point to evidence that the writers of the Eighth Amendment did not view capital punishment as "cruel and unusual," while some liberals argue that the Court should interpret the Eighth Amendment in light of changing standards about punishments.

In recent years there has been a debate on the Court over the use of legislative intent in interpreting statutes. The leading opponent is Justice Scalia, who consistently refuses to refer to legislative history. Most fundamentally, he views it as illegitimate; it is the laws, not the intentions of legislators, that govern. Further, he sees it as an uncertain guide to congressional intent, highly susceptible to being used as justification "for decisions arrived at on other grounds."[30]

Scalia has gained some support from other conservatives on the Court. But more liberal justices—most vocally, Justice Stevens—

continue to favor the use of legislative history. In *Bank One Chicago v. Midwest Bank & Trust Company* (1996), for instance, Stevens strongly contested Scalia's arguments against legislative history. Justice Ginsburg, a moderate liberal, has taken something of a mixed position. "My own approach to legislative history," she has said, "is one of hopeful skepticism. I'm hopeful that I'll find something useful but skeptical that what I find will have any real value."[31]

Precedent. The Supreme Court's own past decisions, its precedents, provide another guide to decision making. A basic doctrine of the law is *stare decisis* (let the decision stand). Under this doctrine a court is expected to adhere to its past interpretations of law as well as those of higher courts. Aside from legal doctrine, precedents have a practical value. By following precedent, a judge relies on past practice rather than taking new and perhaps risky directions in legal interpretation. Following precedent also simplifies the task of decision making.

Technically, a court is bound to follow not everything stated in a relevant precedent but only the rule of law that is necessary for decision in that case—what is called the holding. As Justice Souter said in a 1999 case, "a line of argument unnecessary to the decision of the case remains dictum,"[32] and "dictum" has no legal force. The Court might strike down a special tax on newspapers on the ground that the First Amendment prohibits any tax on publications that does not apply equally to other products. That would be the holding of the case. If the Court's opinion provided examples of other regulations of newspapers that would also violate the First Amendment, those examples—unnecessary for the decision in this case—would be dicta. But the line between holding and dictum is not always easy to draw.

Even if strictly followed, the rule of adhering to precedent would not eliminate all ambiguity in legal interpretation. Most cases before the Supreme Court concern issues that are at least marginally different from those decided in past cases, so precedent seldom determines a decision in a strict way. Justices often "distinguish" precedents, holding that they do not apply in particular situations. They also cut back on precedents, narrowing them without overturning them altogether. Through both methods, the Burger and Rehnquist Courts have limited substantially the reach of major Warren Court decisions on the rights of criminal defendants.

Sometimes the Court simply abandons precedents, and it has done so at an unusually high rate since 1960. By the best count, the Court overturned 162 precedents between 1960 and 1999, an average of four per term.[33] Sometimes the Court overturns precedents after several decades, sometimes after only a few years.

When the Court abandons a relatively recent precedent, it is usually because of a shift in its collective ideological stance. Thus many of the precedents overturned by the Rehnquist Court had been issued by the more liberal Warren and Burger Courts that preceded it. One example concerns government assistance to religious schools. In *Aguilar v. Felton* (1985), the Court ruled by a 5–4 vote that local governments could not use federal funds to pay the salaries of public school employees who taught in religious schools. In *Agostini v. Felton* (1997), a second case arising from the same dispute, the Court overturned the *Aguilar* precedent by another 5–4 vote. The three justices who sat on the Court in both 1985 and 1997 all took the same positions in both cases, but the views of the six justices who joined the Court after 1985 were a bit more conservative than those of the justices they replaced—just enough to produce a majority that favored overturning *Aguilar.*

Justices Rehnquist and O'Connor had been two of the dissenters in *Aguilar.* When *Agostini* came to the Court, they could have changed their position in order to follow the *Aguilar* precedent; instead, they adhered to that position and thereby helped to overturn *Aguilar.* This was not unusual; most of the time, justices refuse to accept a precedent that they had opposed when it was originally established.[34] Indeed, justices often appear selective in their reactions to precedents, emphasizing those that they like and downplaying or rejecting those they dislike. As Justice Scalia suggested in a 1999 case, members of the Court sometimes use precedent "as a weapon rather than a guide."[35]

Yet precedents do have some weight; there is a degree of reluctance—perhaps stronger for some justices than for others—to overturn them directly. To take one example, Chief Justice Rehnquist certainly does not regard precedents as sacred, but in a 1996 case he supported a precedent on state taxing powers while expressing his continuing disagreement with that precedent.[36] Like the law in general, the rule of adhering to precedent hardly controls the Court's decisions, but it does structure and influence them.

Justices' Values

The Influence of Policy Preferences

In 1971 President Richard Nixon nominated Assistant Attorney General William Rehnquist to the Supreme Court. Rehnquist had a long record of conservative positions on political and legal issues—views that he had expressed as a Supreme Court law clerk, a participant in Arizona politics, and a member of the Nixon administration. Rehnquist's nomination drew opposition from liberals who expected that his conservative views would be reflected in his votes and opinions on the Court. Rehnquist told the Senate Judiciary Committee, however, that "my fundamental commitment, if I am confirmed, will be to totally disregard my own personal belief." [37]

Yet Rehnquist's record on the Court has confirmed the expectations of his opponents in 1971. His positions have been strongly conservative, particularly on civil liberties issues, and he seldom surprises observers of the Court. (His opinion upholding the *Miranda* rules in *Dickerson v. United States* in 2000 was a noteworthy exception.) The consistency between the views he indicated before his appointment to the Court and his record on the Court is symbolized by his position that a criminal conviction need not be overturned just because an involuntary confession was introduced as evidence—a position that he expressed in strong terms as a law clerk in 1952 and as chief justice in 1991. [38]

Clearly, Rehnquist's "personal belief" has had a good deal of impact on his record as a justice. And the same is true of his colleagues on the Court. There has been less consistency between the pre-Court records of some other justices and their votes and opinions on the Court, but those who seek to predict the general stance that a nominee will take on the Court have been fairly successful. [39] And when justices express their personal views on policy issues outside the Court, their positions in cases are usually consistent with those views. To take one example, the conservative values that Justice Thomas has expressed in his speeches and writings are reflected in his votes and opinions as a justice. [40]

This should not be surprising. As discussed earlier, the state of the law cannot, and does not, fully control the Court's decisions. For that reason the justices' choices must be based in part on other considerations. Among the other considerations that come into play, the justices' policy preferences are the most powerful; like other policy makers, members of the Supreme Court make decisions largely in terms of their personal attitudes about policy. Indeed, because the Court has a degree of freedom from external pressures, policy preferences may play a larger role in its collective choices than they do in legislatures and administrative agencies.

Some scholars argue that the justices' policy preferences are essentially a complete explanation of the Court's decisions.[41] In contrast, I think that the justices' preferences exert their effects in combination with other important forces, such as the political environment—and, for that matter, the law. But policy preferences certainly provide the best explanation for differences in the positions that the nine justices take in the same cases, because no other factor varies so much from one justice to another.

Of course, the views of Supreme Court justices on policy issues derive from the same variety of sources as do political attitudes generally. Chief Justice Rehnquist meant to be sarcastic when he said that his conservatism "may have something to do with my childhood,"[42] but certainly a justice's upbringing can be an important source of the values expressed on the Court. Powerful experiences such as military service in wartime may affect a justice's reactions to issues such as constitutional protection for flag burning.[43] Career experiences can also have an impact: the years that Justice O'Connor spent as a state legislator and state judge undoubtedly help to explain her support for state powers vis-à-vis those of the federal government. Because justices have different backgrounds and learn different things from those backgrounds, each brings a particular set of attitudes to the Court.

The justices' policy preferences could be reflected in their behavior on the Court in different ways. Justices might simply take the positions that best reflect their views of good policy. Or they might act strategically, adjusting their positions to achieve the best results. In Chapter 3, I discussed strategy in decisions whether to accept cases: to a degree, justices vote to hear cases in which they think that the Court would rule the way they want if it accepted these cases. In decisions on the merits, justices might write opinions that do not fully reflect their own views in order to win the support of other justices. Or the Court collectively could modify its position on an issue in order to reduce the chances that Congress will override the Court's decision and substitute a policy that most justices greatly dislike.

It is not entirely clear to what extent the justices behave strategically and what forms their strategies take.[44] But it appears, on the whole, that strategic considerations do not move justices very far from their own favored positions in cases. Thus the impact of justices' policy preferences can be considered initially without taking strategy into account. In the next two sections, strategy aimed at other justices and at the Court's political environment will be considered.

The Ideological Dimension

Liberal and Conservative Positions. The preferences of justices, as reflected in their votes and opinions, may be understood in ideological terms. On most issues that come to the Supreme Court, opposing positions can be labeled as liberal and conservative. The labeling of positions is straightforward on most civil liberties issues; the position more favorable to legal protection for liberties is considered liberal. Some civil liberties issues involve the right to equal treatment by government and private institutions under the Constitution and federal statutes. The liberal position on these issues is more sympathetic toward challenges to inequality than is the conservative position. Similarly, the liberal position gives greater weight to procedural rights, such as those protecting criminal defendants, and substantive rights, such as freedom of expression and privacy. In contrast, the conservative position gives greater weight to values that compete with these rights, such as the capacity to fight crime effectively.

On economic issues, liberal and conservative positions are more difficult to define. But the liberal position is basically more sympathetic to economic "underdogs" and to government policies intended to benefit those groups. Thus, for example, the conservative position is more favorable to businesses in conflicts with labor unions and more supportive of efforts by businesses to limit government regulation of their operations.

Some cases that come before the Supreme Court do not have obvious liberal and conservative sides. This is true of boundary disputes between two states and most cases involving contracts between busi-

TABLE 4-2

Proportion of Liberal Votes
Cast by Justices, 1998 Term

Justice	Liberal votes
Stevens	75.9
Ginsburg	58.2
Breyer	56.4
Souter	55.7
Kennedy	35.4
O'Connor	34.6
Scalia	34.2
Thomas	25.3
Rehnquist	22.8

Note: Cases are included only if votes could be classified as liberal or conservative by conventional criteria. Cases in which two liberal values or two conservative values conflicted are omitted. Seventy-nine cases are included. Votes in unanimous decisions are classified according to which side is primarily favored by the decision. Votes in nonunanimous decisions are classified according to whether the justice voted for the more liberal or the more conservative outcome favored by members of the Court.

nesses. It is also true of cases in which two civil liberties—freedom of expression and equality, for instance—conflict. In some cases people might disagree about how to label the two sides: is a decision favoring the federal government over other creditors in a bankruptcy case liberal, conservative, or neither? On the whole, ideological lines in American society and thus in the Court have become more complicated. Still, most issues that the Court decides do have clearly defined conservative and liberal sides.

Ideology and Decisions. If opposing positions in most cases can be identified as liberal or conservative, we can describe the justices' voting patterns in terms of the frequency with which they support the conservative side and the liberal side. Table 4-2 shows the ideological patterns of votes for the justices in the 1998 term. As the table shows, every justice cast a good many votes on both sides. But the justices also differed considerably in their ideological tendencies: Justice Stevens supported the liberal side more than three times as often as Chief Justice Rehnquist.

As I have suggested, the votes that justices cast and the opinions they write reflect the influence of several different forces. For that reason we cannot say that Justice Souter is a liberal simply because a majority of his votes supported liberal positions. With a different mix of cases and under different circumstances, Souter might have cast a majority of conservative votes. But because differences in justices' positions reflect primarily differences in their policy preferences, it is appropriate to conclude—at least if the 1998 term is typical—that Souter is more conservative than Stevens and substantially more liberal than Rehnquist. Indeed, the relative positions of the justices tend to remain fairly stable from term to term, though Scalia's proximity to the moderate conservatives Kennedy and O'Connor in the 1998 term was unusual. That stability underlines the importance of policy preferences in shaping the positions that justices take.

It is reasonable to describe the justices in terms of their overall liberalism or conservatism, because there is considerable ideological consistency in their positions across issues. A justice who is strongly conservative on the issue of privacy is also likely to be quite conservative on conflicts between business and labor. In this respect, of course, the justices are similar to other policy makers.

But this consistency is far from absolute. A justice who takes liberal positions on economic issues may be conservative on civil liberties issues. Some members of the current Court give considerably more support to freedom of expression than they do to the rights of criminal defendants.

Within specific areas of policy, the degree of consistency is somewhat greater. The degree of consistency can be measured by what is called a scalogram. If the nine justices can be ranked from most liberal to most conservative in the same way for all the issues that arise in a category such as criminal cases, we would expect a distinctive pattern of votes on cases in that category. Each time the most conservative justice votes for the liberal position in a case, every other justice should do so as well; each time the second most conservative justice casts a liberal vote, the seven more liberal justices should also do so; and so on. Any deviation from that pattern represents an ideological inconsistency. Scalograms, limited to nonunanimous decisions, lay out the actual pattern of liberal and conservative votes to show how closely they follow this expected pattern.

A scalogram depicting a high level of ideological consistency is presented in Figure 4-1, which shows votes in criminal cases during the Court's 1997 term. The justices varied a good deal in their support for criminal defendants, from Stevens at the liberal end of the spectrum (that is, most supportive of defendants) to Thomas at the conservative end. The scalogram shows that to a considerable extent the divisions among the justices in individual cases followed the same ideological lines as the overall rankings of justices. For instance, in the three cases in which the Court divided 8–1 in a conservative direction, Stevens was the dissenter in each case. There were only a few exceptions to perfect ideological consistency.

The scalogram in Figure 4-1 should not be taken as typical. Criminal cases involve unusually sharp ideological divisions, and more substantial deviations from ideological consistency would be found in other areas. For that matter, a scalogram of criminal cases in the 1998 term does not look nearly as neat as that for the 1997 term. Ideological consistency of the sort that scalograms measure is typically high but well short of perfect.

Patterns of Agreement. Analysis of patterns of agreement among justices provides another perspective on the Court's ideological divisions. For each pair of justices who served in the 1997 and 1998 terms, Table 4-3 shows the average percentage of the time that they supported the same opinion in the two terms. While Figure 4-1 focuses on votes, Table 4-3 focuses on doctrine; justices who voted for the same outcome but who could not support the same opinion are treated as disagreeing.

The table shows that some pairs of justices agreed with each other much more often than other pairs. Not surprisingly, the rates of agreement were highest between pairs of justices who are ideologically close to each other (Thomas and Scalia agreed in six of seven cases) and lowest between pairs who are ideologically distant (Stevens agreed with Thomas and Scalia less than half the time). Among the four most liberal justices, Stevens, Breyer, Ginsburg, and Souter, the rates of agreement for each pair were over 70 percent. The same was true of their five more conservative colleagues. The positions of Kennedy and O'Connor in the middle of the Court highlight their importance in casting "swing votes," that is,

FIGURE 4-1

Scalogram of Justices' Votes in Nonunanimous Decisions Arising from Criminal Prosecutions, 1997 Term

Case citation[a]	Justices' votes									Liberal votes
	St	Gi	So	Br	O'C	Ke	Re	Sc	Th	
140–271	+	+	+	+	+	−	+	+	+	8
140–828	+	+	+	+	+	+	+	−	−	7
140–849	+	+	+	+	+	+	+	−	−	7
140–551	+	+	+	+	+	+	+	−	−	7
140–294	+	+	+	+	+	−	−	−	−	5
141–242	+	+	+	+	−	+	−	−	−	5
141–314	+	+	+	+	−	−	−	−	+	5
141–344	+	+	+	+	−	−	−	−	−	4
140–728	+	+	+	+	−	−	−	−	−	4
141–615	+	+	+	−	−	−	−	+	−	4
140–350	+	+	+	−	−	−	−	+	−	4
139–702	+	+	−	+	−	−	−	−	−	3
139–830	+	−	−	+	−	−	−	−	−	2
141–76	+	−	−	−	−	−	−	−	−	1
140–387	+	−	−	−	−	−	−	−	−	1
140–43	+	−	−	−	−	−	−	−	−	1
Total liberal votes	16	12	11	11	5	4	4	3	2	

Note: Cases are those arising from criminal prosecutions. Three cases were excluded because votes for the criminal defendant supported conservative positions on broader issues. Liberal votes (favoring defendants) are designated +, conservative votes (opposing defendants) are designated −. The stepped vertical line divides votes into two groups according to conventional rules of scalogram analysis; − signs to the left of the line and + signs to the right may be interpreted as votes inconsistent with the ideological ordering of the justices.

Key: St = Stevens; Gi = Ginsburg; So = Souter; Br = Breyer; O'C = O'Connor; Ke = Kennedy; Re = Rehnquist; Sc = Scalia; Th = Thomas.

[a] Numbers refer to volumes and pages of citations in *United States Supreme Court Reports, Lawyers' Edition.*

votes that determine whether the Court's decision will be liberal or conservative. Their higher rates of agreement with the justices on their right highlight the Court's recent tendency to reach conservative decisions in cases that divide the justices along ideological lines.

We should be careful not to make too much of the overall patterns of agreement. As the votes in Figure 4-1 illustrate, the justices do not always line up in expected ways. Unusual alliances are especially common in cases in which the liberal and conservative positions are not clear.

More important, we should not assume that patterns of agreement reflect self-conscious alliances or blocs of justices. This is not to say that the justices are unaware of general patterns of agreement among themselves. And like-minded justices sometimes do work together closely; this was true, for instance, of Earl Warren and William Brennan during the 1960s. But ideological allies do not always form close working relationships, and those who agree most often in cases do not necessarily have the closest personal relationships. When alliances do develop, they are chiefly the result of agreement about judicial issues rather than the source of that agreement. Shared preferences, not concerted action, best explain the tendency for certain justices to agree on opinions.

Preferences and Policy Change

The process of policy change in the Supreme Court is difficult to analyze systematically, because the issues before the Court are con-

TABLE 4-3

*Average Percentage of Cases in Which Pairs of Justices
Supported the Same Opinion, 1997 and 1998 Terms*

	Justice							
Justice	Br	Gi	So	Ke	O'C	Re	Th	Sc
Stevens	73	76	72	56	54	51	46	46
Breyer		80	81	69	72	65	56	54
Ginsburg			85	68	64	63	52	56
Souter				69	71	66	59	61
Kennedy					83	85	75	71
O'Connor						84	77	75
Rehnquist							83	78
Thomas								86
Scalia								

Sources: "The Supreme Court, 1997 Term," *Harvard Law Review* 112 (November 1998): 367; "The Supreme Court, 1998 Term," *Harvard Law Review* 113 (November 1999): 401.

Note: Numbers are averages, for the two terms, of the percentages of cases in each term in which a pair of justices agreed on an opinion. Both unanimous and nonunanimous cases are included.

stantly changing. For example, a decline in the proportion of decisions favorable to taxpayers might reflect a change in the Court's policies on tax law or simply a change in the kinds of tax cases that the Court decides, and it is not always easy to distinguish between the two possibilities. Still, at times it is clear that the Court's collective approach to a policy area or a set of policy areas such as civil liberties has changed.

Such changes can occur for many reasons. But shifts in the preferences of the justices as a group are a primary source of policy change in the Court. These shifts could come from change in the views of people already serving on the Court or from change in the Court's membership. In practice, both are significant.

Changes in Views. Close observers of the Supreme Court often try to predict how the Court will decide a pending case; typically, they do rather well in their predictions. The primary reason is that individual justices tend to take stable positions on the issues that arise in various policy areas—positions that reflect their policy preferences. As a result, the views that a justice expressed in past cases about the circumstances under which automobile searches are justified or about application of the antitrust laws to mergers of companies are a good guide to the justice's stance in a future case. In turn, the Court's collective position on such issues generally remains stable so long as its membership remains unchanged.

But as members of the Court, justices are exposed to new influences and confront issues in new forms. As a result, the policy preferences that they express in their votes and opinions may shift. Small changes are common, and occasionally more fundamental changes occur.

A justice who serves on the Court for several years is likely to shift positions on some specific issues, usually because of experience with cases that concern those issues. In his opinion in a 2000 case, Justice Souter took the position that a city seeking to prohibit nude dancing establishments must provide evidence of negative "secondary effects" to meet its burden under the First Amendment. "Careful readers," Souter said,

will of course realize that my partial dissent rests on a demand for an evidentiary basis that I failed to make when I concurred in [a 1991 decision]. I should have demanded the evidence then, too, and my mistake calls to mind Justice Jackson's foolproof explanation of a lapse of his own, when he quoted Samuel Johnson, "'Ignorance, sir, ignorance.'" I may not be less ignorant of nude dancing than I was nine years ago, but after many subsequent occasions to think further about the needs of the First Amendment, I have come to believe that a government must toe the mark more carefully than I first insisted. I hope it is enlightenment on my part, and acceptable even if a little late.[45]

Such shifts are exceptions to the rule, but they do occur from time to time.

Individual issues aside, most justices retain the same basic ideological position throughout their career. A justice who begins as a liberal, such as Thurgood Marshall, generally remains a liberal; the same is usually true of a conservative such as William Rehnquist. When a justice's position shifts relative to that of the Court as a whole, it is usually because new appointments have shifted the Court's ideological center, while the justice has retained the same general views. This appears to be the case with John Paul Stevens, who moved to the liberal end of the Court as more liberal justices were replaced by conservatives.

Justice Blackmun is an example of the relatively rare cases in which a justice's basic views seem to undergo a fundamental shift. Blackmun came to the Court in 1970 as a Nixon appointee, and early in his tenure he aligned himself chiefly with the other conservative justices. He and Chief Justice Burger, boyhood friends from Minnesota, were dubbed the "Minnesota Twins." In the 1973 term, Blackmun agreed with Burger on opinions in 84 percent of the decisions, and with liberal William Brennan in only 49 percent.[46] But gradually Blackmun moved toward the center of the Court, and from the 1980 term on he usually had higher agreement rates with Brennan than with Burger—in 1985, Burger's last term, 30 percentage points higher. By the early 1990s Blackmun had become one of the two most liberal justices on the Court.

This shift to the Court's left resulted in part from the replacement of liberal colleagues with conservatives. But Blackmun's own positions clearly became more liberal. Although the reasons for this change are uncertain, it appears that his experiences in dealing with cases that came to the Court—particularly *Roe v. Wade,* in which he wrote the Court's opinion—were important. And it also seems that Blackmun wanted to help maintain an ideological balance on the Court as it became increasingly conservative.[47]

Perhaps more common than individual ideological shifts are changes in the views of the justices as a group on a particular issue. These shifts typically result from developments in American society that shape the views of the justices along with other groups.

One striking example concerns the legal status of women. The liberal Warren Court gave unprecedented support to the goal of equality under the law, but it did not attack legal rules that treated women and men differently. In contrast, the more conservative Burger and Rehnquist Courts have handed down a series of decisions promoting legal equality for men and women. By the 1990s even the most conservative justices were using a rigorous standard to evaluate laws that treat women and men differently, a standard that might have been unthinkable in the 1960s.[48] The most fundamental cause of this change seems to be the direct and indirect impact of the feminist movement on the Court's agenda and, even more, on justices' views about women's social roles. In any event, this example underlines the potential for significant changes in justices' collective views on policy issues.

Membership Change. Although shifts in the positions of sitting justices can produce major policy changes in the Court, membership change is probably the most important source of policy change in the Court. If Supreme Court policies are largely a product of the justices' preferences, and if those preferences tend to be stable, then change will come most easily through the replacement of one justice with a successor who has a different set of policy preferences.

Change in the Court's membership often alters its positions on specific issues. As noted already, the overturning of a recent precedent usually results from the replacement of justices who helped create that precedent with others who disagree with it. And even when the Court maintains a precedent, a critical shift in membership may ensure that it is extended no further.

More broadly, changes in the Court's overall ideological position through new appointments typically lead to change in the general content of its policies. The Court's civil liberties policies since the 1950s demonstrate this effect of membership change. Table 4-4 shows the proportions of decisions favorable to parties with civil liberties claims during successive periods in the 1958–1998 terms. Because changes in the content of civil liberties cases can make these

TABLE 4-4

*Proportions of Supreme Court Decisions Favoring Parties
with Civil Liberties Claims and Changes in Court Membership,
1958–1998 Terms*

Terms	Proportions of pro–civil liberties decisions		New justices (appointing presidents) and justices leaving the Court
	Actual	*Adjusted*[a]	
1958–1961	57.8	57.8	—
1962–1968	74.1	78.9	*New:* White, Goldberg (Kennedy); Fortas, Marshall (Johnson). *Leaving:* Whittaker, Frankfurter, Goldberg, Clark.
1969–1975[b]	48.8	59.4	*New:* Burger, Blackmun, Powell, Rehnquist (Nixon). *Leaving:* Warren, Fortas, Black, Harlan.
1975–1980[b]	39.1	51.8	*New:* Stevens (Ford). *Leaving:* Douglas.
1981–1985	37.2	50.4	*New:* O'Connor (Reagan). *Leaving:* Stewart.
1986–1989	41.7	49.5	*New:* Scalia, Kennedy (Reagan). *Leaving:* Burger, Powell.
1990–1992	40.1	38.2	*New:* Souter, Thomas (Bush). *Leaving:* Brennan, Marshall.
1993–1998	41.3	37.3	*New:* Ginsburg, Breyer (Clinton). *Leaving:* White, Blackmun.

[a] Adjusted using a statistical technique to control for changes in the content of civil liberties cases decided by the Court. The technique is described in Lawrence Baum, "Measuring Policy Change in the U.S. Supreme Court," *American Political Science Review* 82 (September 1988): 905–912.

[b] 1969–1975 includes the part of the 1975 term with William Douglas on the Court; 1975–1980 includes the part of that term with John Paul Stevens on the Court.

proportions misleading, the table also shows civil liberties support with an adjustment for the content of cases based on a statistical technique.

The early Warren Court was closely divided between liberals and conservatives; from 1958 until 1961 there was a relatively stable division between a four-member liberal bloc and a moderate to conservative bloc of five. By the standards of the 1920s and 1930s, the Court's decisions were quite liberal, but the table shows that parties with civil liberties claims won only a little more than half their cases between 1958 and 1961.

President Kennedy's 1962 appointments created a liberal majority; a law clerk during the 1962 term referred to it as "a turning point in the modern history of the Supreme Court."[49] The Johnson appointments later in the decade maintained that majority. The period from 1962 to 1968 was probably the most liberal in the Court's history. The Court established strikingly liberal positions in a variety of policy areas, and the proportion of pro–civil liberties decisions increased substantially.

Between 1969 and 1992, every appointment to the Court was made by a Republican president, and all but Ford sought to use their appointments to make the Court more conservative. Thus the Court gained a distinctly more conservative set of justices. The impact of these membership changes on the Court's civil liberties policies was somewhat ambiguous. The Court adhered to some policies of the Warren Court and even took new liberal directions on issues such as women's rights. Yet, on the whole, the Burger Court was distinctly less supportive of civil liberties than was the Court of the 1960s, and the Rehnquist Court was even less supportive.

Table 4-4 shows the impact of these Republican appointments on the proportion of decisions favorable to civil liberties. The Nixon appointments reduced that proportion from about three-quarters to about one-half. The replacement of the highly liberal William Douglas with the moderately liberal John Paul Stevens further reduced the level of support for civil liberties. If the content of cases is taken into account, another major decline in support occurred after David Souter and Clarence Thomas replaced the Court's two remaining strong liberals in the early 1990s.

Ruth Bader Ginsburg and Steven Breyer were the first appointees of a Democratic president since 1967. But they have had little impact on the Court's ideological balance: they are best characterized as moderate liberals, and taken together they are not very different from the two justices they succeeded. The proportion of pro–civil liberties decisions has changed little since they joined the Court, and the Court's doctrinal positions continue to be conservative in most respects.

Thus the Court continues to reflect the impact of the Republican appointments from the late 1960s through the early 1990s. These appointments have not had the revolutionary effects that might have been expected, a fact that cautions against exaggerating the impact of membership change. But the change in policies that has occurred is noteworthy, and it strongly suggests that appointments are the most important mechanism by which the Court's policies can be altered.

Role Values

Policy preferences are not the only kinds of values that can affect the Court's decisions. Justices may also be influenced by their role values, their views about what constitutes appropriate behavior for the Supreme Court and its members. In any body, whether it is a court or a legislature, members' conceptions of how they should carry out their jobs structure what they do and affect their policy decisions.

A variety of role values can shape the behavior of justices. Their views about the desirability of unanimous decisions can affect the extent of dissent in the Court's decisions. Their judgments about the legitimacy of "lobbying" colleagues on decisions may determine the outcomes of some cases. But the most important role values concern the considerations that justices take into account in reaching their decisions and the desirability of judicial activism.

It is clear that several different forces shape the justices' votes and opinions in significant ways. The relative weight of these forces depends in part on what justices think they ought to do. In particular, justices have to create a balance between their strong policy preferences on many issues and the expectation that they will decide cases by making accurate interpretations of the law.

There is some evidence that justices differ in the relative weight they give to these legal and policy considerations.[50] These differences are not as sharp as they sometimes appear, however. At any given time, for instance, some justices are considerably more willing than others to uproot some of the Court's precedents. But their attitudes toward precedent as such may be less important than their attitudes toward the policies embodied in particular precedents. In the 1960s, the Court overturned conservative precedents on civil liberties in thirty-two cases, but it overturned liberal precedents only once. In the 1980s and 1990s, in contrast, the Court overturned twenty-two liberal precedents and only six conservative precedents in civil liberties.[51] Not surprisingly, it was conservatives in the 1960s and liberals in the 1980s and 1990s who adhered most strongly to the Court's precedents.

The heart of judicial activism is the making of significant policy changes. Because activism has overtones of illegitimacy, justices often emphasize the value of judicial restraint—the avoidance of activism. But this view has not been unanimous; some justices, such as William Brennan, have made strong defenses of activism. And observers of the Court often label some justices as activists and others as proponents of restraint.

Here, too, however, historical patterns are illuminating. During the 1920s and early 1930s, the laws that the Court struck down were primarily government regulations of business practices. Conservative justices were the most willing to strike down such laws, while liberals on the Court and elsewhere argued for judicial restraint. In contrast, in the 1960s and 1970s the Court struck down primarily laws that conflicted with civil liberties. Liberals were most likely to act against these laws, while conservatives called for judicial restraint. And in the 1980s and 1990s the Court overturned a mix of the two types of laws, with liberals taking the lead in civil liberties and conservatives in economic policy. This history suggests that positions on activism and restraint have served chiefly as justifications of policy choices rather than determining those choices themselves.

This is not to say that the justices' views about activism and other role values have no impact on their behavior. Undoubtedly, such values help to structure the ways in which justices perceive their jobs. But it appears that justices' conceptions of good public policy have a more fundamental impact on their choices.

Group Interaction

In discussing the impact of justices' policy preferences, I presented a simple picture—one in which justices act directly and straightforwardly on their preferences. But justices vote on case outcomes and write and join opinions in a larger context. They are part of a Court that makes decisions as a group, and they are also part of American government and society. As suggested earlier, justices might act strategically by taking into account the possible actions of their colleagues and other institutions. And colleagues and other institutions can shape justices' positions in other ways. Thus both the Court as a group and the Court's environment must be examined.

A Quasi-Collegial Body

In historical accounts of the Supreme Court, some of the most dramatic events concern the interaction among justices in major cases. Newly appointed chief justice Earl Warren, engaging in what Justice Douglas called "a brilliant diplomatic process," moved the Court from sharp division to a unanimous decision in *Brown v. Board of Education* (1954).[52] Members of the Court competed over a period of several months to influence the outcome in *Roe v. Wade* (1973).[53] And the Court's adherence to most of the tenets of *Roe* in *Planned Parenthood v. Casey* (1992) reflected the close collaboration among three justices on a joint opinion that determined the Court's position.[54]

Yet justices and those close to them often describe a quite different picture of the Court, one in which its members work by themselves and make their own judgments. One legal scholar, a former law clerk, wrote that

it's really nine separate courts. The Justices lead separate, even isolated lives. They deal with each other only in quite formalized settings. They vote the way they want to and then retreat to their own chambers.[55]

Contradictory though they may seem, both of these depictions of the Court are accurate; they simply portray different aspects of the same reality. For one thing, the limited personal interaction among justices does not mean that they ignore each other when working out their positions in cases. Rather, the justices now exchange views primarily in writing. According to Justice Breyer, "things take place in writing because that is a mode through which appellate judges are most comfortable communicating."[56]

More fundamentally, the justices do influence each other, but that influence occurs within constraints—constraints that result from their strongly held views on many issues. When they apply their general positions on an issue to a specific case, the resulting judgment about that case may be too firm for colleagues to sway. As Chief Justice Rehnquist wrote, when justices who have prepared themselves "assemble around the conference table on Friday morning to decide an important case presenting constitutional questions that they have all debated and written about before, the outcome may be a foregone conclusion."[57]

Yet the justices also have powerful incentives to work together with each other, even if doing so requires that they take positions in cases that depart from the ones they most prefer. One reason is institutional: justices want to achieve opinions that at least five members endorse, so that the Court is laying down authoritative legal rules. And they generally would like to reach greater consensus, to give more weight to the Court's decisions.

A more powerful reason for working together is the justices' interest in the legal rules that the Court collectively establishes. Justices would like to win the support of colleagues for the rules they prefer, so they have good reason to engage in efforts at persuasion. And they also have reason to show some flexibility in the stances they take in cases, because that flexibility may help them to win the support of colleagues for rules that are at least close to the ones they prefer.

These incentives are reflected in the negotiation described in the first section of this chapter.[58] The most common course of events in a case is for a justice to write a draft opinion for the Court and then to gain the support of a majority for that opinion without serious complications. But a draft opinion frequently attracts requests from colleagues for changes in the opinion, and most of the time justices who make these requests indicate that they cannot sign on to the opinion unless the changes are made. In response, the opinion author usually makes these changes. During the seventeen years of the Burger Court, requests for changes in the draft opinion occurred in 32 percent of all cases, and more often in important cases. Seventy percent of the time, the opinion was modified to make the requested change.[59]

Whether or not colleagues request changes in opinions for the Court, those opinions frequently are revised during the decision process. In the Burger Court, slightly more than half of all cases had at least three drafts of the Court's opinion circulated by the author.[60] While successive drafts may differ only on minor matters, they sometimes differ substantially—and occasionally with important consequences for legal policy.[61]

Beyond the content of opinions, the votes of individual justices on the case outcome can shift during the decision process. During the seventeen years of the Burger Court, 7.5 percent of the justices' individual votes to reverse or affirm shifted from one side to the other, and at least one such shift occurred in 37 percent of the cases. Most vote shifts increase the size of the majority, as the Court works toward consensus. During the Burger Court, the justices who initially voted with the majority switched their votes 5 percent of the time, while those who initially voted with the minority switched 18 percent of the time.[62] But occasionally—in about 9 percent of the cases between 1956 and 1967—shifts of position turn an initial minority into a majority.[63]

The effects of interactions among the justices should not be exaggerated. In the great majority of cases, the side that won in the Court's first vote on the merits of the case wins in the final vote as well. Most of the majority opinions that the Court issues look similar to the original drafts of those opinions. But votes and opinions do change; the Court's decisions are often more than simply an adding together of the positions with which each justice begins.

The group life of the Court has effects on its decisions that are broader and more subtle than shifts of position in individual cases. Interactions among the justices create general patterns of influence within the Court, and the Court's ability to reach consensus is affected by the extent of conflict among its members. Both these effects merit consideration.

Patterns of Influence

Felix Frankfurter and William O. Douglas both joined the Supreme Court in 1939. Frankfurter was a Harvard law professor, one of the most renowned legal scholars in the United States. Douglas, who had been a law professor at Columbia and Yale, was widely regarded as brilliant. Each would serve a long time on the Court—Frankfurter for twenty-two years, Douglas for a record thirty-six years. And each has been included in lists of the greatest justices. Yet neither exerted a great deal of influence over his colleagues on the Supreme Court.

When William Brennan came to the Court in 1956 his work as a lawyer and state judge had given him a reputation for competence, but he was hardly regarded as a great legal thinker. Yet during most of his thirty-four years on the Court, Brennan was probably the most influential justice—even more influential than the chief justices with whom he served. In this sense at least, Brennan was a more successful justice than either Frankfurter or Douglas. How can this result be explained?

In the case of Douglas, the best explanation is a straightforward one: he had only a limited interest in exerting influence over his colleagues. Certainly he devoted some efforts to winning support for his positions, especially in the cases that concerned him most. But in contrast with some other justices, whom he called "evangelists,"[64] he generally preferred to go his own way. One colleague reported, with some overstatement, that "Bill Douglas is positively embarrassed if anyone on the court agrees with him."[65]

Frankfurter is a more complicated case. He came to the Court expecting to play a major leadership role, and he was one of Douglas's "evangelists." But these efforts suffered because of his weak interpersonal skills. Justice Potter Stewart said that Frankfurter "courted" him, but "Felix was so unsubtle and obvious that it was counterproductive."[66] Further, Frankfurter's arrogance caused him to lecture to colleagues, and he reacted sarcastically to opinions with which he disagreed. His behavior alienated several colleagues, with an inevitable impact on his influence within the Court.

Brennan differed from Douglas and Frankfurter in crucial ways. Unlike Douglas, he devoted enormous effort toward influencing his colleagues. He worked hard to gain support from more conservative colleagues, both in individual cases and over the long term. As one commentator described, he

made constant gentle efforts to induce O'Connor and Powell to take his side. He circulated draft opinions to them before sending the drafts to the rest of the Court; he negotiated over language in letters that were not sent to other justices.[67]

Brennan also engaged in what one of Justice Blackmun's law clerks called a "courtship" of Blackmun.[68] In his commitment to winning support from his colleagues and his careful consideration of how to do so, Brennan was among the most strategic-minded justices ever to sit on the Court.[69]

Frankfurter was also strategic, but Brennan was far better suited to win support from his colleagues. Most important, he had the advantage of a personal style that was much warmer than Frankfurter's. "Everybody got along with him," according to one observer, "even those who bitterly opposed him from a doctrinal view."[70] Brennan was also perceptive about how to win majorities; one commentator said that he could "accurately judge his colleagues and figure out what is doable."[71]

Justice Antonin Scalia. His opinions often attack opposing opinions in strong terms.

Brennan's commitment and skills were reflected in the results. As a member of the Warren Court, working closely with Warren, he helped to forge a liberal majority for expansion of civil liberties. In the Burger and Rehnquist Courts, he did much to shape the Court's decisions and thereby to limit its conservative shift.

One justice who seems to stand out on the current Court is John Paul Stevens. One observer concluded that Stevens, like Douglas, "makes little effort to win over other members of the Court."[72] Frequently writing opinions for himself rather than joining his colleagues, he has been called the Court's "Lone Ranger."[73]

Antonin Scalia's situation illustrates the difficulty of determining a justice's influence from outside the Court.[74] Scalia does some things that seem likely to bother his colleagues. His very active role in oral argument creates at least temporary frictions.[75] His communications with colleagues during the decision process are sometimes nasty in tone, and the nastiness comes through in some of his opinions. This quality is illustrated by the opening lines of two concurring opinions in 1998:

I join the opinion of the Court except that portion which takes seriously, and thus encourages in the future, an argument that should be laughed out of court.[76]

"The operation was a success, but the patient died." What such a procedure is to medicine, the Court's opinion in this case is to law.[77]

Scalia's behavior sometimes does annoy his colleagues. Yet he is a gregarious person who has close relationships with some colleagues. Despite their ideological differences, for instance, Scalia and Ruth Bader Ginsburg have what one observer called a "long-time friendship."[78] More important, his intellectual power clearly gives him influence. For instance, he has attracted support for his position that the Court should give no weight to legislative history in interpreting statutes. And federal judge Alex Kozinski, who is close to Scalia, has argued that Scalia "sets the terms of the debate" on issues before the Court and that he is creating a foundation for long-term influence over development of the law.[79] Thus he may be engaging in a patient but effective long-term strategy within the Court.

As the discussion thus far suggests, justices differ a great deal in their influence over the Court's collective decisions. But these differences should not be exaggerated. For one thing, no justice can dominate the strong-minded people who serve on the Court. Under highly unfavorable conditions, even the most influential justice will lose most of the time. Brennan enjoyed a surprising degree of success as the Court became more conservative in the 1970s and 1980s, but he lost more and more battles as new appointments caused the Court to move further away from his views. Further, every justice has considerable power simply by holding one of only nine votes. No matter how unskilled or unpopular a justice might be, that justice still can vote to affirm or reverse, to support one opinion or another.

The Chief Justice

The chief justice is formal head of the Supreme Court, but there are significant limits on the chief's capacity to influence the Court.

One limitation lies in the burden of administrative duties, which reduce the time that the chief can spend on cases. More fundamental is the difficulty of leading colleagues who strongly resist control. As Chief Justice Rehnquist has written, the chief "presides over a conference not of eight subordinates, whom he may direct or instruct, but of eight associates who, like him, have tenure during good behavior, and who are as independent as hogs on ice. He may at most persuade or cajole them."[80] Yet the chief holds significant formal powers, powers that provide considerable potential for leadership.

The Chief Justice's Powers. One important source of power is the role of presiding over the Court in oral argument and in conference. In presiding over the conference, the chief can direct discussion and frame alternatives, thus helping to shape the outcome of the discussion. Most important, the chief ordinarily speaks first on a case in conference. Also significant is the chief's part in creating the discuss list, the set of petitions for hearing that the Court considers fully. The chief, aided by clerks, makes up the initial version of the discuss list. This task gives the chief the largest role in determining which cases are set aside without group judgment.

Opinion Assignment. The power to assign opinions merits more detailed consideration. By custom, the chief justice assigns the Court's opinion whenever the chief is in the majority on the initial vote in conference. (In other cases, the senior justice in the majority makes the assignment.) As a result, the chief justice assigns the great majority of opinions, a little over 80 percent in the period from 1953 to 1990.[81]

In making assignments, chief justices balance different considerations.[82] Administrative considerations relate to spreading workload and opportunities among the justices. Chief justices generally assign about the same number of opinions to each colleague, taking into account assignments from senior associate justices and the workload of opinion writing that a justice already faces at a given time. These considerations have been especially important to Chief Justice Rehnquist, who announced in 1989 that he would be inclined against assigning opinions to colleagues who were behind in their work. One example was justices who had not circulated a draft majority opinion within four weeks of its assignment.[83]

Other considerations relate to the substance of the Court's decisions. The legal rules proclaimed by the Court may depend in part on who writes its opinion. For this reason, chief justices tend to favor themselves and colleagues who have similar ideological positions when assigning opinions in important cases.

The selection of the opinion writer may help to determine whether the initial majority remains a majority. When the initial majority is slim, the chief justice is likely to assign opinions to a relatively moderate member of that majority, even if the assigned justice is ideologically distant from the chief. This practice stems from the belief that a moderate typically has the best chance to write an opinion that will maintain the majority and perhaps win over justices who were initially on the other side.

Because chief justices favor ideological allies in assigning important opinions, in effect they reward the justices who vote with them most often. They might also use the assignment power more directly to reward and punish colleagues, as Chief Justice Burger apparently did. Justice Blackmun said that a justice who was "in the doghouse" with Burger might be assigned one of the "crud" opinions "that nobody wants to write."[84]

Under any chief justice, the assignment power gives other justices something to think about. Asked why he joins Rehnquist in singing carols at the Court's Christmas party, David Souter said, "I have to. Otherwise I get all the tax cases."[85] Souter was joking, but he touched on an important reality.

Variation in Leadership. What particular chief justices make of their formal powers and how much leadership they exert vary a good deal. These differences result from several conditions, including the chief's interest in leading the Court, the chief's skill as a leader, and the willingness of the associate justices to be led.

The two chief justices who preceded William Rehnquist—Earl Warren and Warren Burger—are of particular interest. Earl Warren could not compete with some colleagues as a scholar. He presided over a Court that had several skillful and strong-minded members, such as Douglas and Frankfurter, and that was closely divided between liberals and conservatives during most of his tenure. Under these conditions, Warren hardly could have dominated the Court.

But Warren did have some major assets. Most important, he possessed excellent leadership skills, a product of his personality and his experience as a political leader. He had a good sense of how to build majorities for his positions, and he was effective at persuasion: several of his colleagues told one observer "how hard it had been to withstand the Chief Justice when he was able to operate in a one-on-one setting."[86] Thus Warren was able to play an important leadership role on the Court, albeit one that was shared with and contested by some colleagues.

Warren Burger was ambitious for leadership. He achieved some success in securing administrative changes in the federal courts and procedural changes in the Court itself. Simply by being chief justice, he exerted considerable influence over the Court's decisions. But he was far less effective than Earl Warren.

To a considerable extent, Burger's limited impact on the Court's decisions stemmed from his own qualities and predilections. Colleagues chafed at what they considered a poor style of leadership in conference, and they disliked Burger's practice, apparently unique to him, of casting "false" votes in conference for strategic purposes. "All too damned often," said one justice, "the Chief Justice will vote with the majority so as to assign the opinion, and then he ends up in dissent."[87] He was also accused of bullying his colleagues. One scholar concluded that Potter Stewart "loathed" Burger,[88] and other colleagues also disliked his leadership style. Apparently they were not alone; Justice Marshall's messenger said that when Burger retired, "it was just like Christmas morning."[89]

But Burger also faced obstacles that were beyond his control. Perhaps most important, as a strong conservative he had the disadvantage of standing near one end of the Court's ideological spectrum. In any case, his example shows that even a chief justice who wants to be a powerful leader does not always achieve that goal.

William Rehnquist became chief justice in 1986 after serving on the Court for fifteen years. He brought important strengths to the position, especially his well-respected intellectual abilities and an affable personal style. For these reasons, his promotion was welcomed by colleagues and other Court personnel.[90]

Rehnquist appears to be a very effective chief justice. As early as 1989, Justice Brennan said that Rehnquist was "the most all-around successful" of the last three chiefs.[91] The Court's discussions of cases at conference are shorter and tighter, reflecting his preferences. The sharp decline in the number of cases accepted by the Court has multiple sources, but Rehnquist's leadership almost surely is one of them.

During Rehnquist's tenure as chief justice, the Court's positions on issues such as federalism and the death penalty have moved closer to his own positions. His influence over colleagues has not been the primary source of those shifts; changes in the Court's personnel are considerably more important. As Rehnquist himself has underlined, the chief's impact on the Court's direction is limited. Within those limits, however, Rehnquist's skills and his desire to influence the Court's direction probably give him greater impact than most other justices who have led the Court.

Harmony and Conflict

"From time to time," Justice Kennedy has said, "writings about my own Court circulate in the press and the book trade. We are sometimes portrayed as being hostile and unfriendly to each other."[92] Indeed, the Court has been depicted as rife with conflict. Robert Bork, whose nomination to the Court was defeated in 1987, said four years later that the Court was "a snake pit." According to Bork, "they're locked in that building and they're fighting all the time." [93] And in 1998 a book by a former law clerk portrayed the Court as an institution that was divided into battling ideological camps.[94]

These depictions of the Court are countered by other depictions that characterize the Court as a harmonious group of people whose professional disagreements coexist with a high level of personal amity. The justices themselves sometimes emphasize how well they get along with each other. Justice Scalia, for instance, acknowledged that he and Justice Brennan wrote frequent and sharp dissents from each other's opinions. "I always considered him, however, one of my best friends on the Court, and I think that feeling was reciprocated." [95]

The justices' own descriptions accord with what they would prefer. A harmonious Court is a more pleasant place in which to work, and personal relations can also affect the decisional process. A Court in which conflicts are minimized finds it easier to achieve consensus in decisions. And justices who seek the support of colleagues for the positions they favor want to maintain good relations with those colleagues. Thus the justices have strong incentives to limit frictions.

Yet they cannot always be successful in that effort. The high stakes that justices often have in the Court's decisions, combined with the pressures under which they work, seem likely to breed personal conflicts. And all the sources of strife that exist in other groups can operate in the Court as well. Indeed, there is clear evidence from the past that serious interpersonal conflicts do arise in the Court. At the extreme, some justices have been unable to work with each other.[96]

It is difficult to assess the balance between harmony and conflict in the current Court. On the one hand, there are signs of significant conflict. Justices sometimes state their disagreements in opinions that attack other opinions, or even their authors, in strong terms. Yet the import of such expressions should not be exaggerated, and the Court appears to lack deep personal divisions among justices. At the least, it seems safe to conclude that the Court today is a happier group than it was in some past eras.[97]

The Court's Environment

As members of Congress do their work, they constantly deal with people who want to influence them: constituents who seek help from the government, reporters who look for good stories, lobbyists who argue for the positions of interest groups, and executive branch officials who want to build support for their legislative proposals. Members could try to ignore all these people. But they do not, because their ability to stay in office and their effectiveness as legislators depend on building favorable relationships with constituents, interest groups, and others in their political environment.

The Supreme Court is a very different kind of institution. The justices make their decisions in relative isolation from people outside the Court. As Justice Harold Burton replied when asked about his move from Congress to the Court, "Have you ever gone direct from a circus to a monastery?"[98] This isolation stems in part from norms associated with courts in general and the Supreme Court in particular, norms that require a certain distance between the Court and those who seek to influence its decisions. Unlike members of Congress, the justices do not interact with lobbyists while they consider cases. More important, the life term frees the justices from worries about maintaining their positions. Popular or unpopular, they can continue to do their work on the Court.

But this does not mean that the Court is completely insulated from its political and social environment. For one thing, people outside the Court care about the Court's decisions, and some of them try to influence those decisions. Interest groups submit amicus briefs in cases. Law professors write articles about legal issues that they hope the justices (or their law clerks) will notice. Members of Congress offer their judgments about issues before the Court.

The views of people and institutions outside the Court sometimes do affect the Court's decisions. One reason is strategic. Justices who want to enhance the Court's impact may feel that they can do so by accommodating Congress or the general public. Strategy aside, justices simply may feel better if their actions meet with approval from the legal community or the mass media or other audiences that are important to them. And elements of the Court's environment may influence the justices by affecting their thinking about cases and the issues in them. For these reasons, the various elements of the Court's environment do have a substantial impact on its decisions.

Mass Public Opinion

In 1999 the Supreme Court decided a case in order to resolve an issue that Justice Souter's opinion summarized as follows:

whether a debtor's prebankruptcy equity holders may, over the objection of a senior class of impaired creditors, contribute new capital and receive ownership interests in the reorganized entity, when that opportunity is given exclusively to the old equity holders under a plan adopted without consideration of alternatives.[99]

It is doubtful that a very large share of the public knew of the case before or after it was decided or would have cared about the Court's decision had they known of it. This case was not unique; on many issues that come before the Court, there is no public opinion to speak of.

But many of the Court's decisions address issues that concern a large share of the public, such as crime and civil rights. And some individual decisions, such as the Court's major rulings on abortion, are highly visible and controversial. Thus there is at least the potential for public opinion or potential public reactions to influence the justices.

We might not expect such influence actually to occur, because the justices do not depend on public approval to keep their jobs. But justices, like other people, may enjoy popularity for its own sake. And justices care about public regard for the Court, because high regard can serve as a resource in conflicts between the Court and the other branches of government and can increase people's willingness to carry out the Court's decisions.

Occasionally justices indicate that concern with public opinion did influence them. In *Planned Parenthood v. Casey* (1992), the Court adhered to *Roe v. Wade* in most respects. In their joint opinion that established the Court's collective position in *Casey*, Justices O'Connor, Kennedy, and Souter spoke of the importance of the Court's legitimacy with the general public as a basis for its power. They then said that an overruling of *Roe* would be perceived as "a surrender to political pressure," and "to overrule under fire in the absence of the most compelling reason to reexamine a watershed decision would subvert the Court's legitimacy beyond any serious question."[100]

The depth of feeling about abortion and the divisions within the public make this issue something of a special case. Ordinarily, we would expect public opinion to exert its greatest impact on policy makers when there is a strong majority on one side. Yet the Court does not always side with the majority in those situations. Examples of highly unpopular decisions include the Court's rulings limiting religious exercises in public schools, striking down state and federal laws against flag burning, and holding that states could not establish term limits for members of Congress. In 2000 the Court ruled that student-led prayers at public school football games were unconstitutional even though there was evidence of strong public support for that practice.[101]

The justices sometimes try to present such rulings in ways that would limit criticism, indicating that they do care about public reactions. In *Texas v. Johnson* (1989), one of the flag burning decisions, both Justice Brennan's majority opinion and Justice Kennedy's concurring opinion stressed their authors' reverence for the flag. Still, the Court's majority was willing to take action that ran strongly contrary to public views.

In other instances the Court has sided with strong majority views in the general public. One example is public concern about illegal drugs. Since the 1980s the Court generally has approved of government actions aimed at controlling illegal drugs that are challenged as violations of civil liberties, on issues that range from drug testing to searches and seizures; Table 4-5 describes some of those decisions.

TABLE 4-5

*Selected Supreme Court Decisions Favoring the Government
on Issues Related to Illegal Drugs, 1990–1999*

Employment Division v. Smith (1990)
An Oregon statute that prohibits the use of the drug peyote, when applied to its use in a ceremony of the Native American Church, does not violate the constitutional protection of freedom of religion. (Vote 6–3)

Harmelin v. Michigan (1991)
A state law requiring a sentence of life imprisonment without the possibility of parole for possession of more than 650 grams of cocaine does not violate the Eighth Amendment prohibition of cruel and unusual punishment. (Vote 5–4)

United States v. Alvarez-Machain (1992)
The extradition treaty between the United States and Mexico does not prohibit the kidnapping of a suspect in the murder of a Drug Enforcement Administration agent and the forcible transportation of that suspect from Mexico to the United States for trial. (Vote 6–3)

Vernonia School District No. 47J v. Acton (1995)
A requirement that athletes at a public school take random drug tests even if there is no reason to suspect them as individuals does not constitute an unreasonable search under the Constitution. (Vote 6–3)

Whren v. United States (1996)
Police officers who have probable cause to stop a vehicle for traffic violations can search the vehicle for drugs even if the traffic violations were an excuse for the drug search. (Vote 9–0)

Wyoming v. Houghton (1999)
Police officers who have probable cause to search a car for drugs can search a passenger's belongings even if the passenger is not suspected of criminal activity. (Vote 6–3)

In part, such decisions reflect the Court's growing conservatism on civil liberties issues. But they also reflect the desire of some justices to support government action against what most people view as a major national problem. Dissenting in one of these cases, Justice Thurgood Marshall charged that the majority had been "swept away by society's obsession with stopping the scourge of illegal drugs."[102]

If Marshall was correct, it is uncertain why the Court was "swept away." Perhaps some of the justices sought to take positions that were popular with the general public and with the other branches of government. But it may be that the justices had simply come to share the concern about drugs that pervaded American society as a whole. If so, this line of policy is similar in its source to the Court's growing support for equality between women and men.

Beyond specific issues, the Court might follow general tides of public opinion. As the public moves to the political left or right, so may the Court. Scholars have disagreed about the extent to which the Court follows ideological trends among the public,[103] but it is at least plausible that the Court does so.

In any case, public opinion has much less influence on the Court than it does on Congress, primarily because of the justices' life terms. But the public's views do affect the Court to some degree, and Chief Justice Rehnquist has explained why that impact is inevitable:

Judges, so long as they are relatively normal human beings, can no more escape being influenced by public opinion in the long run than can people working at other jobs. And if a judge on coming to the bench were to decide to hermetically seal himself off from all manifestations of public opinion, he would accomplish very little; he would not be influenced by current public opinion, but instead would be influenced by the state of public opinion at the time he came to the bench.[104]

Elite Opinion: The Mass Media and the Legal Community

Aside from general public opinion, the opinions of particular groups in society may influence justices who pay attention to them and who care about what they think or say. Two groups whose opinions are potentially relevant to all of the justices are the mass media and the legal community.

After his confirmation as a justice, Clarence Thomas reportedly canceled all his newspaper subscriptions.[105] If so, Thomas is unusual: most justices seem to pay attention to the mass media.[106] They read and react to stories about the Court, and they sometimes try to influence media coverage. Some justices meet with reporters, though often in off-the-record sessions.

All this attention to the mass media suggests that they may influence what the justices do. The media are important as the Court's primary source of information on public opinion and on the views of other policy makers, and justices' interest in favorable coverage might influence choices they make in deciding cases.

Some conservatives believe that the media have a more pervasive effect. In their view, Supreme Court reporters are primarily liberals who praise justices for taking liberal positions. Thus some justices are tempted to move to the left to win approval in the short term and a favorable image in history. Conservative commentators who believe that this impact occurs have labeled it the "Greenhouse Effect," after Linda Greenhouse, long-time Court reporter for the *New York Times.* One commentator suggested that Justice Kennedy had become more liberal in his positions because of the Greenhouse Effect.[107]

The legal community is important as a professional reference group. Justices draw many of their acquaintances from this community, and most justices interact a good deal with lawyers and lower court judges. Lawyers are also the primary source of expert evaluation of the Court, especially through articles in the law reviews published by law schools and edited by their students. Scrutiny by the legal community helps to make legal considerations important to the justices in reaching decisions. And if a particular view of legal issues is dominant among lawyers or in a segment of the bar that is important to a justice, that justice may be drawn toward the dominant view.

The law reviews can have another kind of impact as well. Because law review articles are often discussed in briefs and read by justices and clerks, they constitute one source of the information that enters into the Court's decisions. Justices frequently cite law review articles in support of their positions, and on occasion articles may help to determine their positions. For their part, members of the Court sometimes write law review articles to influence the legal community. By doing so, they underline the importance of that community to them.

Litigants and Interest Groups

Simply by bringing cases to the Supreme Court, litigants and interest groups can affect the Court's policies. Once the Court has accepted a case, they may influence its decision on the merits. Because communications to the Court must go through formal channels, the potential for such influence comes primarily through advocacy in written briefs and oral arguments.

Certainly justices pay attention to the material provided by litigants and interest groups. Opinions for the Court address the arguments raised by the parties to the case, and they often refer to positions taken in amicus briefs as well. When justices question lawyers closely during oral argument, they are often looking for responses to strong arguments by the other side. Thus the way lawyers frame arguments in a case can affect the justices' thinking and ultimately their decisions.

More broadly, as discussed in Chapter 3, the quality of advocacy on the two sides of a case has an impact. Once again, the federal government provides a good example. In the Court's decisions on the merits in its 1998 term, the government had a 72 percent success rate, about the same as its overall success rate for the 1990s as a whole.[108] One source of that success, perhaps the most important source, is the expertise of the experienced advocates in the solicitor general's office.[109]

It is possible that justices are influenced by the identities of the litigants or amici in themselves rather than just the arguments they present. Justices who care about their depictions in the mass media might be inclined to favor media organizations when they appear in cases, as one commentator perceived after a 1980 decision protecting the right to attend trials.[110] Conversely, Byron White's distaste for the press may have inclined him in the opposite direction.[111] And one source of success for the federal government in the Court might be the justices' sympathies for the other branches. Still, it seems unlikely that such attitudes play more than a marginal role in the Court's decisions. Almost surely, the justices care much more about the legal and policy issues they decide than about the parties that bring those issues to them.

Congress and the President

Several sets of policy-making institutions are important to the Court. Lower courts and some administrative agencies implement the Court's decisions. The president plays a part in enforcing decisions, helps to shape public attitudes toward the Court, and sometimes interacts with justices. Congress has significant power over the Court as an institution, as well as the power to change Court-made policies. Thus the justices may take these other policy makers into account—especially Congress and the president—when they cast votes and write opinions.

Congress. Congressional powers over the Court range from reversing the Court's interpretations of statutes to control over salary increases for the justices. Because of this array of powers, the justices have good reason to think about congressional reactions to their decisions. Relations with Congress can affect their prestige and their comfort. And justices who think strategically in a broad sense, who care about the ultimate impact of the Court's policies, want to avoid congressional actions that undercut those policies.

Ordinarily, the most likely form of strategy aimed at Congress involves the Court's decisions interpreting federal statutes. These decisions are more vulnerable than the Court's interpretations of the Constitution, since Congress and the president can override them simply by enacting a new statute. Indeed, such overrides are fairly common.

Thus justices might try to calculate whether their preferred interpretation of a statute would make enough members of Congress sufficiently unhappy to produce such an override. If so, the justices would modify their interpretations to avoid such a result. By making this implicit compromise with Congress, the justices could get the best possible result under the circumstances: not the interpretation of a statute that they favor most, but one that is closer to their preferences than the new statute that Congress would have adopted if the Court's decision had triggered an override.

It may be, however, that most justices do not care that much whether Congress overrides their decisions, except on issues that are especially important to them. Or the justices might feel that the likelihood and form of an override are so difficult to predict that there is little to be gained by taking Congress into account when they interpret statutes. In any case, it is not yet clear how often justices pursue this strategic approach.[112]

Sometimes the Court gets into conflicts with Congress that run much deeper than disagreement over the meaning of statutes. During a few periods in the Court's history, its general line of policy aroused dissatisfaction in Congress that was sufficiently broad and deep to generate a serious threat of concrete action against the Court. Such threats may damage the Court, and justices have good reason to act in ways that reduce the chances that the threats actually will be carried out. In several periods, they have done so.

The first such period was the early nineteenth century, when John Marshall's Court faced congressional attacks because of its activist policies. Marshall, as the Court's dominant member, was careful to limit the frequency of decisions that would further anger its opponents.[113] As discussed in Chapter 1, the Court's shift from opposition to support of New Deal legislation in the late 1930s probably reflected some justices' desire to avoid a serious confrontation with the other branches. In the late 1950s, members of Congress reacted to the Court's expansions of civil liberties by seeking to override its policies and limit its jurisdiction; the Court reversed some of its own positions and thereby helped to quiet congressional attacks on the Court.

There have been no clear retreats of this sort since the 1950s. Indeed, the Court has exhibited considerable resistance to congressional pressures. It has been attacked in Congress for its positions on a variety of civil liberties issues, including school desegregation, legislative districting, abortion, school prayer, and flag burning. On each of these issues efforts have been made to overturn the Court's decisions, to limit its jurisdiction, or both. Yet in the face of these attacks the Court has adhered to many of its unpopular policies, and it changed others only when its collective policy preferences became more conservative. Recent history is thus a reminder that the justices do not automatically shy away from decisions that create conflict with Congress.

The President. Presidents have multifaceted relationships with the Supreme Court, and these relationships provide several sources of potential influence. Two of these sources, discussed in earlier chapters, are quite important. The appointment power gives presidents considerable ability to determine the Court's direction. And the president helps to shape the federal government's litigation policy, and thus affects the Court's decisions, through appointment of the solicitor general and occasional intervention in specific cases.

Personal relationships between justices and presidents are a third source of influence. Some members of the Court were close associates of the presidents who later selected them. And justices may interact with presidents while serving on the bench. Some, such as Abe Fortas, have been frequent visitors to the White House for advisory or social purposes. Such relationships hardly compel justices to support the president's position in litigation, but they may affect a justice's responses to cases with which the president is concerned.

Finally, presidents can help to shape the Court's impact by influencing both the public's view of the Court and responses of other institutions to the Court's decisions. Because presidents may exert such influence, justices have reason to keep the peace with the president just as they do with Congress. As a result, presidents undoubtedly exert a subtle influence on the Court's policy choices.

But this does not mean that presidents can get what they want from the Court simply by pressuring it. During the Reagan administration, both the president and Justice Department officials criticized the Court and some of its justices, but it does not appear that these attacks caused the Court to retreat at all. And Dwight Eisenhower was unsuccessful in a rare presidential attempt to influence a justice directly, when he argued with his appointee Earl Warren against mandating school desegregation. At one point Warren reportedly responded, "You mind your business, and I'll mind mine."[114] This example illustrates a general point: while the president and Congress hold considerable power over the Supreme Court, ordinarily that power produces something far short of control over the Court's policies.

Conclusion

Of all the considerations that may influence the Supreme Court's decisions, I have given primary emphasis to the justices' policy preferences. The application of the law to the Court's cases is usually ambiguous, and environmental constraints are generally weak. As a result, the justices have considerable freedom to choose positions in accord with their own conceptions of good policy. Thus the Court's membership and the process of selecting the justices have the greatest impact on the Court's direction.

If justices' preferences explain a great deal, they do not explain everything. The law and the political environment rule out some possible options for the Court, and they influence the justices' choices among the options that remain. The group life of the Court affects the behavior of individual justices and thus the Court's collective decisions. In particular, the justices regularly adjust their positions to win support from colleagues and help build majorities. These forces are reflected in results that might seem surprising: strikingly liberal decisions from a seemingly conservative Court, and the maintenance of precedents even when most justices no longer favor the policies they embody.

Thus what the Court does is a product of multiple, intertwined forces. We can discuss specific factors one at a time, but ultimately they operate together in complicated ways to shape the Court's decisions. Those who want to understand why the Court does what it does must accept the complexity of the process by which justices make their choices.

NOTES

1. *Grupo Mexicano de Desarrollo, S.A. v. Alliance Bond Fund, Inc.*, 527 U.S. 308, 333 (1999).
2. Joan Biskupic, "The Quirks of the Highest Order," *Washington Post*, May 3, 1999, A23.
3. "Judicial Conference, Second Judicial Circuit of the United States," 178 *Federal Rules Decisions* 210, 281 (1997).
4. Joan Biskupic, "Nine Supreme Individualists: A Guide to the Conversation," *Washington Post*, April 28, 1998, A15.
5. Joan Biskupic, "Justices Growing Impatient with Imprecision," *Washington Post*, May 5, 1997, A17.
6. Biskupic, "Nine Supreme Individualists."
7. David Savage, "Hate Speech, Hate Crimes, and the First Amendment," in *A Year in the Life of the Supreme Court*, ed. Rodney A. Smolla (Durham: Duke University Press, 1995), 195.
8. Thomas F. Spaulding, "A Lawyer's Day at the United States Supreme Court," *Alaska Bar Rag*, July–August 1999, 11.
9. Joan Biskupic, "Supreme Court Film Offers Glimpse Behind Justices' Closed Doors," *Washington Post*, June 17, 1997, A15.
10. William H. Rehnquist, *The Supreme Court: How It Was, How It Is* (New York: Morrow, 1987), 277.
11. Tony Mauro, "Rehnquist Compartmentalizes," *Legal Times*, January 18, 1999, 8–9. The cases were, respectively, *Saenz v. Roe* (1999) and *Davis v. Monroe County Board of Education* (1999).
12. This discussion of the conference is based in part on Rehnquist, *The Supreme Court*, 289–295.
13. Bernard Schwartz, *Decision: How the Supreme Court Decides Cases* (New York: Oxford University Press, 1996), 42.
14. Rehnquist, *The Supreme Court*, 295.
15. *Allentown Mack Sales and Service, Inc. v. National Labor Relations Board* (1998).
16. Antonin Scalia, "The Dissenting Opinion," *Journal of Supreme Court History*, 1994, 42.
17. *U.S. Department of Justice v. Reporters Committee for Freedom of the Press*, 489 U.S. 749, 780 (1989).
18. David G. Savage, *Turning Right: The Making of the Rehnquist Supreme Court* (New York: Wiley, 1992), 328.
19. Linda Greenhouse, "States Are Given New Legal Shield by Supreme Court," *New York Times*, June 24, 1999, A1.
20. Robert L. Stern, Eugene Gressman, Stephen M. Shapiro, and Kenneth S. Geller, *Supreme Court Practice*, 7th ed. (Washington, D.C.: Bureau of National Affairs, 1993), 620–621.
21. Leah Garchik, "Freedom of Conversation," *San Francisco Chronicle*, October 25, 1999, E11.

22. Tony Mauro, "Solicitor General Has Subpar Season," *Legal Times*, September 4, 1995, 9.
23. Walter Murphy, *Elements of Judicial Strategy* (Chicago: University of Chicago Press, 1964), 44 n.*. See Jack Knight and Lee Epstein, "The Norm of *Stare Decisis*," *American Journal of Political Science* 40 (November 1996): 1018–1035.
24. *Bennis v. Michigan*, 516 U.S. 442, 454 (1996).
25. Lori Hausegger and Lawrence Baum, "Inviting Congressional Action: A Study of Supreme Court Motivations in Statutory Interpretation," *American Journal of Political Science* 43 (January 1999): 162–185.
26. Cass R. Sunstein, "The Spirit of the Laws," *New Republic*, March 11, 1991, 32.
27. Fred Barbash, "Congress Didn't, So the Supreme Court Did," *Washington Post*, July 5, 1998, C1.
28. 18 *U.S. Code* sec. 924(c)(1). See Carlos E. Gonzales, "Reinterpreting Statutory Interpretation," *North Carolina Law Review* 74 (March 1996): 588–590.
29. *Smith v. United States* (1993); *Bailey v. United States* (1995); *Muscarello v. United States* (1998).
30. *Thunder Basin Coal Co. v. Reich*, 510 U.S. 200, 219 (1994). See Antonin Scalia, *A Matter of Interpretation: Federal Courts and the Law* (Princeton: Princeton University Press, 1997), 14–37.
31. "Judicial Conference," 178 *Federal Rules Decisions* 210, 280–281.
32. *Reno v. American-Arab Anti-Discrimination Committee*, 525 U.S. 471, 511 (1999).
33. This count is based on the list in Saul Brenner and Harold J. Spaeth, *Stare Indecisis: The Alteration of Precedent on the Supreme Court, 1946–1992* (New York: Cambridge University Press, 1995), 112–121, supplemented by the lists in the annual *Supreme Court Yearbook*, written by Kenneth Jost and published by CQ Press.
34. Harold J. Spaeth and Jeffrey A. Segal, *Majority Rule or Minority Will: Adherence to Precedent on the U.S. Supreme Court* (New York: Cambridge University Press, 1999).
35. *College Savings Bank v. Florida Prepaid Postsecondary Education Expense Board*, 527 U.S. 666, 689 (1999).
36. *Fulton Corporation v. Faulkner* (1996).
37. Quoted in Alpheus Thomas Mason, *The Supreme Court from Taft to Burger* (Baton Rouge: Louisiana State University Press, 1979), 293.
38. Savage, *Turning Right*, 381–382. The 1991 case was *Arizona v. Fulminante*.
39. Jeffrey A. Segal and Albert D. Cover, "Ideological Values and the Votes of U.S. Supreme Court Justices," *American Political Science Review* 83 (June 1989): 557–565; Jeffrey A. Segal, Lee Epstein, Charles M. Cameron, and Harold J. Spaeth, "Ideological Values and the Votes of Justices Revisited," *Journal of Politics* 57 (August 1995): 812–823.
40. Scott Douglas Gerber, *First Principles: The Jurisprudence of Clarence Thomas* (New York: New York University Press, 1999).
41. A good example is Jeffrey A. Segal and Harold J. Spaeth, *The Supreme Court and the Attitudinal Model* (New York: Cambridge University Press, 1993).
42. John A. Jenkins, "The Partisan: A Talk with Justice Rehnquist," *New York Times Magazine*, March 3, 1985, 31.
43. Savage, *Turning Right*, 260.
44. See Lee Epstein and Jack Knight, *The Choices Justices Make* (Washington, D.C.: CQ Press, 1998); and Jeffrey A. Segal, "Separation-of-Powers Games

in the Positive Theory of Congress and Courts," *American Political Science Review* 91 (March 1997): 28–44.

45. *City of Erie v. Pap's A. M.* (2000). A case citation is omitted from the opinion excerpt.

46. Figures on agreement between Blackmun and his colleagues are taken from the annual statistics on the Supreme Court term in the November issues of *Harvard Law Review,* vols. 85–100 (1972–1987). See also "The Changing Social Vision of Justice Blackmun," *Harvard Law Review* 96 (1983): 717–736.

47. Joseph F. Kobylka, "The Judicial Odyssey of Harry Blackmun: The Dynamics of Individual-Level Change on the U.S. Supreme Court" (Paper presented at the annual conference of the Midwest Political Science Association, Chicago, April 1992); Stephen L. Wasby, "Justice Harry A. Blackmun: Transformation from 'Minnesota Twin' to Independent Voice," in *The Burger Court: Political and Judicial Profiles,* ed. Charles M. Lamb and Stephen C. Halpern (Urbana: University of Illinois Press, 1991), 63–99.

48. *United States v. Virginia* (1996).

49. Richard A. Posner, "A Tribute to Justice William J. Brennan, Jr.," *Harvard Law Review* 104 (November 1990): 13.

50. Spaeth and Segal, *Majority Rule or Minority Will,* 290–301.

51. "Civil liberties" is defined broadly. These figures were calculated by the author from the lists of overturnings in Congressional Research Service, *The Constitution of the United States: Analysis and Interpretation* (Washington, D.C.: Government Printing Office, 1996), 2250–2256, and *1998 Supplement* (Washington, D.C.: Government Printing Office, 1999), 127, updated from Kenneth Jost, *The Supreme Court Yearbook, 1998–1999* (Washington, D.C.: CQ Press, 2000), 24. These lists differ somewhat from that in Brenner and Spaeth, *Stare Indecisis,* discussed earlier.

52. See Richard Kluger, *Simple Justice: The History of Brown v. Board of Education and Black America's Struggle for Equality* (New York: Knopf, 1976), 582–699. The quotation is from William O. Douglas, *The Court Years, 1939–1975: The Autobiography of William O. Douglas* (New York: Random House, 1980), 115.

53. See David J. Garrow, *Liberty and Sexuality: The Right to Privacy and the Making of Roe v. Wade* (New York: Macmillan, 1994), 473–599.

54. David G. Savage, "The Rescue of Roe vs. Wade," *Los Angeles Times,* December 13, 1992, A1, A28, A29.

55. Linda Greenhouse, "Name-Calling in the Supreme Court: When the Justices Vent Their Spleen, Is There a Social Cost?" *New York Times,* July 28, 1989, B10.

56. "Justice Stephen Breyer Visits IGS for an Informal Talk About the Supreme Court," *Public Affairs Report* (Institute of Governmental Studies, University of California, Berkeley), 38 (May 1997): 10.

57. William H. Rehnquist, "Chief Justices I Never Knew," *Hastings Constitutional Law Quarterly* 3 (Summer 1976): 647.

58. See Forrest Maltzman, James F. Spriggs II, and Paul J. Wahlbeck, *Crafting Law on the Supreme Court: The Collegial Game* (New York: Cambridge University Press, 2000).

59. Sandra L. Wood, "Negotiating on the Burger Court" (Paper presented at the annual meeting of the Midwest Political Science Association, Chicago, April 1999), 22–23.

60. Paul J. Wahlbeck, James F. Spriggs II, and Forrest Maltzman, "Marshalling the Court: Bargaining and Accommodation on the U.S. Supreme Court"

(Paper presented at the annual meeting of the Western Political Science Association, San Francisco, March 1996), 18–19.

61. Bernard Schwartz, *The Unpublished Opinions of the Burger Court* (New York: Oxford University Press, 1988); Schwartz, *The Unpublished Opinions of the Rehnquist Court* (New York: Oxford University Press, 1996).

62. Forrest Maltzman and Paul J. Wahlbeck, "Strategic Policy Considerations and Voting Fluidity on the Burger Court," *American Political Science Review* 90 (September 1996): 587.

63. Saul Brenner, "Fluidity on the Supreme Court: 1956–1967," *American Journal of Political Science* 26 (May 1982): 390.

64. Douglas, *The Court Years,* 18.

65. "The Court's Uncompromising Libertarian," *Time Magazine,* November 24, 1975, 69. See also Melvin I. Urofsky, "Getting the Job Done: William O. Douglas and Collegiality in the Supreme Court," in *He Shall Not Pass This Way Again: The Legacy of Justice William O. Douglas,* ed. Stephen L. Wasby (Pittsburgh: University of Pittsburgh Press, 1990), 33–37.

66. James F. Simon, *The Antagonists: Hugo Black, Felix Frankfurter and Civil Liberties in Modern America* (New York: Simon & Schuster, 1989), 249.

67. Mark V. Tushnet, *Making Constitutional Law: Thurgood Marshall and the Supreme Court, 1961–1991* (New York: Oxford University Press, 1997), 42.

68. Ruth Wedgwood, "Constitutional Equity," *Yale Law Journal* 104 (October 1994): 33.

69. Hunter R. Clark, *Justice Brennan: The Great Conciliator* (New York: Birch Lane Press, 1995); Kim Isaac Eisler, *A Justice for All: William J. Brennan, Jr., and the Decisions That Transformed America* (New York: Simon & Schuster, 1993).

70. Alexander Wohl, "What's Left," *American Bar Association Journal* 77 (February 1991): 42.

71. Nina Totenberg, "A Tribute to Justice William J. Brennan, Jr.," *Harvard Law Review* 104 (November 1990): 37.

72. Bernard Schwartz, *A History of the Supreme Court* (New York: Oxford University Press, 1993), 318.

73. Bradley C. Canon, "Justice John Paul Stevens: The Lone Ranger in a Black Robe," in *The Burger Court,* ed. Lamb and Halpern, 373.

74. See Christopher E. Smith, *Justice Antonin Scalia and the Supreme Court's Conservative Moment* (Westport, Conn.: Praeger, 1993).

75. John C. Jeffries, Jr., *Justice Lewis F. Powell, Jr.* (New York: Scribner's, 1994), 534.

76. *United States v. Estate of Romani,* 523 U.S. 517, 535 (1998).

77. *National Endowment for the Arts v. Finley,* 524 U.S. 569, 590 (1998).

78. Jeffrey Rosen, "The New Look of Liberalism on the Court," *New York Times Magazine,* October 5, 1997, 90.

79. Alex Kozinski, "My Pizza with Nino," *Cardozo Law Review* 12 (June 1991): 1583–1591. The quotation is on page 1588.

80. Rehnquist, "Chief Justices I Never Knew," 637.

81. Forrest Maltzman and Paul J. Wahlbeck, "Hail to the Chief: Opinion Assignment on the Supreme Court" (Paper presented at the annual meeting of the American Political Science Association, Chicago, August–September 1995), 11.

82. This discussion of criteria for opinion assignment is based largely on the findings for the 1953–1990 period in Maltzman and Wahlbeck, "Hail to the Chief"; and Maltzman and Wahlbeck, "May It Please the Chief? Opin-

ion Assignments in the Rehnquist Court," *American Journal of Political Science* 40 (May 1996): 421–443.

83. David J. Garrow, "The Rehnquist Reins," *New York Times Magazine*, October 6, 1996, 68.

84. Ruth Marcus, "Alumni Brennan, Blackmun Greet Harvard Law Freshmen," *Washington Post*, September 6, 1986, 2.

85. Tony Mauro, "The Highs and Lows of the 1992 Court," *Legal Times*, December 28, 1993, 14.

86. Bernard Schwartz, *Behind Bakke: Affirmative Action and the Supreme Court* (New York: New York University Press, 1988), 99.

87. Bernard Schwartz, *The Ascent of Pragmatism: The Burger Court in Action* (Reading, Mass.: Addison-Wesley, 1990), 14.

88. Garrow, *Liberty and Sexuality*, 558.

89. Jeffries, *Justice Lewis F. Powell, Jr.*, 545.

90. This discussion of Rehnquist is based in part on Schwartz, *A History of the Supreme Court*, 364–367; Savage, *Turning Right*; David G. Savage, "The Rehnquist Court," *Los Angeles Times Magazine*, September 29, 1991, 12–16, 38, 40; Garrow, "The Rehnquist Reins," 65–71, 82, 85; and Sue Davis, "The Chief Justice and Judicial Decision-Making: The Institutional Basis for Leadership on the Supreme Court," in *Supreme Court Decision-Making: New Institutionalist Approaches*, ed. Cornell W. Clayton and Howard Gillman (Chicago: University of Chicago Press, 1999), 141–149.

91. Henry J. Abraham, *Justices, Presidents, and Senators: A History of the U.S. Supreme Court Appointments from Washington to Clinton*, rev. ed. (Lanham, Md.: Rowman & Littlefield, 1999), 293.

92. Anthony M. Kennedy, "Judicial Ethics and the Rule of Law," *Saint Louis University Law Journal* 40 (Summer 1996): 1071.

93. Scott Winokur, "Justice and Balance," *San Francisco Examiner*, March 3, 1991, E-5.

94. Edward Lazarus, *Closed Chambers* (New York: Times Books, 1998).

95. Scalia, "The Dissenting Opinion," 41.

96. Phillip J. Cooper, *Battles on the Court: Conflict Inside the Supreme Court* (Lawrence: University Press of Kansas, 1995).

97. See Joan Biskupic, "High Court's Uncommon Bond," *USA Today*, June 30–July 2, 2000, 1A, 2A.

98. Mary Frances Berry, *Stability, Security, and Continuity: Mr. Justice Burton and Decision-Making in the Supreme Court, 1945–1958* (Westport, Conn.: Greenwood Press, 1978), 27.

99. *Bank of America National Trust and Savings Association v. 203 North LaSalle Street Partnership*, 526 U.S. 434, 437 (1999).

100. *Planned Parenthood v. Casey*, 505 U.S. 833, 867.

101. Richard Carelli, "Court Bans Student-Led Public Prayer," *Chicago Sun-Times*, June 19, 2000, 1. The decision was *Santa Fe Independent School District v. Doe* (2000).

102. *Skinner v. Railway Labor Executives' Association*, 489 U.S. 602, 654 (1989).

103. See William Mishler and Reginald S. Sheehan, "The Supreme Court as a Countermajoritarian Institution? The Impact of Public Opinion on Supreme Court Decisions," *American Political Science Review* 87 (March 1993): 87–101; Helmut Norpoth and Jeffrey A. Segal, "Popular Impact on Supreme Court Decisions: Comment," *American Political Science Review* 88 (September 1994): 711–716; and Roy B. Flemming and B. Dan Wood, "The Public and the Supreme Court: Individual Justice Responsiveness to

American Policy Moods," *American Journal of Political Science* 41 (April 1997): 468–498.

104. William H. Rehnquist, "Constitutional Law and Public Opinion" (Talk presented at Suffolk University School of Law, Boston, April 10, 1986), 40–41.

105. Mauro, "The Highs and Lows of the 1992 Court," 14.

106. This discussion of the mass media is based in part on Richard Davis, *Decisions and Images: The Supreme Court and the Press* (Englewood Cliffs, N.J.: Prentice-Hall, 1994).

107. Terry Eastland, "The Tempting of Justice Kennedy," *American Spectator* 26 (February 1993): 32–37. See Thomas Sowell, "Blackmun Plays to the Crowd," *St. Louis Post Dispatch*, March 4, 1994, 7B; and Robert H. Bork, "Again, a Struggle for the Soul of the Court," *New York Times*, July 8, 1992, A19.

108. These figures are based on data provided by the Office of the Solicitor General.

109. Kevin T. McGuire, "Explaining Executive Success in the U.S. Supreme Court," *Political Research Quarterly* 51 (June 1998): 505–526.

110. Anthony Lewis, "A Public Right to Know About Public Institutions: The First Amendment as Sword," in *The Supreme Court Review 1980,* ed. Philip B. Kurland and Gerhard Casper (Chicago: University of Chicago Press, 1981), 2.

111. See Dennis J. Hutchinson, *The Man Who Once Was Whizzer White: A Portrait of Justice Byron R. White* (New York: Free Press, 1998), 4–5, 383, 449.

112. For contrasting arguments and evidence, see Pablo T. Spiller and Rafael Gely, "Congressional Control or Judicial Independence: The Determinants of U.S. Supreme Court Labor-Relations Decisions, 1949–1988," *RAND Journal of Economics* 23 (1992): 463–492; and Segal, "Separation-of-Powers Games."

113. Mark A. Graber, "The Problematic Establishment of Judicial Review," in *The Supreme Court in American Politics: New Institutionalist Interpretations,* ed. Howard Gillman and Cornell Clayton (Lawrence: University Press of Kansas, 1999), 28–42.

114. Juan Williams, "The Triumph of Thurgood Marshall," *Washington Post Magazine,* January 7, 1990, 19.

Chapter 5

Policy Outputs

I n the last two chapters I discussed how the Supreme Court determines which cases it will hear and what decisions it will reach in those cases. But it is the substance of the Court's work that people care most about. What kinds of issues does the Court address? How active is it as a policy maker? What is the content of the policies it makes? This chapter examines those questions by looking at the Court's policy outputs in the current era and in the past. It concludes by developing an explanation for historical patterns in the Court's outputs.

Areas of Activity: What the Court Addresses

The Court's Current Activity

During any given term, the Supreme Court resolves a broad range of issues in fields as varied as antitrust, environmental protection, and freedom of speech. In this sense the Court's agenda is highly diverse. But the Court generally devotes most of its efforts to a few policy fields. To a considerable degree, then, the Court is a specialist.

The content of the Court's agenda can be illustrated with the cases that it heard in the 1998 term. It is useful first to describe the issues in a fairly representative sample of cases decided during that term:

> 1. Whether Congress has power under Article I of the Constitution to subject states to private lawsuits for monetary damages in the states' courts (*Alden v. Maine*, 1999).
> 2. Whether a student may bring a private lawsuit against a public school board in a complaint of sexual harassment by

another student (*Davis v. Monroe County Board of Education*, 1999).

3. Whether the Sixth Amendment right of criminal defendants to be confronted with the witnesses against them is violated by the admission into evidence of the confession of an accomplice who does not testify at trial (*Lilly v. Virginia*, 1999).

4. Whether the Fourth Amendment requires police officers to obtain a warrant before seizing an automobile from a public place when the police have probable cause to believe that the vehicle is subject to forfeiture (*Florida v. White*, 1999).

5. Whether an administrative body, the federal courts, or both have jurisdiction to review an insurance company's refusal to reopen a decision concerning reimbursement of a health care provider (*Your Home Visiting Nurse Services v. Shalala*, 1999).

6. Whether the Federal Communications Commission has authority to make rules to carry out provisions of a federal statute providing for local telephone competition (*AT&T Corporation v. Iowa Utilities Board*, 1999).

7. Whether the First Amendment is violated by statutes that impose certain requirements on people who circulate petitions to put initiative measures on the ballot (*Buckley v. American Constitutional Law Foundation*, 1999).

8. Whether the rule that group boycotts automatically violate the Sherman antitrust law applies to a group action affecting a single company's decision to buy from one supplier rather than another (*NYNEX Corp. v. Discon, Inc.*, 1998).

9. Whether the federal Equal Employment Opportunity Commission has legal authority to require a federal agency to pay compensatory damages for employment discrimination that violates the Civil Rights Act of 1964 (*West v. Gibson*, 1999).

10. Whether the Administrative Procedure Act waives the immunity of the federal government from enforcement of liens on government property (*Department of the Army v. Blue Fox, Inc.*, 1999).

Table 5-1 provides a more systematic picture of the Court's agenda in the 1998 term by summarizing the characteristics of the eighty-two decisions with full opinions in that term. The distribution of cases by category is similar to the distribution in other recent terms.

TABLE 5-1

*Characteristics of Decisions by the Supreme Court
with Full Opinions, 1998 Term*

Characteristic	Number	Percentage
Number of decisions	81	—
Cases from lower federal courts	70	86
Cases from state courts	11	14
Original cases	1	0
Federal government party[a]	30	37
State or local government party[a]	28	35
No government party	23	28
Constitutional issue present[b]	37	46
No constitutional issue	44	54
Civil liberties issue present[b]	44	54
No civil liberties issue	37	46
Criminal cases[c]	20	25
Civil cases	61	75

Note: The data are based on listings of cases in *United States Supreme Court Reports, Lawyer's Edition.* Consolidated cases decided with one set of opinions were counted once.

[a] Cases with both a federal government party and another government party were listed as federal government. Government as party includes agencies and individual government officials.

[b] Cases were counted as having constitutional or civil liberties issues if the parties raised those issues, even if the Court decided them on the basis of other issues.

[c] Includes actions brought by prisoners to challenge the legality of their convictions but excludes cases concerning rights of prisoners.

The federal government or one of its agencies was a party in a large minority of cases, and in many other cases a state or local government was a party. Moreover, most of the disputes between private parties were based directly on government policy, such as regulation of labor-management relations and protection against discrimination.

There were about equal numbers of constitutional and nonconstitutional cases. Observers of the Court tend to focus on its interpretations of the Constitution, which often involve fundamental issues about the structure and power of government. But the Court also acts as interpreter of federal statutes, adjudicating what are often important disputes about their meaning.

In the 1998 term, as has been true for three decades, the Court's primary area of activity was civil liberties. As in earlier discussions, the term *civil liberties* refers here to three general types of rights: procedural rights of people involved in government proceedings; the right of disadvantaged groups to equal treatment; and certain "substantive" rights, the most important of which are freedom of expression and freedom of religion.

Related to the Court's civil liberties emphasis is an interest in criminal law and procedure. In recent years more than one-quarter of the Court's decisions have fallen in this area. Some criminal cases involve statutory interpretation, but a large majority concern constitutional rights of due process.

The list of representative cases from the 1998 term illustrates two other areas in which the Court is active. Outside of civil liberties, the largest number of cases concern economic issues. While most civil liberties cases are based on constitutional questions, economic cases generally involve statutory interpretation. Most of these cases arise from government regulation of economic activity, such as labor-management relations, antitrust, and environmental protection. Issues related to tax law are also common.

Another major subject of Court activity is federalism, the division of power between federal and state governments. Federalism overlaps with other categories, and most federalism cases concern economic issues. This concern was prominent in the 1998 term.

Thus the Court deals with a wide range of matters, from the procedural rights of criminal defendants to the meaning of provisions in the federal tax laws. But the Court gives particular attention to some areas of policy. Most striking is its concentration on civil liberties. Although civil liberties cases are quite varied, the fact that half of the Court's decisions concern this single kind of issue is an indication of the Court's specialization.

Change in the Court's Agenda

The Court's agenda is far from static. Even in the short run, the Court's attention to specific categories of cases sometimes increases or decreases substantially. The shape of its agenda as a whole changes more slowly, but over long periods it may undergo fundamental change.[1]

Signing ceremony for the Civil Rights Act of 1964, which has been the source of several dozen Supreme Court cases.

Changes in Specific Areas.   Until 1980, the Supreme Court seldom dealt with issues concerning employees' pension plans. But in the two decades since then the Court has decided about forty cases concerning these issues. The source of this change is simple: Congress enacted the Employee Retirement Income Security Act of 1974. This regulation of pension plans raised a variety of legal questions that the courts had to address, and the justices have seen a need to resolve many of these questions themselves. As a result, pensions have become a staple of the Court's work.

This is a common kind of history. When it adopts legislation that creates new legal questions and legal rights, Congress often increases the Court's attention to the issues involved. An especially striking example is employment discrimination. Until Congress legislated in this area, there was little basis for bringing discrimination cases to court. But the Civil Rights Act of 1964 included a provision prohibiting employment discrimination on the basis of race, sex, or

Ruth Bader Ginsburg in 1977. As head of the Women's Rights Project of the American Civil Liberties Union, she brought a number of sex discrimination cases to the Supreme Court in the 1970s.

religion. Large numbers of cases were filed in federal court under this provision, inevitably creating questions for the Court to address. Other statutes relating to employment discrimination have created their own questions of interpretation. As a result, the Court has heard more than one hundred cases in this field over the past three decades.

The Court itself can open up new areas on its agenda with decisions that create legal rights or add to existing rights. When the Court held in *Roe v. Wade* (1973) that the abortion laws of most states violated the constitutional right to privacy, it ensured that it would have to decide a stream of cases involving challenges to new abortion laws. The same was true of *Furman v. Georgia* (1972), which invalidated existing death penalty laws and virtually required the Court to address a wide array of issues arising under the successors to those laws. Since then, capital punishment has featured prominently on the Court's agenda.

Of course, when Congress or the Court takes action that might open up a new area, the opening will actually occur only if litigants bring cases to the Court. Often, interest groups play a key role in this process. In *Reed v. Reed* (1971) the Court signalled that it was newly receptive to challenges to laws that treat women and men differently. The Women's Rights Project of the American Civil Liberties Union and other groups then acted to ensure that challenges to such laws would reach the Court.

Just as issues can rise on the Court's agenda, they can recede as well. Often, a new statute or Court decision raises a series of issues that the Court resolves. Once they are resolved, the Court need not decide as many cases in this area. To a degree, this has been true of cases involving employment discrimination statutes and the Fourteenth Amendment's protection against sex discrimination. Congress can cut off an area by changing the law, as it did with cases involving the military draft when it ended the draft in 1973. The justices may simply decide that they will devote less attention to a field of policy, a path they took in patent law.

Changes in the Agenda as a Whole. Beyond these changes in specific areas, the overall pattern of the Court's agenda may change over a period of several decades. Indeed, comparison of the Court's 1998 agenda with the agendas of the early 1930s indicates that there has been a fundamental change in the kinds of issues and cases the Court addresses. This change is documented by findings from Richard Pacelle's study of the Court's agenda during the 1933–1995 terms, summarized in Table 5-2. Pacelle has also illuminated the process by which this change occurred, and the discussion that follows is based primarily on his analysis.

The Court's agenda in the 1930s was similar to its agenda throughout the preceding half century.[2] Issues of procedural due process constituted a small proportion of the agenda, and other civil liberties issues were barely present. Far more numerous were cases that concerned economic issues, arising primarily from government economic policies. Also important but clearly secondary were cases about federalism.

By the 1960s, civil liberties had replaced economics as the Court's primary concern, and this broad category has remained

TABLE 5-2

*Percentages of Supreme Court Agenda Devoted to
Selected Issue Areas, in Selected Periods, 1933–1995 Terms*

	Terms				
Issue area	1933– 1942	1948– 1957	1963– 1972	1978– 1987	1991– 1995
Civil liberties[a]	10.0	28.9	53.3	53.1	49.8
Racial equality[b]	0.5	1.8	6.3	4.6	2.6
Criminal procedure[b]	4.8	14.2	23.4	22.6	20.4
Federal taxation	16.8	7.4	4.0	2.8	3.0
Federalism	13.9	10.8	6.2	10.6	10.3

Sources: Richard L. Pacelle, Jr., *The Transformation of the Supreme Court's Agenda From the New Deal to the Reagan Administration* (Boulder: Westview Press, 1991), 56–57, 147, 159. Data for 1991–1995 were provided by Professor Pacelle.

Note: Only cases with opinions of at least one page in length are included.

[a] Includes due process, equality, and substantive rights such as freedom of expression and freedom of religion.
[b] Included within civil liberties category.

dominant since then. Most categories of economic cases, including challenges to federal taxes and state regulatory policies, have declined precipitously in number. Federal economic regulation has become a much smaller component of the agenda, though the number of cases arising in such areas as securities and environmental regulation has actually increased. Federalism cases are also less common than they were in the 1930s, but this category has had something of a resurgence since the 1970s and may continue to grow. Federalism aside, the major trend is clear: the Court has evolved from an institution concerned primarily with economic issues to one that gives attention primarily to individual liberties.

Many forces contributed to this change in the Court's agenda, ranging from public opinion to federal legislation. But actions by the Court itself had the most direct effect. Perhaps most important, the justices were increasingly interested in protecting civil liberties and thus in hearing challenges to government policies that allegedly infringed on liberties. Because they had to make room on the agenda for civil liberties cases and because they were less interested in scrutinizing economic policies, the justices gave more limited attention to fields other than civil liberties.

But the shift in emphasis from economics to civil liberties was gradual rather than swift. The Court had to continue addressing important economic issues, particularly those that had caused conflicts between lower courts. Litigants also needed time to respond to the Court's growing support for civil liberties by bringing additional cases to the Court. And massive change in the agenda inevitably takes time; the Court could not have moved simultaneously into all the diverse areas of civil liberties that have occupied a place on its agenda since the 1960s. Of course, the shift was not total: the Court decides a great many cases that concern economic issues, even while its agenda emphasizes civil liberties.

A Broader View of the Agenda

If the Supreme Court's current agenda differs from the agendas of previous Courts, it also differs from those of other policy makers. In turn, those differences provide some perspective on the Court's role.

Comparison with Other Institutions. In some respects, the Supreme Court's agenda is similar to that of other appellate courts, especially state supreme courts and federal courts of appeals. To a considerable extent, all of these courts focus on government parties and government policy. Criminal cases are prominent on the agendas of virtually all appellate courts. Except for the rights of criminal defendants, however, civil liberties issues are relatively rare in lower appellate courts. The Supreme Court stands alone in the prominence of issues involving rights to equal treatment and freedom of expression.

Like the Court, the president is something of a specialist. But the president's agenda has its own emphases: foreign policy and maintenance of the nation's economic health. In contrast, the Court makes few decisions about foreign policy, and its decisions on economic policy barely touch the function of managing the economy.

In contrast, Congress is something of a generalist, spreading its activity across a large set of issues. One result is that the congressional agenda covers virtually all the types of policy that the Supreme Court deals with. But some of the issues that are central to the Court, especially in civil liberties, receive much less attention from Congress. And Congress gives substantial attention to many areas, ranging from foreign policy to agriculture, that are less important to the Court.

The Court's Position. These comparisons of agendas underline the limited range of the Court's work. Its jurisdiction is very broad, but the bulk of its decisions are made in a few policy areas.

The Court's specialization affects its role in policy making. Even in civil liberties, the Court can address only a small portion of the policy issues that arise. But by deciding as many cases as it does in this area, the Court maximizes its opportunities to shape law and public policy on civil liberties.

In contrast, the Court's relative lack of activity in several major areas of policy severely limits its potential impact in those fields. It cannot have much effect on development of the law in such fields as contracts and personal injuries. The Court today has little impact on government management of the economy and even less impact on foreign policy;[3] many people consider these the two most important areas of government policy.

These realities should give pause to those who believe that the Supreme Court is the most important policy maker in the United States. The Court should not be regarded as preeminent when the range of its activities is so limited. It could not possibly be dominant as a policy maker except in federalism, civil liberties, and some limited areas of economic policy. For reasons that are discussed in the rest of this chapter and in Chapter 6, even here the Court's dominance is far from certain.

The Court's Activism

The Court's attention or inattention to various areas of policy tells us something about where it is likely to play a significant role. But its role, in a single area or more generally, also depends on the extent to which it uses its decisions to make significant changes in government policy, engaging in what is often called judicial activism.

Of the various forms of judicial activism, perhaps the most important is making decisions that conflict with policies of the other branches. This form of activism is often gauged by the Court's use of judicial review, its power to overturn acts of other policy makers on the ground that they violate the Constitution. The Court intervenes in the policy-making process most directly and most clearly through its use of judicial review. And judicial review, unlike some other forms of activism, is easy to measure. For these reasons it is a good focus for analysis of activism.

Overturning Acts of Congress

The most familiar use of judicial review comes in decisions holding that federal statutes are unconstitutional. Such rulings represent a striking assertion of power by the Court. When the Court overturns a federal law on constitutional grounds, it directly negates a decision by another branch of the federal government.

There is sometimes disagreement about whether a statute actually has been struck down by the Court. By one count, however, by the end of 1999 the Court had overturned 148 federal laws completely or in part.[4] This number in itself is significant. On the one hand, it indicates that the Court has made fairly frequent use of its review power — on average, more than once every two years. On the other hand, the laws struck down by the Court constitute a minute fraction of the more than sixty thousand laws that Congress has adopted. A closer look at these decisions provides a better sense of their significance.[5]

One question is the importance of the statutes that the Court has overturned. The Court has struck down some statutes of major significance. Among these were the Missouri Compromise of 1820, concerning slavery in the territories, which the Court declared unconstitutional in the *Dred Scott* case in 1857; the laws prohibiting child labor that were struck down in 1918 and 1922; and the New Deal economic legislation that was overturned in 1935 and 1936.[6] In contrast, many of the Court's decisions declaring statutes unconstitutional have been unimportant to the policy goals of Congress and the president, either because the statutes were minor or because they were struck down only as they applied to particular circumstances.

A related question is the timing of judicial review. The Court's decisions striking down federal statutes fall into three groups of nearly equal size: those that came no more than four calendar years after a statute's enactment, those that came five to twelve years later, and those that occurred at least thirteen years later. Congress sometimes retains a strong commitment to a statute from an earlier period. But often it collectively cares little if an older law is overturned: the statute becomes less relevant over time, or the collective point of view in Congress becomes less favorable to the provision in question. For that reason, many of the decisions that struck down older statutes were unlikely to arouse much concern in the legislative branch.

Thus the Court's frequent use of its power to invalidate congressional acts is somewhat misleading. Any decision that strikes down a federal statute might seem likely to bring about a major conflict between the Court and Congress, but that is not necessarily the case. Conflict is most likely when the Court invalidates an important congressional policy within a few years of its enactment, but most of the time those criteria are not met.

Another way to gauge the significance of judicial review is in terms of the historical pattern of its use. As Table 5-3 shows, the Court has not overturned federal statutes at a consistent rate. It struck down only two statutes before 1865. But at that point the Court began to exercise its judicial review power more actively, overturning thirty-five federal laws between 1865 and 1919. Two more increases, even more dramatic, followed: the Court struck down fifteen federal laws during the 1920s, and twelve from 1934 through 1936. Over the next quarter century, the Court employed this power sparingly. But from 1960 through 1999 it overturned seventy-six statutes, far more than in any previous period of the same length and more than half of the total for the Court's entire history.

The years 1918 to 1936 were the period of greatest conflict between the Court and Congress. During that period the Court overturned twenty-nine federal laws. More important, much of the legislation that the Court declared unconstitutional in this period was significant. Between 1918 and 1928, the Court struck down two child labor laws and a minimum wage law, along with several less important statutes. Then, between 1933 and 1936, a majority of the Court engaged in a frontal attack on the New Deal program, an attack that ended with the Court's retreat in 1937.

As noted earlier, the Court overturned legislation at a record pace from the 1960s through the 1990s. But it struck down few laws of major importance, and many were fairly old. Typically, the Court invalidated a minor law or an unessential provision of a major law. Altogether, at least until the latter half of the 1990s, the Court's decisions overturning federal laws did not reshape major areas of national policy.

TABLE 5-3
*Number of Federal Statutes Held Unconstitutional
by the Supreme Court, 1790–1999*

Period	Number	Period	Number
1790–1799	0	1900–1909	9
1800–1809	1	1910–1919	6
1810–1819	0	1920–1929	15
1820–1829	0	1930–1939	13
1830–1839	0	1940–1949	2
1840–1849	0	1950–1959	5
1850–1859	1	1960–1969	16
1860–1869	4	1970–1979	20
1870–1879	7	1980–1989	16
1880–1889	4	1990–1999	24
1890–1899	5	Total	148

Source: Congressional Research Service, *The Constitution of the United States of America: Analysis and Interpretation* and *1998 Supplement* (Washington, D.C.: Government Printing Office, 1996, 1999); Kenneth Jost, *The Supreme Court Yearbook, 1998–1999* (Washington, D.C.: CQ Press, 2000).

Some of the provisions that the Court struck down between 1960 and 1995 clearly *were* important. *Buckley v. Valeo* (1976) and several later decisions invalidated some major provisions of the Federal Election Campaign Act on First Amendment grounds and thereby made it impossible to regulate campaign finance comprehensively. In *Immigration and Naturalization Service v. Chadha* (1983) the Court struck down a relatively minor provision of an immigration law. But its ruling indicated that the legislative veto, a widely used mechanism for congressional control of the executive branch, violated the constitutional separation of powers. In general, however, the legislation overturned by the Court in this period was not nearly as significant as the economic legislation that it struck down in the 1930s. Indeed, most of the Court's decisions striking down federal laws received little attention from the mass media or the general public.

Between 1995 and 1999 the Court invalidated twenty-one laws, an unusually large number for a five-year period. During this period too, most of the laws involved were relatively minor. But in *Clinton v. City of New York* (1998), the Court ruled that Congress could not give presidents the power to veto individual items within budget bills, thus ending a major innovation in policy making. And it reached several decisions that limited the constitutional power of Congress to regulate states and the private sector through the commerce clause and the Fourteenth Amendment.[7] Then in 2000, the Court struck down one federal statute, struck down a second statute in part, and interpreted a third narrowly, each on the basis of limits on federal power.[8] Should this trend continue, the Court may establish very substantial constraints on congressional power. As yet, however, the period from 1918 through 1936 stands alone as a time when the Court acted in a sustained way to disturb a major aspect of federal policy.

Overturning State and Local Laws

The Supreme Court's exercise of judicial review over state and local laws has less of an activist element than does its use of that power over federal laws. When the Court strikes down a state law, it does not put itself in conflict with the other branches of the federal government. Indeed, it may be supporting their powers over those of the states. Still, by striking down a state or local law, the Court invalidates the action of another policy maker. For that reason, this form of judicial review is significant.

From 1790 to 1999, by one count, the Court overturned 1,249 state statutes and local ordinances. Most were struck down on the ground that they directly violated the Constitution, the others because they were superseded by federal law under the constitutional principle of federal supremacy. That is more than eight times the number of federal statutes struck down by the Court (see Table 5-3). The disparity is even greater than this figure suggests, because many of the Court's decisions overturning particular state and local laws also applied to similar laws in other states.

As shown in Table 5-4, the rate at which the Court invalidates state and local laws has increased tremendously over time. One jump came in the 1860s, another early in this century. The highest rate of decisions striking down state and local laws occurred from the 1960s through the 1980s. In that period, the Court declared unconstitutional an average of seventeen such laws per year. The rate of invalidations was much lower in the 1990s, returning to the level of the 1940s and 1950s. That decline probably reflected the support

TABLE 5-4

Number of State Laws and Local Ordinances
Held Unconstitutional by the Supreme Court, 1790–1999

Period	Number	Period	Number
1790–1799	0	1900–1909	40
1800–1809	1	1910–1919	118
1810–1819	7	1920–1929	139
1820–1829	8	1930–1939	93
1830–1839	3	1940–1949	57
1840–1849	9	1950–1959	61
1850–1859	7	1960–1969	149
1860–1869	23	1970–1979	193
1870–1879	36	1980–1989	162
1880–1889	46	1990–1999	61
1890–1899	36	Total	1,249

Sources: Congressional Research Service, *The Constitution of the United States of America: Analysis and Interpretation* and *1998 Supplement* (Washington, D.C.: Government Printing Office, 1996, 1999); Kenneth Jost, *The Supreme Court Yearbook, 1998–1999* (Washington, D.C.: CQ Press, 2000).

of several Rehnquist Court justices for enhanced state power and autonomy.

While the Court struck down relatively few state laws before 1860, its decisions during that period were important because they limited state powers under the Constitution. For instance, under John Marshall (1801–1835) the Court weakened the states with decisions such as *McCulloch v. Maryland* (1819), which denied the states power to tax federal agencies, and *Gibbons v. Ogden* (1824), which narrowed state power to regulate commerce.

The state and local laws overturned by the Court in more recent periods have been a mixture of the important and the minor. In the aggregate, the Court's decisions have been sufficiently important to give it a significant role in shaping state policy. During the late nineteenth century and the first third of the twentieth, the Court struck down a great deal of important state economic legislation, including many laws regulating business practices and labor relations. The net effect was to turn back much of a major tide of public policy.

Some of the Court's decisions since the mid-1950s have also impinged on important elements of state policy. A series of rulings helped to break down the legal bases of racial segregation and discrimination in southern states. In 1973 the Court overturned the broad prohibitions of abortion that existed in most states, thereby requiring a general legalization of abortion, and it has struck down a large number of new laws regulating abortion since then. And through a long series of decisions, the Court limited state power to regulate the economy in areas that Congress has preempted under its constitutional supremacy. In doing so, the Court shifted power further toward the federal government and away from the states. The current Court is reversing this shift to a degree, but it is not yet clear how far this reversal will extend.

Other Targets of Judicial Review

The Supreme Court can declare unconstitutional any government policy or practice, not just laws enacted by legislative bodies. The number of nonstatutory policies and practices that the Court has struck down is probably much larger than the 1,400 laws it has overturned. In recent years the Court has overturned such actions as a county board's termination of a trash hauler's contract in retaliation for criticism of the board and a federal court injunction that imposed certain limits on picketing at an abortion clinic.[9] The Court is especially active in scrutinizing criminal procedure under the Constitution, and it frequently holds that actions by police officers or trial judges violate the rights of defendants. By playing this role, the Court has had a major impact on the criminal justice process.

Of particular interest is the Court's scrutiny of orders and other actions by the president. Decisions of presidents, or of officials acting on their behalf, can be challenged on the grounds that they are unauthorized by the Constitution or that they directly violate a constitutional rule. It is difficult to say how frequently the Court strikes down presidential actions as unconstitutional, because it is often unclear whether an action by the executive branch should be considered "presidential." But such decisions by the Court seem to be relatively rare.[10]

The Court has invalidated a few major actions by presidents, however. In *Ex parte Milligan* (1866), it held that President Abraham Lincoln had lacked the power to suspend the writ of habeas corpus for military prisoners during the Civil War. And in *Youngstown Sheet and Tube Co. v. Sawyer* (1952), it declared that President Harry Truman had acted illegally when he ordered the federal government to seize major steel mills whose workers were on strike during the Korean War. Those two decisions underline the importance of the Court's power to scrutinize presidential actions.

Judicial Review: The General Picture

The Supreme Court's record in using judicial review is uneven. The extent of activism has varied during the Court's history, with a general increase over time. One reason for that increase is growth in the level of government activity, including the number of statutes; there are more policies and practices to challenge. The use of judicial review has also differed between levels of government. The Court has overturned considerably more state and local policies than federal policies, and it has done more to limit the freedom of action of state and local governments on important issues.

Taken as a whole, the Court's record is ambiguous. Certainly the justices have made considerable use of the power of judicial review. By striking down many government decisions, including some important ones, the Supreme Court has established itself as a major participant in the policy-making process.

From another perspective, however, the Court's use of judicial review seems limited. The Court generally has been quite selective in employing its power to strike down laws. Partly as a result, the great majority of public policies at all levels of government have continued without Court interference. While judicial review allows the Court to play a major role in policy making, it certainly has not made the Court the dominant national policy maker.

Statutory Interpretation

Only a minority of the Supreme Court's decisions determine whether some government practice is unconstitutional. Most of the Court's work involves the interpretation of federal statutes. Statutory interpretation can involve activism in at least two senses.

First, the Court's statutory decisions often involve the question of whether the executive branch has interpreted a provision correctly in adopting a regulation or carrying out a practice. If the Court concludes that an administrative agency has erred, it strikes down the agency's action as unauthorized by statute. For example, a federal statute allows people to join credit unions if they belong "to groups having a common bond of occupation or association." The National Credit Union Administration, the federal agency that administers this statute, interpreted its language to mean that a single credit union could have members who worked for multiple employers. But in *National Credit Union Administration v. First National Bank and Trust Co.* (1998), the Court ruled that a credit union was restricted to members who worked for a single employer and thus nullified the agency's rule.

Another example underlines the importance of the Court's review of administrative decisions. In 1996 the federal Food and Drug Administration decided that a statute giving the FDA power to regulate drugs and devices affecting the body extended to cigarettes and smokeless tobacco, and it issued a set of sweeping regulations as a means to reduce tobacco use by young people. Tobacco companies, manufacturers, and advertisers challenged the regulations, and in *Food and Drug Administration v. Brown & Williamson Tobacco Corporation* (2000) the Court ruled that the statute did not give the FDA power to regulate tobacco products and thus blocked a major anti-tobacco campaign.

Second, the Court often puts its own stamp on a statute through its interpretations of that statute over the years. Certainly this has been true of its decisions on antitrust, labor relations, and environmental protection. In particular periods the Court's decisions in these areas have shaped or reshaped the coverage and operation of major statutes.

This process is exemplified by Title VII of the Civil Rights Act of 1964, the major federal law prohibiting employment discrimination; its effect on the Court's agenda was discussed earlier. As is typical of statutes, Congress laid out the broad outlines of the law and left it to administrators and ultimately courts to fill in the gaps. Over the years the Court has addressed a number of major issues that Congress did not resolve, including such fundamental issues as the rules for determining whether discrimination has occurred and whether an employer who did not intend to discriminate could be in violation of the statute.[11] It has also addressed new questions such as whether sexual harassment constitutes sex discrimination.[12] Until the late 1980s the Court's decisions on Title VII generally broadened protection of racial minority groups and women. Since then, its position has been more mixed.[13] In both periods the Court has done much to determine the use and impact of this statute.

The Content of Policy

In the preceding sections of this chapter I have examined the areas in which the Supreme Court concentrates its efforts and the extent of its activism. To complete the picture of the Court as a policy maker, I will now turn to the content of the Court's policies. These policies can best be understood in terms of their ideological direction and their beneficiaries.

The 1890s to the 1930s

Scrutinizing Economic Regulation. In 1915 the Supreme Court decided *South Covington & Cincinnati Street Railway Co. v. City of Covington.* The company, which ran streetcars between Covington, Kentucky, and Cincinnati, Ohio, challenged several provisions of a Covington ordinance regulating its operations. The Court struck down some provisions on the ground that they constituted a burden on interstate commerce between Ohio and Kentucky. The Court also declared invalid a regulation stipulating that the temperature in the cars never be permitted to go below fifty degrees Fahrenheit: "We therefore think . . . this feature of the ordinance is unreasonable and cannot be sustained"—apparently on the ground that the regulation violated the Fourteenth Amendment by depriving the company of its property without due process of law.

The *South Covington* case illustrates some important characteristics of the Court's decisions during the period from the 1890s to the late 1930s. In that period the Court dealt primarily with economic issues, especially government policies that affected private businesses. Most important, it ruled on challenges to growing government regulation of business practices.

The Court frequently ruled in favor of government in these cases, rejecting most challenges to federal and state policies and giving broad interpretations to some government powers.[14] But the Court also established important limits on government regulatory powers under the Constitution, and over time it created increasingly strong barriers to regulation. This development is reflected in the number of laws involving economic policy that the Court struck down each decade: 44 from 1900 to 1909, 112 from 1910 to 1919, and 133 from 1920 to 1929.[15] The Court attacked government regulation most directly in the mid-1930s, when it declared unconstitutional most of the major statutes in President

Franklin Roosevelt's New Deal program to deal with the Great Depression.

The theme of limiting government regulatory powers was reflected in the Court's constitutional doctrines. At the national level, the Court gave narrow interpretations to congressional powers over taxation and interstate commerce. In contrast, the Court read the general limitation on federal power in the Tenth Amendment broadly as a bar to some federal action on the ground that it interfered with state prerogatives. At the state level, the Court ruled in 1886 that corporations were "persons" whose rights were protected by the Fourteenth Amendment.[16] Further, it interpreted the Fourteenth Amendment requirement that state governments provide "due process of law" in making decisions as an absolute prohibition of regulations that interfered unduly with the liberty and property rights of businesses. The Court's ruling against the Covington temperature rule was one of many such decisions.

The Court's Beneficiaries. The business community benefited from the Court's policies during this period, and major corporations benefited the most. Much of the regulatory legislation that the Court overturned or limited was aimed at the activities of large businesses, because legislators believed that these businesses abused their great economic power. The railroads were the most prominent example.[17] In the decade from 1910 to 1919, the Court overturned forty-one state laws in cases brought by railroad companies. Thus major corporations such as railroads might be considered the clientele of the Court from the 1890s to the 1930s.

Large corporations did not simply benefit from the Court's policies; they helped to bring them about.[18] Beginning in the late nineteenth century, the corporate community employed much of the best legal talent in the United States to challenge the validity of regulatory statutes, and the effective advocacy of these attorneys laid some of the groundwork for the Court's policies favoring business.

The corporate interests that brought their claims to the Supreme Court came to the judiciary because of their defeats elsewhere in government. On the whole, Congress and the state legislatures were friendly to business interests, but they did enact a good many regulations of private enterprise. In giving close scrutiny to these regulations, the Court served as a court of last resort for corporations in a political sense as well as the legal sense.

Civil Liberties: A Limited Concern. Civil liberties as I have defined them were a minor concern of the Court between 1890 and the mid-1930s. Only occasionally did it hear cases dealing with issues such as the procedural rights of criminal defendants and discrimination against disadvantaged groups.

The Court issued a number of specific decisions that favored civil liberties in this period.[19] But the justices gave individual rights far less protection than they accorded the economic rights of businesses. The absence of wholehearted support for racial equality was exemplified by *Plessy v. Ferguson* (1896), in which the Court upheld the legitimacy of racial segregation by ruling that state governments could mandate "separate but equal" facilities for different racial groups. In 1908 the Court held that only a limited set of the procedural rights for criminal defendants in the Bill of Rights were "incorporated" into the due process clause of the Fourteenth Amendment and thus were applicable to proceedings in state courts.[20] Late in that era, the Court ruled that the due process clause protected freedom of speech and freedom of the press from state violations. But in a series of decisions it held that the federal government could prosecute people whose expressions allegedly endangered military recruitment and other national security interests.[21]

Overview. In ideological terms, the Court of this period was predominately conservative. It generally interpreted the law in ways that protected advantaged interests in society, such as business corporations. It did little to protect disadvantaged groups, such as racial minorities.

This conservatism was not new; the dominant themes of the Court's work in earlier periods were also conservative. The Court provided considerable support for the rights of property holders and much less support for liberal values such as civil liberties.

Thus, an observer of the Supreme Court during this era had good reason to conclude that the Court was a fundamentally conservative institution. Indeed, this was the position of two distinguished observers as late as the early 1940s. Henry Steele Commager argued in 1943 that, with one possible exception, the Court had never intervened on behalf of the underprivileged; in fact, it frequently had blocked efforts by Congress to protect the underprivileged.[22] Two years earlier, Attorney General and future

Supreme Court justice Robert Jackson reached this stark conclusion: "Never in its entire history can the Supreme Court be said to have for a single hour been representative of anything except the relatively conservative forces of its day."[23]

1937 to 1969

At the beginning of 1937, the Court's conservatism seemed to be deeply rooted. But later that year the Court began a shift in its direction that one historian has called "the Constitutional Revolution of 1937." That revolution, he said,

altered fundamentally the character of the Court's business, the nature of its decisions, and the alignment of its friends and foes. From the Marshall Court to the Hughes Court, the judiciary had been largely concerned with questions of property rights. After 1937, the most significant matters on the docket were civil liberties and other personal rights. . . . While from 1800 to 1937 the principal critics of the Supreme Court were social reformers and the main supporters people of means who were the principal beneficiaries of the Court's decisions, after 1937 roles were reversed, with liberals commending and conservatives censuring the Court.[24]

Acceptance of Government Economic Policy. In the first stage of the revolution, the Court abandoned its opposition to government intervention in economic matters. That step came quickly. In a series of decisions beginning in 1937, majorities accepted the constitutional power of government—particularly the federal government—to regulate and to manage the economy. The culmination of this shift was *Wickard v. Filburn* (1942), in which the Court held that federal power to regulate interstate commerce extended so far that it applied to a farmer growing wheat for his own livestock.

This collective change of heart proved to be of long duration. The Court consistently upheld major economic legislation against constitutional challenge, striking down only one minor provision of federal law regulating business in the period from the 1940s through the 1960s.[25] Supporting federal supremacy in economic matters, the Court struck down many state laws on the ground that they impinged on the constitutional powers of the federal government or that they were preempted by federal statutes. But in other respects state governments were also given more freedom to make economic policy.

The Court continued to address nonconstitutional economic issues involving interpretations of federal statutes. In some instances it overrode decisions of regulatory agencies such as the Interstate Commerce Commission and the National Labor Relations Board, holding that those decisions misinterpreted statutes. Some of these interventions were significant, but the Court did not challenge the basic economic programs of the federal government.

Support for Civil Liberties. In a 1938 decision, *United States v. Carolene Products Co.,* the Court signaled that there might be a second stage of the revolution. This was simply one of many cases in which the Court upheld federal economic policies. But in what would become a famous footnote, Justice Harlan Stone's opinion for the Court argued that the Court was justified in taking a tolerant view of government economic policies while it gave "more exacting judicial scrutiny" to policies that infringed on civil liberties.

This second stage took much longer to develop than the first stage. In the 1940s and 1950s the Court gave more attention and support to civil liberties than it had in earlier eras, but it did not make a strong and consistent commitment to the expansion of individual liberties. This stage of the revolution finally came to full fruition in the 1960s. In that decade civil liberties issues dominated the Court's agenda for the first time and the Court's decisions expanded liberties in many fields, from civil rights of racial minority groups to procedural rights of criminal defendants to freedom of expression.

As in the preceding era, the Court's policy position was reflected in the constitutional doctrines it adopted. Departing from its earlier view, the Court of the 1960s ruled that nearly all the rights of criminal defendants in the Bill of Rights were incorporated in the Fourteenth Amendment and thus applied to state proceedings. In interpreting the equal protection clause of the Fourteenth Amendment, the Court held that some government policies challenged as discriminatory would be given "strict scrutiny," if the groups treated differently were especially vulnerable or if the rights that the policies affected were especially important.

The Court's sympathies for civil liberties were symbolized by *Griswold v. Connecticut* (1965), which established a new constitutional right to privacy. A majority of the justices discovered this right in provisions of the Bill of Rights nearly two centuries after those provisions were written.

The Court's direction after 1937 is illustrated by the pattern of decisions declaring laws unconstitutional. Figure 5-1 shows the number of economic statutes and statutes limiting civil liberties that the Court overturned in successive decades, from 1900 to the 1990s. The number of economic laws that the Court struck down declined precipitously between the 1920s and the 1940s and remained relatively low in the 1950s and 1960s. In contrast, the number of statutes struck down on civil liberties grounds became significant in the 1940s and 1950s and increased sharply in the 1960s. That increase reflected the Court's increasing liberalism. The reversal of these trends in the 1980s is also noteworthy; I discuss its implications later in this section.

The Court's Beneficiaries. The groups that benefited most from the Court's policies, of course, were those that brought civil liberties claims to the Court. Among them were socially and economically disadvantaged groups, criminal defendants, and people who took unpopular political stands. In 1967, during the Court's most liberal period, an unsympathetic editorial cartoonist depicted the Court as a Santa Claus whose list of gift recipients included Communists, pornographers, extremists, drug pushers, criminals, and perverts.[26] Whatever one may think of this characterization, it underlines the change in the Court.

The segment of the population that the Court supported most strongly was black citizens, particularly in the fields of education and voting rights. The Court also made great efforts to protect the civil rights movement when it came under attack by southern states in the late 1950s and 1960s. Like the Court's policies favoring corporations in an earlier era, this support reflected effective litigation efforts, particularly by the Legal Defense Fund of the NAACP.

The Court did not support all the civil liberties claims brought to it, but it was usually more favorable to liberties than the other branches of government. Congress did not adopt a strong civil rights bill attacking racial discrimination until 1964, ten years after *Brown v. Board of Education.* The Court's support for some other liberties diverged even more from the positions of the other branches. The procedural rights of criminal defendants had few advocates in the executive and legislative branches. Political activities of leftist political groups such as the Communist party were attacked a good deal by Congress. As it had done when it favored business interests, the Court provided relief for groups that fared less well elsewhere in government.

FIGURE 5-1
*Number of Economic and Civil Liberties Laws (Federal, State, and Local)
Overturned by the Supreme Court by Decade, 1900s–1990s*

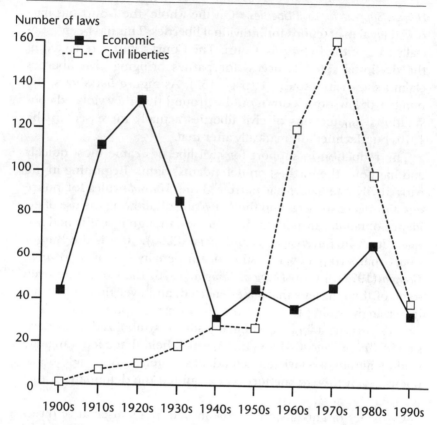

Number of laws

Legend:
— ■ — Economic
-- □ -- Civil liberties

X-axis: 1900s 1910s 1920s 1930s 1940s 1950s 1960s 1970s 1980s 1990s

Y-axis: 0, 20, 40, 60, 80, 100, 120, 140, 160

Sources: Congressional Research Service, *The Constitution of the United States of America: Analysis and Interpretation* and *1998 Supplement* (Washington, D.C.: Government Printing Office, 1996, 1999); Kenneth Jost, *The Supreme Court Yearbook, 1998–1999* (Washington, D.C.: CQ Press, 2000); coded by the author.

Note: Civil liberties category does not include laws supportive of civil liberties.

The Burger and Rehnquist Courts

In the three decades since 1969, a clear trend of increasing conservatism has emerged in the Supreme Court's policies. There is considerable disagreement about the strength of this trend: some commentators see the current Court as highly conservative, while others argue that the Court remains relatively liberal.[27] Thus, as is often the case, it is more difficult to characterize the Court in the current era than in prior eras.

Uneven Support for Civil Liberties.   On the whole, the Court has narrowed legal protections for individual liberties. This has been especially true of the Rehnquist Court. The Court's shift is reflected in the declining rate of success for parties bringing civil liberties claims, shown in Table 4-4 (page 155). As Figure 5-1 shows, the number of laws struck down on the ground that they violated constitutional protections of civil liberties actually increased in the 1970s but declined dramatically after that.

The reduction in support for civil liberties came most quickly and has gone the furthest on defendants' rights. Beginning in the early 1970s, the Court has narrowed the *Miranda* rules for police questioning of suspects and the *Mapp* rule disallowing the use of evidence obtained through illegal searches, though it reaffirmed *Miranda* itself in *Dickerson v. United States* (2000). It was the Burger Court that struck down existing death penalty laws in *Furman v. Georgia* (1972). But in *Gregg v. Georgia* (1976) the Court approved some of the new laws that states enacted, and over time it became increasingly willing to accept the use of capital punishment. The Court's current stance in criminal justice is symbolized by its decision in *United States v. Watts* (1997), which held that a federal judge could lengthen a convicted defendant's sentence for an additional offense even though the jury had acquitted the defendant of that offense.

On issues of equality, the Court moved in a conservative direction more slowly and unevenly. The Burger Court was the first to strike down laws under the equal protection clause on the ground that they discriminated against women, it held that Northern-style school segregation could be unconstitutional, and it approved the use of affirmative action in employment. By and large, it gave broad interpretations to federal laws against discrimination. But it also limited the use of the Fourteenth Amendment to challenge discrimination by private institutions that are connected to government.

The Rehnquist Court has interpreted anti-discrimination laws more narrowly than its predecessor. It has also given government less room to engage in affirmative action, at least in programs that favor businesses owned by members of racial minority groups. At the same time, the Court generally has been sympathetic to discrimination claims by women under the Constitution and under federal statutes. This position is reflected in *United States v. Virginia* (1996), in which the Court required that the Virginia Military Institute admit female students.

Freedom of expression is the only area in which the Court has directly overruled major Warren Court decisions favoring civil liberties—specifically, in standards determining obscenity.[28] The Court has narrowed some other First Amendment protections as well. But it has supported freedom of expression in other areas. Most noteworthy are its protections for commercial speech such as advertising and its limits on government power to regulate spending in political campaigns.

More Limits on Economic Regulation.   In interpreting federal statutes that regulate economic practices, the Burger and Rehnquist Courts have taken more conservative positions than the Warren Court. For example, in antitrust law the Court has moved away from Warren Court rulings that had made certain business practices automatically illegal.[29] In labor law the Court has given more support to employers, and for the most part it has interpreted environmental laws narrowly.

The Burger Court maintained the Court's broad interpretation of government powers under the Constitution to regulate economic activity. In contrast, the Rehnquist Court has taken some steps to limit those powers. It has expanded the right of property owners to monetary compensation when government regulates the use of their property.[30] Beginning with *United States v. Lopez* (1995), it has narrowed somewhat congressional power to regulate activities related to interstate commerce. The Rehnquist Court has also limited federal power over state governments in the economic arena.

The Court's shifts in economic policy generally have favored the business community by limiting regulation of its practices. The same is true of freedom of expression, where the Court has loosened restraints on commercial speech and the use of money by businesses for political purposes. If there is a single beneficiary of recent trends in the Court's policies, it is business. But the complexity of these policies cautions against broad generalizations. All that can be said confidently is that the Court, having moved in a liberal direction from the 1930s to the 1960s, has reversed direction since that time.

Explaining the Court's Policies

In the preceding section I have described the very substantial changes in the content of the Supreme Court's policies over the past century. The Court's agenda and its activism also have changed a good deal over time. All these changes are summarized in Table 5-5.

The magnitude of these changes underlines the need to explain the Court's policies. What forces can account for shifts in the kinds of cases that the Court hears, in the extent of its activism, in the ideological content of its policies? I have discussed these forces at several points earlier in the book, but in this section I will pull them together and apply them to the broad patterns described in this chapter.

The Court's Environment

Freedom from External Pressures.   The life terms of Supreme Court justices give them considerable freedom from the other branches of government and from the general public. This freedom is reinforced by the reluctance of the other branches to use their powers to attack the Court as an institution. The Court's relative freedom from external pressures distinguishes it from the other branches of government.

The Court's freedom is reflected in some of the positions that it takes in individual decisions. Neither Congress nor a state legislature could adopt a resolution supporting the right to burn the American flag as a form of political protest, nor could they enact a statute that prohibits student-led prayers at public schools' football games. But the Court could and did make such decisions.

More important, the Court has adopted broad lines of policy that often run counter to the majority view in the general public and elsewhere in government. To a considerable degree, it resisted the widespread support for regulation of business in the early twentieth century. Even more striking was the Court's expansion of the procedural rights of criminal defendants in the 1960s. No elected body, even a court, could have adopted so many rules favoring so unpopular a segment of society.

TABLE 5-5
Summary of the Supreme Court's Policies During Three Historical Periods

Period	Predominant Area on Agenda	Extent of Activism	Content of Policy
1890s to 1930s	Economic regulation	Variable, increasingly inclined to strike down legislation	Mixed, primarily conservative
1937 to 1969	Economic regulation, then civil liberties	Initially low, becoming higher and then very high in 1960s	Generally liberal, very liberal in 1960s
Burger and Rehnquist Courts	Civil liberties	High, declining somewhat in 1990s	Moderate in 1970s, then increasingly conservative

Note: Characterizations of each period are approximate and subject to disagreement. Extent of activism is gauged primarily by striking down of government policies.

Influence from the Other Branches.   The Court's freedom from external pressures is only relative. Congress and the president hold considerable power over the Court. Through legislation the other branches can raise the justices' salaries or leave them as they are, allow the Court's interpretations of statutes to stand or override them, and control its jurisdiction. They also can shape the implementation of the Court's decisions.

While the other branches have been reluctant to use some of these powers against the Court, members of Congress often threaten to use them when the Court's actions displease them. Because such threats and criticisms are unpleasant in themselves, and because they might affect the Court's public standing, the justices have an incentive to minimize direct conflicts with Congress.

It is difficult to ascertain the impact of this incentive on the Court's policies. There are some specific instances when the justices seemed to avoid or minimize conflict with the other branches; its retreat from some of its expansions of civil liberties in the late 1950s and its refusal to decide whether American participation in the Vietnam War was unconstitutional are two examples. More broadly, the Court has limited its use of judicial review to strike down significant national policies. As I have noted, only between 1918 and 1936 did the Court overturn a large set of major congressional policies. And the Court has been far more active in striking down state and local laws than national laws, in part because Congress has much more power to attack the Court as an institution than do state and local policy makers.[31]

Societal Influence.   The justices are also influenced by developments in society as a whole. Those developments can affect the justices' attitudes toward issues such as women's rights and illegal drugs. They can exert an influence on their own as well.

One form of influence concerns what might be called a requirement of minimum support: the justices are unlikely to take a sustained policy position that lacks significant support outside the Court, especially from the segments of society whose judgment is most important to them. In part, this is because the justices want to avoid a situation in which their adoption of highly unpopular positions over time creates increasing antipathy toward the Court and its members. On a different level, a position for which there was little support might be difficult for the justices themselves to take seriously.

Another form of influence derives from the litigation process. The Court acts on the cases that come to it, and substantial litigation on a set of issues usually requires considerable activity by interest groups. Thus the Court cannot reshape its agenda without action by litigants and, more generally, by broad social movements that support interest group litigation.

These influences are reflected in the two most distinctive patterns in the Court's policies during the twentieth century. Arguably, the Court's resistance to government regulation of the economy before 1937 had only minority support in society. But that position was strongly approved by most of the business community and much of the legal community, clearly meeting the requirement of minimum support. And corporations and their representatives engaged in a concerted litigation campaign, bringing to the Court a steady flow of litigation and strong legal arguments against government economic policies.

The Court's expansions of civil liberties from the 1940s to the 1970s also benefited from social support. If these expansions were not always popular, they were favored by significant portions of society as a whole, including political elites and the legal community. And the development of organizations such as the NAACP and the ACLU and other social changes made it possible for civil liberties to take a more prominent place on the Court's agenda and for the Court to adopt broadened interpretations of constitutional rights.[32]

Lines of policy that lack substantial backing in society may be very difficult for the Court to adopt. Since the 1970s increased conservatism in American society and a growth in litigation by conservative groups have facilitated the Court's reduced support for civil liberties and its increased activism on behalf of business interests. But it would probably be impossible for the Court in the early twenty-first century to reverse fully the expansions of government regulatory power that it adopted in the 1930s and 1940s or the expansions of civil liberties that it adopted in the 1960s and 1970s: there simply is too little support for such reversals. The Court has considerable freedom from societal opinion and social trends, but its freedom is not total.[33]

Policy Preferences and the Appointment Power

The Importance of Policy Preferences.   The freedom that the justices do possess enables them generally to make their own judgments about the choices they face. Those judgments are based in part on their assessments of cases in legal terms. But because the questions before the Court seldom have clear legal answers, justices' policy preferences are the strongest determinant of the positions they take.

The importance of policy preferences suggests that a great deal about the Court's policies can be explained simply and directly: during any given period in the Court's history, its policies have reflected the collective preferences of its members. Most of the justices who served from the 1890s to the 1930s were political conservatives who accepted government restrictions on civil liberties but who were skeptical of government regulation of business enterprises. In contrast, the justices who came to the Court from the late 1930s to the late 1960s were predominately liberals who supported government management of the economy and, in most instances, broader protections of civil liberties.

But this explanation is not entirely satisfying, because it does not show why certain preferences predominated on the Court during particular periods. One reason is that some national values were dominant during the periods in which justices were developing their attitudes. Another is that the justices came from backgrounds that instilled particular values in them; thus, the higher status backgrounds that predominated during most of the Court's history helped to produce a sympathy for the views and interests of segments of society that had high status. Further, the prevailing ideology in elite segments of the legal profession shapes the views of its members, including future Supreme Court justices. But the most direct source of the Court's collective preferences is the decisions that presidents make in appointing justices.

The Impact of Appointments.   The predominant pattern of Supreme Court policy at any given time reflects the appointments that presidents make. If a series of appointees is politically conservative, the Court is likely to become a conservative body. And because vacancies occur on the Court with some frequency—on the average, once every two years—most presidents can have a significant impact on the Court's direction.

Robert Dahl argued that for this reason, "the policy views dominant on the Court are never for long out of line with the policy views dominant among the lawmaking majorities of the United States."[34] In Dahl's judgment, the president's power to make appointments has limited the frequency with which the Court overturns major federal statutes: justices generally take the same view of policy as members of Congress and the president, so they seldom upset the policies of these branches. I think there is much to Dahl's argument. But the appointment power produces only imperfect control by "lawmaking majorities" because of several complicating factors.

One factor is time lag. Most justices serve for many years, so the Court nearly always reflects the views of past presidents and Senates at least as much as those of the current president and Senate. For this reason Fred Rodell suggested that the aphorism, "the Supreme Court follows the election returns" be amended to refer to the returns "of ten or twelve years before."[35]

The lag varies, chiefly because presidents have differing opportunities to make appointments. Richard Nixon could select four justices during his first term in office, while Franklin Roosevelt and Jimmy Carter made none in the four years after they took office. Roosevelt's bad luck in this respect led to his conflict with the Court over its handling of New Deal legislation. Had he been able to replace two conservative justices early in his first term, the Court probably would not have acted as a major roadblock to his program. Carter's luck was even worse; the absence of vacancies during his term, combined with his failed reelection bid in 1980, made him the first president to serve at least four years without appointing any justices. As a result, he had no opportunity to make the Court more liberal. Of course, a president's influence on the Court's direction depends only in part on the number of appointments to be made. It also depends on the ideological configuration of the Court and on which members leave it.

Another complicating factor is the deviation of justices from presidential expectations. Presidents usually get most of what they want from their appointees, but this is not a certainty. The unprecedented liberalism of the Court in the 1960s resulted largely from Dwight Eisenhower's miscalculations in nominating Earl Warren and William Brennan. The current Court would be more conservative if David Souter and, to a lesser degree, Sandra Day

O'Connor and Anthony Kennedy had not diverged from the expectations of the Republican presidents who chose them.

For these reasons, Dahl's argument is valid only as a statement of a general tendency. The element of chance in shaping the Court's general direction also merits emphasis. Chance plays a part in the timing of Court vacancies and in the performance of justices relative to their appointers' expectations. For that matter, the identity of the president who fills vacancies on the Court sometimes reflects chance. The close victories of John Kennedy in 1960 and Richard Nixon in 1968, each with major effects on the Court's direction, were hardly inevitable.

The two policy orientations that prevailed on the Supreme Court between the 1890s and the 1960s reflected the existence of strong lawmaking majorities during two periods: the conservative Republican governments that dominated much of the period from the Civil War to the Great Depression, and the unprecedented twelve-year tenure of Franklin Roosevelt. But these orientations also reflected patterns of resignations and deaths, unexpected behavior on the part of justices, and other factors that were a good deal less systematic. And under somewhat different circumstances the Court would not have become as conservative as it is today. The forces that shape the Court's policy positions, like so much about the Court, are highly complex.

Conclusion

In this chapter I have examined a wide range of subjects concerning the Supreme Court's policy outputs. A few conclusions merit emphasis.

First, in some periods the Court's policy making has had fairly obvious themes. During the first part of the twentieth century, the dominant theme was scrutiny of government economic policies. Later, the primary theme was scrutiny of practices that infringed on individual civil liberties. In each instance, the theme was evident in both the Court's agenda and the content of its decisions.

Second, these themes and the Court's work as a whole reflect both the justices' policy preferences and the influence of the Court's environment. In large part the Court's policies are what its members would like them to be. But the Court is subject to environmental influences that limit the divergence between Supreme

Court decisions and the policies adopted by the other branches of government. In a different way, the president's appointment power establishes a direct link between the justices' policy preferences and their political environment.

Finally, the Court's role as a policy maker—though clearly significant—is a limited one. The Court gives considerable attention to some areas of policy, but there are several major policy areas that it scarcely touches. Some critical matters, such as foreign policy, are left almost entirely to the other two branches. Even in the areas that the Court gives the most attention, it seldom disturbs the basic features of national policy.

The significance of the Supreme Court as a policy maker ultimately depends on the impact of its decisions, the subject of Chapter 6. After examining the effect of the Court's decisions, I can make a fuller assessment of the Supreme Court's role in the policy-making process.

NOTES

1. This discussion of agenda change is drawn in part from Richard L. Pacelle, Jr., *The Transformation of the Supreme Court's Agenda from the New Deal to the Reagan Administration* (Boulder: Westview Press, 1991); and Pacelle, "The Dynamics and Determinants of Agenda Change in the Rehnquist Court," in *Contemplating Courts,* ed. Lee Epstein (Washington, D.C.: CQ Press, 1995), 251–274. Numbers of cases involving particular issues or statutes were calculated from data in the U.S. Supreme Court Judicial Database created by Harold Spaeth, updated by the author.
2. Sandra L. Wood, Linda Camp Keith, Drew Noble Lanier, and Ayo Ogundele, "The Supreme Court, 1888–1940: An Empirical Overview," *Social Science History* 22 (Summer 1998): 212–213.
3. On the Court and foreign policy, see Thomas M. Franck, *Political Questions/Judicial Answers: Does the Rule of Law Apply to Foreign Affairs?* (Princeton: Princeton University Press, 1992).
4. Because of ambiguities, different observers have obtained different numbers of laws overturned. The numbers of federal and state laws struck down by the Court that are presented in this chapter are based on data in Congressional Research Service, *The Constitution of the United States of America: Analysis and Interpretation and 1998 Supplement* (Washington, D.C.: Government Printing Office, 1996, 1999), and Kenneth Jost, *The Supreme Court Yearbook, 1998–1999* (Washington, D.C.: CQ Press, 2000). There are two unusual features of the compilation of laws struck down in the book by the Congressional Research Service. First, although the count is of statutes, when the Court overturned different sections of the same statute in different decisions, the book counts these as two different statutes. The second unusual feature concerns decisions that nullify state laws on the ground that they are preempted by federal laws: apparently most, but not all, of these decisions are treated as declarations that the state law is unconstitutional.

5. The distinctions made in the paragraphs that follow are drawn chiefly from Robert A. Dahl, "Decision-Making in a Democracy: The Supreme Court as a National Policy-Maker," *Journal of Public Law* 6 (Fall 1957): 279–295.
6. *Scott v. Sandford* (1857); *Hammer v. Dagenhart* (1918); *Bailey v. Drexel Furniture Co.* (1922). Decisions overturning New Deal economic legislation include *United States v. Butler* (1936) and *Schechter Poultry Corp. v. United States* (1935).
7. Among these decisions are *United States v. Lopez* (1995); *City of Boerne v. Flores* (1997); *Printz v. United States* (1998); and *Alden v. Maine* (1999).
8. The decisions were, respectively, *Kimel v. Florida Board of Regents* (2000); *United States v. Morrison* (2000); and *Jones v. United States* (2000).
9. The cases were, respectively, *Board of County Commissioners v. Umbehr* (1996) and *Schenck v. Pro-Choice Network* (1997).
10. Glendon A. Schubert, Jr., *The Presidency in the Courts* (Minneapolis: University of Minnesota Press, 1957); Robert Scigliano, "The Presidency and the Judiciary," in *The Presidency and the Political System*, 3d ed., ed. Michael Nelson (Washington, D.C.: CQ Press, 1990), 471–499.
11. *McDonnell Douglas Corp. v. Green* (1973); *Griggs v. Duke Power Co.* (1971).
12. *Meritor Savings Bank v. Vinson* (1986).
13. See, for example, *St. Mary's Honor Center v. Hicks* (1993) and *United Auto Workers v. Johnson Controls* (1991).
14. Wood et al., "The Supreme Court, 1888–1940," 215–216; William G. Ross, *A Muted Fury: Populists, Progressives, and Labor Unions Confront the Courts, 1890–1937* (Princeton: Princeton University Press, 1994).
15. To obtain these figures and others to be presented later in the chapter, I categorized decisions that struck down laws according to whether they pertained to economics, civil liberties, or other subjects. The criteria that I used were necessarily arbitrary; other criteria would have resulted in slightly different totals.
16. *Santa Clara County v. Southern Pacific Railroad Co.* (1886).
17. See Richard C. Cortner, *The Iron Horse and the Constitution: The Railroads and the Transformation of the Fourteenth Amendment* (Westport, Conn.: Greenwood Press, 1993).
18. Benjamin Twiss, *Lawyers and the Constitution* (Princeton: Princeton University Press, 1942).
19. John Braeman, *Before the Civil Rights Revolution: The Old Court and Individual Rights* (Westport, Conn.: Greenwood Press, 1988).
20. *Twining v. New Jersey* (1908).
21. See *Schenck v. United States* (1917). See also David Rabban, *Free Speech in Its Forgotten Years* (New York: Cambridge University Press, 1997).
22. Henry Steele Commager, "Judicial Review and Democracy," *Virginia Quarterly Review* 19 (Summer 1943): 428.
23. Robert H. Jackson, *The Struggle for Judicial Supremacy* (New York: Knopf, 1941), 187.
24. William E. Leuchtenburg, *The Supreme Court Reborn: The Constitutional Revolution in the Age of Roosevelt* (New York: Oxford University Press, 1995), 235.
25. *United States v. Cardiff* (1952).
26. *San Francisco Examiner*, December 14, 1967, 42.
27. Frederick P. Lewis, *The Context of Judicial Activism: The Endurance of the Warren Court Legacy in a Conservative Age* (Lanham, Md.: Rowman & Littlefield, 1999).

28. *Miller v. California* (1973).
29. Lino A. Graglia, "Economic Rights," in *The Burger Court: Counter-Revolution or Confirmation?*, ed. Bernard Schwartz (New York: Oxford University Press, 1998), 154–165.
30. *Lucas v. South Carolina Coastal Council* (1992); *Dolan v. City of Tigard* (1994).
31. See William Lasser, *The Limits of Judicial Power: The Supreme Court in American Politics* (Chapel Hill: University of North Carolina Press, 1988), 262–270.
32. Charles R. Epp, *The Rights Revolution: Lawyers, Activists, and Supreme Courts in Comparative Perspective* (Chicago: University of Chicago Press, 1998), chaps. 3–4.
33. See John R. Howard, *The Shifting Wind: The Supreme Court and Civil Rights from Reconstruction to Brown* (Albany: State University of New York Press, 1999).
34. Dahl, "Decision-Making in a Democracy," 285.
35. Fred Rodell, *Nine Men* (New York: Random House, 1955), 9. The original aphorism was coined by author Finley Peter Dunne and put in the mouth of his character Mr. Dooley in 1901. See Finley Peter Dunne, *Mr. Dooley on Ivrything and Ivrybody,* selected by Robert Hutchinson (New York: Dover Publications, 1963), 160.

Chapter 6

The Court's Impact

I n two decisions in 1962 and 1963 the Supreme Court ruled that prayer and Bible reading exercises in public schools violate the constitutional prohibition of an establishment of religion.[1] These decisions seemed to resolve the issue of organized religious observances in public schools.

Four decades later, the issue is a long way from settled. For one thing, the Court's decisions attracted strong criticism, criticism that has strengthened in recent years. Some of the strongest denunciations of the Court have come from members of Congress. Senator Jesse Helms of North Carolina said that "the decline of this country" began with "the lawsuit that resulted in the first Supreme Court decision banning prayer."[2] Members have introduced several hundred resolutions to overturn the Court's school prayer decisions through a constitutional amendment. Other proposals would eliminate the Court's jurisdiction to hear cases on this subject.

A good many school districts had engaged in the religious observances that the Court prohibited in 1962 and 1963. After the Court's rulings, many districts eliminated these observances. But many others retained them, and it does not appear that compliance has increased over the years. Some states enacted laws that were intended to get around the Court's rulings, such as a requirement of a "moment of silence" that could be used by teachers as an occasion for prayer. Other states simply mandated prayer in contradiction of the Supreme Court.

Some schools have sought to maintain prayers as part of graduations or athletic events. The Court ruled in 1992 that schools could not present prayers at graduation ceremonies,[3] but many schools continued such prayers or allowed student-initiated prayers as a substitute. In 2000 the Court held that schools could not have student-led prayers at football games,[4] but the responses to its earlier rulings on school religion suggested that there would not be full compliance with this decision either.

While some noncompliant districts and state governments have continued their practices without challenge, others have been taken to court. On the whole, federal judges have struck down practices that conflicted with the Court's rulings. But one district judge in Alabama announced in an opinion that the Supreme Court had "erred" and refused to apply its rulings.[5]

As that opinion illustrates, the most dramatic defiance of the Court's decisions on school religion has occurred in Alabama. The state legislature has enacted five laws to reinstate school prayer. When the fourth law was struck down by a federal judge in 1997, Governor Fob James said he would resist the judge's order "by every legal and political means, with every ounce of strength I possess." He also seemed to say that public officials need not follow Supreme Court decisions that they view as inconsistent with the Constitution.[6] This is an extraordinary series of events. But Alabama is typical of the country as a whole in one important respect: the Supreme Court's decisions have not resolved the matter of school religious observances in the political world or in the schools themselves.

The Court is the highest interpreter of federal law, and people often think of it as the final arbiter of the issues it addresses. But the school prayer controversy shows that this image of the Court is misleading. It is more useful to think of the Court as one of many institutions that participate in a fluid process of policy making. Often the Court's decisions decide only one aspect of an issue or offer general guidelines that other policy makers have to fill in. Even when the Court rules decisively on an issue, other institutions may limit the impact of that ruling or negate it altogether. Congress and the president can write a new statute to override the Court's interpretation of an old one. Congress and the states can amend the Constitution to overcome a constitutional decision. Judges and administrators can carry out a Supreme Court policy as they see fit. And the Court's ultimate impact on society depends on the actions of other institutions in and out of government. The Court influences the strength of the labor movement and the status of women, but so do many other forces—including some that are likely to be far more powerful than the Court.

This chapter explores the impact of Supreme Court decisions. I begin by looking at what happens to the litigants themselves. The remainder of the chapter examines the broader effects of the Court's policies: their implementation, responses to them by legislatures and chief executives, and their effects on society as a whole.

Outcomes for the Parties

Whatever else it does, a Supreme Court decision affects the parties in the case. But the Court's ruling does not always determine the final outcome for the two sides. Indeed, a great deal can happen to the parties after the Court rules in their case.

If the Court affirms a lower court decision, that decision usually becomes final. If the Court reverses, modifies, or vacates a decision, it almost always remands (sends back) the case to the lower court for "further proceedings consistent with this opinion," or the like. When it remands a case, the Court sometimes gives the lower court little leeway about what to do. This was true of a 1998 case in which the Court instructed a federal court of appeals to dismiss the case in question.[7] More often, however, the lower court has wide discretion about how to apply the Court's ruling. As a result, as the Court said in one decision, "we do not foreclose the possibility that the Court of Appeals may reach the same conclusion it did earlier"—a conclusion favoring the party who had won in the court of appeals but lost in the Supreme Court.[8] Sometimes the court to which the case is remanded sends it to the original trial court for retrial. This is a common path when the Court overturns a criminal conviction because of procedural errors.

Lower court judges occasionally respond to remands in questionable ways, using the leeway that the Supreme Court provides to reach a result that conflicts with the Court's intent. A litigant who feels that a lower court has failed to follow the Supreme Court's directions after a remand can bring the case back to the Court for a second ruling. The Court may then reach a final decision itself, but more often it issues a decision and remands the case again with more specific instructions to the lower court. When it decided the complicated *Amchem* case on procedures for class action lawsuits in 1997, the Court remanded a second case to the federal Fifth Circuit Court of Appeals for further consideration in light of *Amchem*. The court of appeals reinstated its original judgment over the objections of a dissenting judge who said that it was failing to follow *Amchem*. A commentator said that the court was "thumbing its nose at the Supreme Court." [9] The losing party came back to the Supreme Court, and its brief was equally pointed about the Fifth Circuit's action: "Some people just can't take a hint." [10] The Court accepted the case, and not surprisingly it reversed the court of appeals and remanded the case a second time. In chiding the lower court, Justice Souter's majority opinion was itself a bit pointed: "The Fifth Circuit fell short in its attention to *Amchem*'s explanation of the governing legal standards." [11]

A more extreme step is to issue a writ of mandamus to the lower court, ordering it to take specified action in the case. If the writ is disobeyed, the judges can be cited for contempt of the Supreme Court. But the Court is very reluctant to take these steps. Indeed, it has never held a judge in contempt. Lower court judges who strongly oppose the Court's position in a case can refuse to comply with the terms of the remand, knowing that they will have ample warning if the Court contemplates the use of strong measures to deal with their resistance.

The ultimate outcome for the parties is often determined outside of court. Sometimes the parties settle the case, with the Court's decision serving as leverage for the party that it favored. This was the case, for instance, in *Harris v. Forklift Systems* (1993), in which the Court ruled in favor of an employee's sexual harassment claim. Two years later, the employee won a settlement from her former employer.[12]

Sometimes other branches of government become involved after the Supreme Court rules in a case, either by necessity or voluntarily. When the Court rules that a state's districting plan for the House of Representatives is unconstitutional, the state legislature has no choice but to enact a new plan. This was true, for instance, of the Court's decision in 1996 that a black-majority district in North Carolina established after the 1990 census had been drawn in a way that violated the Fourteenth Amendment. The legislature then drew up a new plan, which also was challenged in federal court; in 2000 the Court agreed to address that challenge for a second time, with its decision to come after the 2000 census had been completed.[13]

In New York, state legislators took it upon themselves to intervene after the Court's decision in *Board of Education v. Grumet* (1994). In that decision the Court struck down a New York statute that had created a school district for a religious enclave, allowing children from the enclave to receive publicly funded special education services while remaining separate from students outside the group. In response the governor and legislature enacted three successive statutes, each designed to meet the Court's objections to the original statute while maintaining the same separate district. New York's highest court ruled that the first two of these statutes were also unconstitutional. As of mid-2000 it had not yet ruled on the third.[14]

Implementation of Supreme Court Policies

More important than the outcome of a case for the litigants are the broader effects of the legal rules that the Supreme Court lays down in its opinions. Like statutes or presidential orders, these rules have to be implemented—put into effect—by administrators and judges. Judges' task is to apply the Court's interpretations of law whenever they are relevant to a case. For administrators, ranging from cabinet officers to police officers, the task is to follow Court-created rules that are relevant to their work.

The responses of judges and administrators to the Court's rules of law can be examined in terms of their compliance and noncompliance with these rules. But the Court's decisions may evoke responses ranging from complete rejection to enthusiastic acceptance and extension, and the concept of compliance does not capture all the possible variations.

The Effectiveness of Implementation

Implementation is an imperfect process. People sometimes assume that when Congress enacts a statute, other policy makers automatically do what is required to make the statute effective. In reality, implementation of statutes is far from automatic. Indeed, congressional policies frequently fail to achieve their objectives because they are carried out poorly. The same is true of Supreme Court decisions: judges and administrators may not carry them out fully, thereby creating a gap between the Court's goals and the actual results.

This does not mean that implementation always works badly; any policy maker is likely to have a mixed record in getting its policies put into effect. This certainly is true of the Supreme Court. Some of the Court's decisions are carried out more effectively than others, and specific decisions are implemented better in some places or situations than in others.

On the whole, the Court achieves considerable success in getting its policies carried out by lower courts, especially appellate courts. When the Court issues a decision with a new rule of law, judges generally do their best to follow its lead, even on issues as controversial as abortion. And when a series of decisions in a field of law indicates a broader change in the Court's position in that field, lower courts tend to follow the new trend.[15]

Certainly outright refusal to follow the Court's doctrines is unusual. The disobedience of an Alabama federal judge on school prayer, discussed at the beginning of the chapter, received considerable attention because it was so rare. More common is what might be called implicit noncompliance, in which a court purports to follow the Supreme Court's lead but actually evades the implications of the Court's rulings for the case in question. To take one example, lower federal courts have engaged in some implicit noncompliance with the Court's decisions on the administration of public welfare programs.[16]

Implementation problems seem more common among administrators than among judges. Problems at the federal level are illustrated by the long period in which the Patent and Trademark Office failed to carry out Supreme Court rulings on the standards to be used in awarding or denying patents to applicants. At the state level, major examples include school religious exercises, discussed earlier, and school desegregation and police investigations, to be considered shortly.

There have also been widespread implementation problems on procedural matters in state trial courts, which resemble administrative agencies in some respects. Many courts have complied only in part with several of the Warren and Burger Court decisions on criminal procedure, such as the ruling that juvenile defendants are entitled to basic procedural rights.[17] The Court's decision in *Tate v. Short* (1971), holding that an indigent person cannot be sentenced to jail because of inability to pay a fine, has been subverted by judges who fail to inquire into a defendant's ability to pay.[18]

Two Case Studies of Implementation

School Desegregation. Before the Supreme Court's 1954 decision in *Brown v. Board of Education,* separate schools for black and white students existed throughout the Deep South and in most districts of border states such as Oklahoma and Maryland. The Court's decision required that these dual school systems be eliminated. Full desegregation in the border states took time, but considerable compliance with the Court's ruling came within a few years. In contrast, policies in the Deep South changed very slowly. As late as 1964–1965, there was no Deep South state in which even 10 percent of the black students went to school with any white students—a minimal definition of desegregation.[19] This resistance requires a closer look.

Judges and school officials in the Deep South responded to the *Brown* decision in an atmosphere hostile to desegregation. Visible opinion among white citizens was strongly opposed to desegregation; the opinion of black citizens was far less important because a large proportion of them were prevented from voting. Throughout the South, public officials encouraged resistance to the Supreme Court. In 1956, ninety-six southern members of Congress signed a "Southern Manifesto" that attacked the *Brown* decision. Governors and legislatures expressed a strong distaste for desegregation and took official action to prevent it. Governor Orval Faubus of Arkansas, for instance, intervened to block desegregation in Little Rock in 1957.

In this atmosphere school officials generally sought to maintain the status quo. Most administrators personally favored segregation and did everything possible to preserve it. Those administrators who wanted to comply with the Court's ruling were deterred from doing so by pressure from state officials and local citizens.

In places where the schools did not act on their own, parents could file suits in the federal district courts to challenge the continuation of segregated systems. In many districts no suits ever were brought; one reason was fear of retaliation.

Even where suits were brought, their success was hardly guaranteed. In its second decision in *Brown* in 1955, the Supreme Court gave federal district judges substantial freedom to determine the appropriate schedule for desegregation in a school district. Many judges themselves disagreed with the *Brown* decision, and all felt local pressure to proceed slowly if at all. As a result, few demanded speedy desegregation of the schools, and many supported school officials in resisting change. In Dallas, for instance, two district judges struggled mightily to maintain segregation. Some judges did

TABLE 6-1

Percentage of Black Elementary and Secondary Students Going to School with Any Whites, in Eleven Southern States, 1954–1973

School year	Percentage	School year	Percentage
1954–1955	0.001	1964–1965	2.25
1956–1957	0.14	1966–1967	15.9
1958–1959	0.13	1968–1969	32.0
1960–1961	0.16	1970–1971	85.6
1962–1963	0.45	1972–1973	91.3

Sources: Southern Education Reporting Service, *A Statistical Summary, State by State, of School Segregation-Desegregation in the Southern and Border Area from 1954 to the Present* (Nashville: Southern Education Reporting Service, 1967) (for 1954–1967); U.S. Bureau of the Census, *Statistical Abstract of the United States* (Washington, D.C.: Government Printing Office, 1971 and 1975) (for 1968–1973).

Note: The states are Alabama, Arkansas, Florida, Georgia, Louisiana, Mississippi, North Carolina, South Carolina, Tennessee, Texas, and Virginia.

support the Court wholeheartedly, but they found it difficult to overcome delaying tactics by school administrators and elected officials.

After a long period of resistance, officials in the southern states began to comply. In the second decade after *Brown,* most dual school systems in the South were finally dismantled. Although school segregation was not eliminated altogether, the proportion of black students attending school with whites increased tremendously, as shown in Table 6-1.

The initial and key impetus for this change came from Congress. The Civil Rights Act of 1964 allowed federal funds to be withheld from institutions that practiced racial discrimination. In carrying out that provision, the Department of Health, Education, and Welfare required that schools make a "good-faith start" toward desegregation in order to receive federal aid. Faced with a threat to important financial interests, school officials felt some compulsion to go along. The 1964 act also allowed the Justice Department to bring desegregation suits where local residents were unable to do so, and this provision greatly increased the potential for litigation against school districts that refused to change their policies.

This congressional action was reinforced by the Court, whose decisions in 1968 and 1969 demanded effective desegregation without further delay.[20]

In the 1970s the Court turned its attention to the North. In many northern cities, a combination of housing patterns and school board policies had created a situation in which white and nonwhite students generally went to different schools. In a Denver case, *Keyes v. School District No. 1* (1973), the Court held that segregation caused by government in such cities violated the Fourteenth Amendment and required a remedy. In a series of decisions over the next decade, the Court spelled out rules with which to identify segregation that violated the Constitution and to devise remedies for such segregation.

On the whole, federal district judges in the North supported the Court more than had their southern counterparts. Many were willing to order sweeping remedies for segregation in the face of strong local opposition to those remedies, especially busing. One judge ordered the imposition of higher property taxes to pay for school improvements that might facilitate desegregation in Kansas City. Another held a city in New York State and some of its council members in contempt for failing to approve new public housing for a similar purpose.[21] Ironically, the Court found some of these remedies *too* sweeping.

Few northern school districts took significant steps to eliminate segregation until they were faced with a court order or pressure from federal administrators. For the most part, however, northern districts complied with desegregation orders rather than resisting. Compliance was increased by the willingness of some district judges to supervise school desegregation directly and closely.

Congress did not support northern desegregation. Beginning in 1968 it enacted several legal provisions to prohibit federal agencies from requiring school busing for desegregation, and it took some limited and ineffective steps to limit the issuance of busing orders by federal courts. The Reagan administration sought to restrict the scope of court-imposed remedies for segregation.

The record of implementation in school desegregation is quite variable. In the Deep South, the Court's decisions ultimately were implemented, but only with considerable help from the other two branches. In the border states, the Court achieved substantial change even before receiving outside assistance. In the North, the

Court was able to bring about major changes in school practices despite some opposition from the other branches.

Police Investigation. The Warren Court imposed substantial procedural requirements on the police in two areas of criminal investigation, issuing a landmark decision in each. In search and seizure, *Mapp v. Ohio* (1961) extended to the states the "exclusionary rule," under which evidence illegally seized by the police cannot be used against a defendant in court. The *Mapp* decision thus provided an incentive for police to follow rules for legal searches that the Court established in other decisions. In the area of interrogation, *Miranda v. Arizona* (1966) required that suspects be given a series of warnings before police questioning if their statements were to be used as evidence. How have judges and police officers responded to those rules?

Lower court responses to *Mapp* and *Miranda* have been mixed. Some state supreme courts criticized the decisions and interpreted them narrowly. At the trial level, many judges who sympathize with the police are reluctant to exclude evidence from trials on the basis of Supreme Court rules. But some lower court judges have applied the Court's rulings vigorously.

While the basic rules of *Mapp* and *Miranda* remain standing, the Burger and Rehnquist Courts have narrowed their protections of suspects. Many lower courts have followed this new direction enthusiastically. Indeed, in 1999 the federal court of appeals for the Fourth Circuit ruled that a statute enacted by Congress in 1968 had effectively overturned *Miranda* for federal cases. The judges who made this ruling may have believed that the Supreme Court would agree with them and perhaps would overturn *Miranda* altogether. Instead, the Court used the case to reaffirm *Miranda*.[22]

Meanwhile, some state supreme courts that support the rulings of the 1960s have found a legitimate means to establish broader protections of procedural rights by declaring that rights denied by the Court under the U.S. Constitution are protected independently by state constitutions. The most important example concerns the Court's ruling in *United States v. Leon* (1984). In *Leon,* the Court held that evidence seized on the basis of a search warrant that had been improperly issued could be used in court if the officers engaging in the search had a "good faith" belief that the warrant was justified. At least nine state supreme courts have held that there is no good faith exception to the search rules in their own constitutions.[23]

Inevitably, *Mapp* and *Miranda* were unpopular in the law enforcement community. Most police officers want maximum freedom for their investigative activities and resent court decisions that impose constraints on them. But they also want their evidence to stand up in court. The result has been a complex pattern of police behavior.

In the case of police questioning, it appears that reading the *Miranda* warning to suspects gradually has become standard practice in most places. For instance, a scholar who observed nearly two hundred interrogations in three California cities in the 1990s found no instances in which detectives were required to provide *Miranda* warnings and failed to do so.[24]

Despite the warnings, most suspects waive their rights and answer questions. One reason is that police officers structure the situation to induce a waiver. One common approach is exemplified by this statement from a detective to a suspect:

> In order for me to talk to you specifically about the injury with [the victim], I need to advise you of your rights. It's a formality. I'm sure you've watched television with the cop shows right and you hear them say their rights and so you can probably recite this better than I can, but it's something I need to do and we can get this out of the way before we talk about what's happened.[25]

Officers sometimes continue to question suspects who have invoked their right to remain silent or to wait for a lawyer. Indeed, a training manual used in Los Angeles and Santa Monica encourages detectives to undertake this practice.[26] Although information obtained through such questioning cannot be admitted directly in court, under a 1971 Supreme Court decision that evidence can be used to impeach a defendant's testimony.[27]

This noncompliance indicates that police officers find the *Miranda* warnings to be a hindrance despite the high rate of waivers by suspects. But the Court's ruling serves them well in other respects: departments that have suspects sign a form in which they waive their *Miranda* rights have a very strong defense against claims of improper practices. For this reason, many police officers have come to accept *Miranda*.[28]

By threatening that evidence would be excluded from court proceedings, *Mapp* gave police officers an incentive to comply with the body of judicial rules for searches and seizures. Prior to that time, according to one scholar, officers "*systematically*" ignored the

requirements of the Fourth Amendment because there was no reason to pay attention to it." [29] In effect, then, *Mapp* was an effort to
bring about a revolution in police practices.

In those terms, *Mapp* has been partially successful. It produced
significant changes in police behavior, including a substantial increase in the use of search warrants in some departments.[30] It appears, as we would expect, that *Mapp*'s effects have increased over
time as police adjusted to it. Sociologist Jerome Skolnick observed
police search practices in one large city in the 1960s and then in the
1980s, and he concluded that compliance with legal rules "improved significantly."[31]

But compliance is far from perfect. Studies indicate that in a relatively small but significant number of cases, prosecutors drop
charges because of illegally seized evidence or judges grant motions
to suppress illegal evidence. Such actions occur most often in cases
involving "search-intensive" crimes such as drug offenses.[32] Some
noncompliance is inadvertent, reflecting the complexity and ambiguity of the body of rules that police are asked to follow in searches
and seizures. According to one judge, "the law is so muddy that the
police can't find out what they are allowed to do even if they wanted
to."[33] Intentional noncompliance reflects the conflict that police
officers often perceive: if they follow the applicable legal rules, they
cannot obtain evidence that they see as critical.

Explaining the Implementation Process

It should be clear by now that the effectiveness with which Supreme
Court policies are implemented can vary a great deal. That effectiveness depends on several conditions: communication of policies
to relevant officials, the motivations of those officials to follow or resist the Court's policies, the Court's authority, and the sanctions it
can use to deter noncompliance.

Communication. Judges and administrators can carry out Supreme
Court decisions well only if they know what the Court wants them
to do. The communication process begins with the Court's opinions. Ideally, an opinion would state the Court's legal rules with sufficient precision and specificity that an official who reads the opinion would know how to apply those rules to any other case or
situation. Frequently, however, opinions fall far short of that ideal:
there is considerable ambiguity in the Court's messages.

Much of this ambiguity is unavoidable. The Court's opinions proclaim general legal principles in the context of specific cases. As the example of police searches indicates, the application of those principles to other cases or situations often is uncertain. Ambiguity sometimes results when a majority opinion writer inserts language in an opinion to obtain agreement from other justices or when a concurring opinion interprets the Court's decision.

Because of the Court's ambiguity, lower courts frequently diverge in their interpretation and application of its rulings. This divergence is symbolized by a 1994 decision of one federal court of appeals, which split 7–6 in its reading of a Court decision on entrapment of suspects in criminal cases. Viewing the disarray in his court, one dissenter asked the Supreme Court to revisit the issue and clarify its position.[34]

Officials who are uncertain about what the Court wants may not carry out the Court's intent properly even if they would like to do so. When officials do *not* want to carry out the Court's intent, ambiguity gives them leeway to interpret decisions as they see fit. Thus the Court's vague timetable for school desegregation gave southern judges and school administrators an excuse to delay desegregation.

Whether the Court's position on an issue is clear or ambiguous, its decisions must be transmitted to relevant judges and administrators. This is not an automatic process. Even judges seldom monitor the Supreme Court's output systematically to identify relevant decisions. Instead, decisions come to the attention of officials through other channels.

One channel is the mass media. A few Supreme Court decisions are sufficiently interesting that they receive heavy publicity in newspapers and on television. But most decisions garner much less attention from the mass media. Americans collectively get more news from television than from any other source, but only a minority of decisions get any coverage on the network news programs. And that coverage is typically quite limited and sometimes misleading.[35]

Attorneys communicate decisions to some officials. Through their arguments in court proceedings and administrative hearings, lawyers bring favorable precedents to the attention of judges and administrators. Staff lawyers in administrative agencies often inform agency personnel of relevant decisions. But administrators such as teachers and public welfare workers lack that source of information.

Another channel of information is professional hierarchies. State trial judges often become aware of the Court's decisions when they are cited by state appellate courts. Police officers learn of decisions from departmental superiors. Here, too, there is considerable potential for misinformation, especially when the communicator disagrees with a decision. Many state supreme courts and most police officials conveyed negative views of liberal criminal justice decisions by the Warren Court when they informed their subordinates of those decisions.

Effective communication of decisions depends on the receivers as well as the channels of transmission. Legally trained officials are the most capable of understanding decisions and their implications. Police officers and other nonlawyers who work regularly with the law also have some advantage in interpreting decisions. On the whole, administrators who work outside the legal system have the greatest difficulty in interpreting what they learn about Supreme Court rulings.

Where transmission problems exist, they have an obvious and significant impact. Policy makers who do not know of a decision cannot implement it. By the same token, those who misunderstand the Court's requirements will not follow them as intended. Police officers who do not fully understand the complex body of rules for searches cannot fully comply with those rules. In sum, effective transmission of the Court's policies, like clarity in the policies themselves, is needed for their effective implementation.

Motivations for Resistance. If policy makers know of a Supreme Court policy that is relevant to a choice they face, they must decide what to do with that policy. As we would expect, officials are likely to carry out a policy faithfully if they think it is a good policy and that they will benefit from doing so. But if that policy conflicts with their policy preferences or their self-interest, they may resist the Court's lead.

When appellate judges fail to implement Supreme Court decisions fully, the most common reason is a conflict between those decisions and their policy preferences. When the Court adopts a new policy, lower court judges may conclude that it has made a serious mistake. Those judges sometimes rebel against the Court's policy, though their rebellion is usually quiet.

Disagreement about judicial policy tends to follow ideological lines. That tendency is illustrated by conflict between the Supreme

Court and the Ninth Circuit Court of Appeals on the West Coast. For the last two decades the Ninth Circuit generally has been the most liberal court of appeals. Although it has become more conservative over that period, the Ninth Circuit as a whole remains more liberal than the Supreme Court, and some of its three-judge panels that hear specific cases are far more liberal than the Court. Largely as a result, the Ninth Circuit sometimes takes positions that are at least arguably inconsistent with those of the Supreme Court. In a 1996 decision, for instance, Justice Ginsburg wrote that the Ninth Circuit "did not attend to this Court's reading of [a federal statute] in a controlling decision." [36]

Of course, trial judges and administrators may also disagree with Supreme Court decisions. A great many teachers and school administrators disapprove of the Court's decisions limiting religious observances in public schools. Similarly, most police officers regard decisions that limit their investigative powers as bad policy. This disagreement has produced widespread noncompliance and partial compliance with both sets of decisions.

Supreme Court policies may conflict with officials' self-interest if they threaten existing practices that serve important purposes. Elected administrators who solidify their political strength by giving government jobs to supporters can be expected to resist Court decisions that limit their power to make such hirings.[37] In 1972 the Supreme Court ruled that mayors could not serve as judges in traffic court if their towns receive a substantial portion of their revenue from traffic fines. But precisely because they *do* benefit enormously from that revenue, some Ohio towns have ignored the Court's decision.[38]

Elected officials sometimes have good reason not to carry out highly unpopular decisions. In recent years conservative groups have enjoyed some success in campaigning against elected judges who give broad interpretations to the rights of criminal defendants. For that reason, judges may avoid following Supreme Court policies that require such broad interpretations. For the same reason, school board members in conservative areas are unlikely to take strong stands against school prayers.

Because their positions are secure, federal judges might seem to be immune from these political concerns. But they too may wish to avoid incurring public wrath. Full adherence to *Brown v. Board of Education* would have made the lives of district judges less pleasant because of the reactions of their friends and neighbors. J. Skelly Wright of Louisiana, who did adhere to *Brown,* found that his life was greatly affected. "You never know whether people really want to talk with you and I don't see a lot of people anymore." [39] Wright also had to endure public attacks, including a demonstration in which white parents and children from integrated New Orleans schools brought an effigy of Wright in a coffin into the state capitol, to the applause of legislators.[40]

Wright and a few other judges were willing to accept the costs of supporting the Supreme Court, and several northern federal judges ordered school desegregation despite the prospect of severe public criticism. But they are exceptions. If officials expect to suffer serious consequences for carrying out a decision fully, few will do so.

Differences in the implementation of Supreme Court policies result chiefly from differences in the policy preferences and self-interest of implementers. Police departments tend to resist decisions that limit their powers but follow with alacrity those that expand them. They have carried out *Miranda* more faithfully than limitations on searches because *Miranda* causes them fewer difficulties in practice. The Deep South and the border states responded differently to the *Brown* decision because attitudes toward race and segregation differed between the two regions.

The Court's Authority. In *Singleton v. Norris* (1997), Judge Gerald Heaney of the federal court of appeals for the Eighth Circuit in St. Louis wrote an opinion "to add my voice to those who oppose the death penalty as violative of the United States Constitution." Having taken that position, Heaney nonetheless voted to uphold the death sentence in this case. He explained the seeming contradiction simply: "I am compelled to adhere to the law"—apparently, the Supreme Court's position that capital punishment is constitutionally acceptable.[41]

Judge Heaney is hardly unique. A year earlier, another court of appeals judge criticized a Supreme Court decision as "unsound when decided" and "inconsistent with later decisions" of the Court, but he felt compelled to follow that decision.[42] And several years before that a Texas judge wrote his court's opinion striking down the state's anti-flag burning statute, despite his conservatism and his fear that the opinion might jeopardize his re-election, because he saw the Supreme Court's precedents as dictating that result.[43]

These judges were accepting both the Supreme Court's authority to make authoritative judgments about the law and their own obligation to comply with the Court's decisions. This acceptance is an important force in the implementation of those decisions, because it motivates public officials to carry out policies that they view negatively.

The Court's authority is strongest for judges, because they have been socialized to accept the leadership of higher courts and because as judges they also benefit from acceptance of judicial authority. But judges may give narrow interpretations to Court decisions with which they strongly disagree, thereby limiting the impact of those decisions while acknowledging the Court's authority. And some judges accord its decisions less authority.

The Court's authority extends to administrators. Some school officials eliminate religious observances that they would prefer to maintain because they accept their duty to follow Supreme Court rulings.[44] On the whole, however, the Court's authority is weaker for administrators than it is for judges. Administrative agencies are somewhat removed from the judicial system and its norm of obedience to higher court, and relatively few administrators have had the law school training that supports this norm. As a result, administrative officials find it somewhat easier to justify deviation from Supreme Court policies than do judges.

The Court's authority tends to decline as organizational distance from the Court increases. Officials at the grass-roots level may not feel obliged to adjust their policies to the Court's decisions. State trial judges typically orient themselves more closely to appellate courts in their state than to the Supreme Court, several steps away from them in the judicial hierarchy.

The Court's authority is an important motivation for acceptance of its policies. Especially within the judiciary, the authority attached to Supreme Court decisions reduces noncompliance with those decisions. But the Court's authority is not so powerful that it produces full compliance by officials who have strong reasons not to comply.

Sanctions for Disobedience. In 1906 the Supreme Court ordered a stay of execution for a Tennessee prisoner. The local sheriff responded by allowing the prisoner to be lynched. In response, the Court held the sheriff in contempt of court and ordered him to jail.[45]

This episode was the only time that the Court has held an official in contempt for failure to comply with its decisions, but it illustrates the Court's power to punish noncompliance through sanctions. Such sanctions can give judges and administrators an incentive to follow the Court's lead, an incentive more concrete than the Court's authority.

For judges, the most common sanction is reversal. If a judge does not follow an applicable Supreme Court policy, the losing litigant may appeal the case and secure a reversal of the judge's decision. This sanction is significant, in part because people often evaluate judicial performance by the frequency of reversals. Judges express a variety of attitudes toward reversal, but few are indifferent toward it. "Do I wince when a decision of mine is reversed by an appeals court?" one judge asked. "You bet I do." [46]

But reversal has its limits as a sanction. A judge who feels strongly about an issue may be willing to accept a few reversals on that issue as the price of following personal convictions. The relative liberalism of the federal court of appeals for the Ninth Circuit has led the Court to reverse an unusually large number of its decisions in the last several years. The 1999 term was fairly typical: the Court affirmed only one of the ten Ninth Circuit decisions that it reviewed.[47] But those reversals have not caused a retreat by the Ninth Circuit's liberals. One of those judges, Stephen Reinhardt, was asked whether the Court's reversals of his decisions bothered him. "'Not in the slightest!' he boomed. 'If they want to take away rights, that's their privilege. But I'm not going to help them do it.'"[48] And failure to follow the Supreme Court's lead does not always lead to reversal. The losing litigant may not appeal. Moreover, the great majority of judges are reviewed by a court other than the Supreme Court, and the reviewing court may share their opposition to the Court's policies.

For administrators, the most common sanction is a court order that directs compliance with a decision. If a public welfare agency fails to follow an applicable Supreme Court policy, someone who is injured by its failure may bring a lawsuit to compel compliance with the Court's decision. Such a suit in itself hurts the agency because of the trouble and expense it entails. A successful suit is even worse, because an order to comply with a Supreme Court rule puts an agency under judicial scrutiny and may embarrass agency officials. The agency may also be required to pay monetary damages to the person who brought the lawsuit.

But this sanction has weaknesses. Most important, it requires that people bring litigation challenging agency behavior, and they do not always do so. To take one example, school religious observances that violate the Supreme Court's rulings have gone unchallenged in many communities. And if a lawsuit is threatened or actually brought, agencies can usually change their practices in time to avoid serious costs. Thus the possibility of a lawsuit, in the abstract, is not always a strong deterrent against noncompliance.

Still, to follow a policy that conflicts with a Supreme Court ruling carries risks that most officials prefer to avoid. This attitude helps to account for the frequency with which administrative organizations on their own initiative eliminate practices prohibited by the Court. And administrators whose actions require court enforcement, such as officials in some regulatory agencies, have even more reason to avoid noncompliance that may cost them judicial support.

Police practices in searches and seizures illustrate both the strength and limitations of this sanction. Under *Mapp,* noncompliance with rules for searches jeopardizes the use of evidence in court. As a result, officers engage in a good deal of compliance with rules that they would prefer to ignore. On the other hand, officers seldom receive any personal sanctions for practices that cause evidence to be thrown out. Moreover, illegal searches may not prevent convictions. Most defendants plead guilty, and by doing so they generally waive their right to challenge the legality of searches. Trial judges often give the benefit of the doubt to police officers on borderline evidentiary questions. And evidence that is ruled illegal may not be necessary for a conviction. Thus police officers have a strong incentive to avoid illegal searches, but not so strong that they always try to follow the applicable rules.

This discussion suggests two conditions that affect the implementation process. First, interest groups play an important part in enforcement of Supreme Court decisions. The American Civil Liberties Union brings frequent challenges to school religious observances that would otherwise continue unchallenged, and by doing so it has enhanced compliance with the Court's rules. Second, the Court's decisions are easiest to enforce when the affected policy makers are few in number and highly visible. It has been relatively simple for the Court to oversee the fifty state governments that must carry out its decisions on the drawing of legislative districts. It is a far more difficult matter for the Court to oversee the day-to-day activities of the thousands of police officers who investigate crimes.

In general, the sanctions available to the Court are fairly weak. The Court can do relatively little to overcome resistance to its policies. Thus help from Congress and the president can make a great deal of difference when the Court faces widespread non-compliance. In enforcing school desegregation, that help was a necessity.

Summary. The Supreme Court's policies are implemented more effectively in some settings than in others. Judges generally carry out the Court's policies more fully than administrators because communication of decisions to judges is relatively good, most judges accord the Court considerable authority, and their self-interest is less likely to conflict with the implementation of decisions. For some of the same reasons, federal judges and administrators are probably better implementers of decisions than are their state counterparts. The Court's decisions are communicated to them more effectively, and its authority and sanctions affect them more directly.

On the whole, the Court's policies are implemented fairly well, but the gap between the rules of law that the Court establishes and the actions taken by judges and administrators is often considerable. To a degree, this gap reflects the Court's weaknesses as a policy maker, in that it can exert little control over the implementation process. Most important, the sanctions that it can apply to disobedient officials are relatively weak compared with those available to Congress or the president. But more striking than this difference is the similarity in the basic positions of Court, Congress, and president: each proclaims policies that have uncertain and often unhappy fates in the implementation process.

Responses by Legislatures and Chief Executives

After the Supreme Court hands down its decisions, Congress, the president, and their state counterparts can respond in various ways. They may help or hinder the implementation of decisions, they may act to change the Court's interpretations of the law, and they may attack the Court or its members.

Congress

Statutory Interpretation. As discussed in Chapter 5, the Supreme Court in 1998 ruled that a federal regulatory agency had misinterpreted a statute in allowing individual credit unions to enroll as

Curt Flood, star center fielder for the St. Louis Cardinals, lost his challenge to base-ball's exemption from the antitrust laws in the Supreme Court in *Flood v. Kuhn* (1972). Congress overturned that ruling in part with a bill labeled the "Curt Flood Act of 1998."

members people who work for different employers. Five months later, after considerable lobbying by the credit unions, Congress enacted a new statute that largely overruled the Court's decision.[49]

There was nothing illegitimate about this congressional action, because Congress is supreme in statutory law: it can override the Supreme Court's interpretation of a statute simply by adopting a new statute with different language that supersedes the Court's reading of the old statute. Congress can also ratify or extend the Court's interpretation of a statute, but overrides of statutory decisions are especially significant.

A substantial proportion of statutory decisions receive some congressional scrutiny, and proposals to override decisions are common. Most of these proposals fail, for the same reasons that most bills of any type fail: legislation must navigate successfully through several decision points at which it can be killed, and there is usually a presumption in favor of the status quo. Still, overrides are far from rare. Over the past three decades, on average, more than ten statutory decisions have been overturned in each two-year Congress. Of the statutory decisions in the Court's 1978–1989 terms, Congress had overridden more than five percent by 1996.[50] Some overrides, such as the 1998 action involving credit union membership, follow quickly after a decision. Others come considerably later. One 1998 statute removed part of the exemption of major-league baseball from the antitrust laws, an exemption that the Court first established in a 1922 decision.[51]

In most respects, the politics of congressional response to the Court's statutory decisions resembles congressional politics generally.[52] The initiative for bills to overturn decisions often comes from interest groups. Just as groups that fail to achieve their goals in Congress frequently turn to the courts for relief, groups whose interests suffer in the Supreme Court frequently turn to Congress.

The success of efforts to overturn statutory decisions depends on the same broad array of factors that influence the fates of other bills in Congress. The political strength of the groups that favor or oppose overrides is important. Not surprisingly, the federal executive branch enjoys considerable success in getting Congress to overturn unfavorable decisions, while nearly all decisions that work to the detriment of criminal defendants are left standing.[53] When a significant group favors action and organized opposition does not exist, Congress may override a decision quickly and easily. Many successful overrides are enacted not as separate bills but as provisions of broader bills such as appropriations, and members of Congress who vote for those bills are not always aware that they are overriding a Supreme Court decision.

Congress does not always have the last word when it overrides a statute, because the new statute is subject to judicial interpretation. In *Westfall v. Erwin* (1988), the Court held that federal officials could be sued for personal injuries under some circumstances. A few months later Congress overrode *Westfall* by allowing the attorney general to certify that an employee who had been sued was acting as a federal official and thereby substituting the federal government for the employee as a defendant. But in *Gutierrez de Martinez v. Lamagno* (1995), the Court weakened the override by holding that the attorney general's certification could be challenged in court. The Court sometimes goes even further. In *Plaut v. Spendthrift Farm* (1995), it held that a congressional override of a 1991 decision on the statute of limitations in securities fraud cases was unconstitutional because it violated the constitutional separation of powers between the legislative and judicial branches.

Constitutional Interpretation. When the Court interprets the Constitution, the most direct and decisive way to overturn its decision is through a constitutional amendment. But that is a very difficult route, because the amending process is arduous and there is a widespread reluctance to tamper with the Constitution. It is far easier to adopt a new statute, but a constitutional decision cannot be overturned directly by a statute. Under some circumstances, however, a statute can negate or limit the effects of a constitutional decision.

If the Court has nullified or limited a statute on constitutional grounds, Congress can enact a second statute to try to meet the Court's objections. Congress frequently takes such action.[54] One example is the response to *Reno v. American Civil Liberties Union* (1997), in which the Court struck down on First Amendment grounds a 1996 statute aimed at limiting children's exposure to sexually oriented material on the Internet. A year later Congress included in a spending bill a new provision aimed at achieving the same goal. Avoiding the language that the Court had cited as vague and unduly broad in its 1997 decision, Congress required operators of websites to obtain proof that someone is an adult before giving access to material that is "harmful to minors."[55] The Court has not yet ruled on whether the new law is acceptable.

When the Court holds that a right is not protected by the Constitution, Congress often can protect that right by enacting a statute. Congress has taken that action on issues such as the use of search warrants to gather information from newsrooms. In one recent instance, however, the Court ruled that such congressional action was invalid. In *Employment Division v. Smith* (1990), the Court gave a narrow interpretation to the protections of freedom of religion in the First and Fourteenth Amendments, making it easier for governments to justify rules that treat religion neutrally but that have the effect of putting a burden on a particular religious practice. A broad set of religious groups attacked the decision. In response, Congress enacted the Religious Freedom Restoration Act in 1993 to restore the broader pre-*Smith* standard of protection for religion. But in *City of Boerne v. Flores* (1997), the Court held that the 1993 act was unconstitutional as applied to state and local govern-

TABLE 6-2

Selected Resolutions Introduced in Congress for Constitutional
Amendments to Overturn Supreme Court Decisions, 1999–2000

Purpose	Decisions that would be overturned
Giving states power to impose term limits on members of Congress	*U.S. Term Limits v. Thornton* (1995)
Giving Congress power to limit campaign spending	*Buckley v. Valeo* (1976), later decisions
Allowing organized prayer in public schools	*Engel v. Vitale* (1962)
Giving federal and state governments power to prohibit flag desecration	*Texas v. Johnson* (1989), *United States v. Eichman* (1990)
Prohibiting abortion under most circumstances	*Roe v. Wade* (1973), *Planned Parenthood v. Casey* (1992), other decisions
Allowing the president to veto individual items in spending bills	*Clinton v. City of New York* (1998)

ments because it went beyond congressional power to enforce the Fourteenth Amendment.

In situations where constitutional decisions cannot be negated by statute, members of Congress often introduce resolutions to overturn them with constitutional amendments. In recent years, resolutions have been submitted on a variety of issues. The range of these issues is suggested by a sampling of resolutions introduced in the 106th Congress (1999–2000), shown in Table 6-2.

Not surprisingly, few of these efforts to propose amendments have achieved the necessary two-thirds votes in both houses. Only five times has Congress proposed an amendment that was aimed directly at Supreme Court decisions. And one of these, proposed in 1924 to give Congress the power to regulate child labor, was not ratified by the states. (A few amendments have indirectly negated Supreme Court decisions.) Since the child labor proposal, the only amendment that Congress has proposed in order to overturn a decision was the Twenty-sixth Amendment, adopted in 1971. In *Oregon v. Mitchell* (1970), the Court had ruled that Congress could not regulate the voting age in elections to state office; Congress acted quickly to propose an amendment overturning the decision, and the states quickly ratified it.

In contrast with the Twenty-sixth Amendment, the most prominent failed campaigns for amendments in recent years were aimed at decisions that increased legal protections for civil liberties. Even highly unpopular decisions, such as prohibitions of school prayer, stood up against efforts to overturn them. In these instances, the general reluctance to amend the Constitution was compounded by a special reluctance to limit the protections of rights in the Bill of Rights.

That reluctance is illustrated by the effort to propose an anti-flag-desecration amendment. In *Texas v. Johnson* (1989), the Supreme Court struck down a state statute prohibiting flag burning on the ground that it punished people for political expression. Four months later Congress enacted a federal statute against flag burning, written in an effort to meet the Court's objections to the Texas statute. But in *United States v. Eichman* (1990), the Court held that the new statute was also unconstitutional.

Members of Congress then sought a constitutional amendment to allow prohibition of flag desecration. Its passage seemed inevitable, because most members of Congress share an abhorrence of flag burning and because a member's vote against the amendment might provide an election opponent with a powerful issue. But both houses defeated a flag-desecration amendment in 1990. Similar amendments won approval in the House in 1995, 1997, and 1999, but each time they failed in the Senate. Most recently, the version approved by the House in 1999 fell four votes short of the required two-thirds majority in the Senate in 2000. These repeated failures underline the difficulty of amending the Constitution, especially in ways that might limit civil liberties.

Affecting the Implementation of Decisions. By passing legislation, Congress can influence the implementation of Supreme Court decisions by other institutions. Its most important tool is budgetary. Congress can provide or fail to provide funds to carry out a decision. It can also help the Court by withholding federal funds from state and local governments that refuse to comply with the Court's decisions. Congressional use of the latter power was critical in achieving school desegregation in the Deep South.

Occasionally a Supreme Court decision requires implementation by Congress itself. In these situations Congress generally has accepted its obligation with little resistance. The legislative veto is an exception. In *Immigration and Naturalization Service v. Chadha* (1983), the Court indicated that any statutes allowing Congress or one of its units to "veto" proposed executive branch actions are invalid. After the decision, Congress eliminated legislative veto provisions from several statutes. But it maintained others, and since 1983 it has adopted more than two hundred new legislative veto provisions— most requiring that specific congressional committees approve action by administrative agencies. Agency officials are willing to accept these provisions rather than challenging their legality, in order to maintain good relations with congressional committees and to avoid even more stringent congressional controls. Thus political realities have allowed noncompliance with *Chadha* to continue.[56]

Attacks on the Court and Its Members. When members of Congress are dissatisfied with the Supreme Court's behavior, they may attack the Court or the justices directly. The easiest way to do so is verbal, and members of Congress frequently express their disapproval of the Court by denouncing it publicly. More concretely, Congress can take formal legislative action of several types.

One type of action concerns jurisdiction. The Constitution allows Congress to alter the Court's appellate jurisdiction through legislation, though there is some question about whether Congress can narrow the Court's jurisdiction to prevent it from protecting constitutional rights. Congress has used its power over jurisdiction to control the Court only once, in an unusual situation: in 1869 it withdrew the Court's right to hear appeals in habeas corpus actions in order to prevent it from deciding a pending challenge to the post–Civil War Reconstruction legislation. In *Ex parte McCardle* (1869), the Court ruled that this congressional action was constitutionally acceptable.

In recent years, Congress has considered several bills that would have limited the Court's jurisdiction in areas of civil liberties activism. In 1964, the House did pass a bill to eliminate the jurisdiction of all federal courts over the drawing of state legislative districts, and in 1979 the Senate approved a provision to eliminate federal court jurisdiction over cases that concerned school prayer. Both of these bills died in the other house. Since the early 1980s, bills and amendments have been introduced to limit the Court's jurisdiction over such issues as abortion, school busing, and prayer. But none have passed either house.

The most extreme action that Congress can take against individual justices is to remove them through impeachment. Members of Congress sometimes talk of impeachment when they dislike a justice's policy positions. In 1997, for instance, House Majority Whip Tom DeLay of Texas reportedly used the Court's 1979 decision upholding affirmative action by employers as an example of judicial activism that would justify impeachment.[57] But impeachment based on disagreement over policy is extremely unlikely.

Congress controls the Court budget, limited only by the constitutional prohibition against reducing the justices' salaries. Congressional dissatisfaction with the Court's policies sometimes reduces its willingness to increase the justices' salaries and approve the Court's budget requests. The clearest example occurred during the 1960s, a time when many members were displeased with the Court's civil liberties policies. In 1964 Congress singled out the justices by increasing their salaries by $3000 less than those of other federal judges. A year later the House defeated a proposal to restore the $3000, after a debate in which several members attacked the Court and Robert Dole of Kansas suggested that this pay increase be contingent on the Court's reversing a legislative districting decision that he disliked.[58]

It is striking how little use Congress actually made of its enormous powers over the Court during the twentieth century. The variety of actions that were threatened against the conservative Court in the early part of the century, culminating in Franklin Roosevelt's Court-packing plan, were never carried out.[59] And all the attacks on the liberal Court in the second half of the century resulted in nothing more serious than the salary "punishment" of 1964 and 1965. Why has Congress been so hesitant to employ its powers, even at times when most members are unhappy about the Court's direction?

To begin with, there are always some members of Congress who agree with the Court's policies and lead its defense. Further, serious forms of attack against the Court, such as impeachment and reducing its jurisdiction, seem illegitimate to many people. Finally, when threatened with serious attack, the Court sometimes retreats to reduce the impetus for congressional action. For these reasons, the congressional bark at the Supreme Court has been a good deal worse than its bite.

The President

Influencing Congressional Response. The president can influence congressional responses to the Supreme Court by taking a position on proposals for action. Sometimes it is the president who first proposes anti-Court action. The most dramatic example in the twentieth century is Roosevelt's Court-packing plan.

Since the 1960s, conservative presidents have encouraged efforts in Congress to limit or overturn some of the Court's liberal rulings on civil liberties. For instance, George Bush led the effort to overturn the Court's flag-burning decisions in 1989 and 1990.

Bill Clinton also sought action to reverse the effects of some decisions. In *United States v. Lopez* (1995) the Court held that a federal statute prohibiting guns in and around schools had gone beyond congressional power to regulate interstate commerce. Clinton then proposed narrower legislation that was tied more directly to interstate commerce, and that legislation was enacted in 1996. After the Supreme Court's ruling in 2000 that the federal Food and Drug Administration lacked authority from Congress to regulate tobacco, Clinton threw his support behind a pending bill to provide that authority.[60]

Using Executive Power. As chief executive, the president has a number of means to shape the implementation of Supreme Court decisions. For one thing, presidents can decide whether to support the Court with the power of the federal government when its decisions encounter open resistance from officials with the responsibility to carry them out.

The most coercive form of federal power is deployment of the military. When southern states began to defy *Brown v. Board of Education,* President Dwight Eisenhower indicated that he would not use troops to enforce the decision. But in 1957, when a combination of state interference and mob action prevented court-ordered desegregation of the schools in Little Rock, Arkansas, Eisenhower abandoned his earlier position and brought in troops. In 1962 President John Kennedy used federal troops to enforce desegregation at the University of Mississippi.

Presidents can also use litigation and their control over federal funds. The Johnson administration's vigorous use of both these mechanisms was directly responsible for breaking down segregated school systems in the Deep South. More recent presidents have differed in their readiness to use federal money and initiate lawsuits in conflicts over school desegregation.

President Ronald Reagan's use of his executive powers helped to spur a major change in labor-management relations. In *National Labor Relations Board v. Mackay Radio & Telegraph Company* (1938), the Court ruled that under a federal labor law, companies could hire new employees as permanent replacements for workers who were on strike. For several decades companies made little use of the Court's ruling. But after federal air traffic controllers went on strike in 1981, Reagan ordered the strikers replaced. The strike failed, and this episode encouraged employers to take similar action. By doing so, they accelerated a decline in the power of organized labor.

President Clinton also used his executive powers in response to the Court's decisions. In 1995 he tried to reverse the effects of Reagan's firing of air controllers through an executive order under which companies receiving substantial amounts of money from federal contracts were prohibited from hiring permanent replacement workers. But the next year a federal court of appeals ruled that the order violated the statute that the Court had interpreted in *Mackay*.[61] In 1998 Clinton acted to limit the effects of a 1995 decision that had struck down a federal program giving minority-owned businesses an advantage in winning government contracts; by executive order, Clinton established a more limited program that might meet the Court's objections to the earlier program.[62] The Court has not yet ruled on the validity of this order.

Presidential Compliance. Occasionally a Supreme Court decision requires compliance by the president, either as a party in the case or—more often—as head of the executive branch. Some presidents and commentators have argued that the president need not obey an order of the Supreme Court, which is a coequal body rather than a legal superior. In any case, presidents would seem sufficiently powerful to disobey the Court with impunity.

But in reality their position is not that strong. The president's political power is based largely on the ability to obtain support from other policy makers. This ability, in turn, depends in part on perceptions of the president's legitimacy. Because disobedience of the Court would threaten this legitimacy, Samuel Krislov argued, presidents "cannot afford to defy the Court." [63]

That conclusion is supported by presidential responses to two highly visible Court orders. In *Youngstown Sheet and Tube Co. v. Sawyer* (1952), the Court ruled that President Harry Truman had acted illegally in seizing steel mills to keep them operating during a wartime strike and ordered that they be released. Truman immediately complied.

Even more striking is *United States v. Nixon* (1974). During investigation of the Watergate scandal, President Richard Nixon withheld recordings of certain conversations in his offices that were sought by special prosecutor Leon Jaworski. In July 1974, the Supreme Court ruled unanimously that Nixon must yield the tapes.

In oral argument before the Court, the president's lawyer had indicated that Nixon might not comply with an adverse decision. Immediately after the decision was handed down, Nixon apparently considered noncompliance. By the end of that day, however, Nixon released a statement indicating that he would comply. At the least, this compliance speeded Nixon's departure from office: he released transcripts of some of the tapes, whose content provided strong evidence of presidential misdeeds, and opposition to impeachment evaporated. Fifteen days after the Court's ruling, Nixon announced his resignation.

In light of that result, why did Nixon comply with the Court order? He apparently did not realize how damaging the evidence in the tapes actually was. Perhaps more important, noncompliance would have damaged his remaining legitimacy fatally. For many members of Congress noncompliance in itself would have constituted an impeachable offense, one on which there would be no dispute about the evidence. Under the circumstances compliance may have been the better of two unattractive choices.

State Legislatures and Governors

State governments have no direct power over the Supreme Court as an institution. But state legislatures and governors, like Congress and the president, can influence the impact of the Court's decisions in a variety of ways.

Any legislature can rewrite a statute to try to meet the Court's constitutional objections to it. The Chicago city council did so in 2000 when it crafted a new ordinance against loitering by gang members after the Court struck down an earlier version on First Amendment grounds.[64] The same kind of action by state legislatures restored capital punishment after the Court struck down existing death penalty laws in *Furman v. Georgia* (1972). In the next few years, thirty-five state legislatures wrote new laws that were designed to avoid arbitrary use of capital punishment and thus meet the objections raised by the pivotal justices in *Furman*. In a series of decisions from 1976 on, the Court upheld some of the new statutes and overturned others. States whose laws were rejected by the Court then adopted the forms that the Court had found acceptable, and by doing so they nearly nullified the impact of *Furman*.

In the case of term limits, voters rather than legislators have sought to limit the Court's impact.[65] After a 1995 decision that the states could not impose term limits on members of Congress, voters in ten states adopted initiatives that would punish any member of Congress who did not support a constitutional amendment establishing term limits by putting on the ballot next to that member's name, "DISREGARDED VOTERS' INSTRUCTION ON TERM LIMITS." Lower courts uniformly struck down these initiatives. The Supreme Court in 2000 agreed to rule on their validity,[66] but meanwhile supporters of term limits took a new approach: three western states adopted initiatives that allow congressional candidates to sign pledges to serve a limited number of terms and have that pledge indicated on the ballot. If a successful candidate later violates the pledge, this fact will be noted on the ballot.

More frequently than Congress, state legislatures have adopted statutes that seem clearly to violate the Court's decisions. In the decade after *Brown v. Board of Education,* southern states passed a large number of statutes to prevent school desegregation, and some states have enacted laws to restore school religious observances that the Court invalidated. Most such statutes are overturned quickly by the federal courts, but they still allow legislators to express their opposition to the Court's rulings.

Occasionally state legislatures act to protect rights that the Supreme Court has held to be unprotected by the Constitution. As discussed earlier, the Court ruled in *City of Boerne v. Flores* (1997) that Congress lacked the power to expand protection for religious practices against state regulation. Since then, several legislatures have enacted similar laws to provide expanded protection in their own states.

Like presidents, governors can influence both legislative responses to the Court's decisions and their implementation.

Southern governors helped to block school desegregation in the 1950s and 1960s through their efforts to stir up resistance. More recently, governors have been prominent in state controversies over issues such as school prayer and criminal procedure, sometimes supporting and sometimes opposing the Court's decisions.

Legislatures, governors, and their local counterparts must act to put some Supreme Court decisions into effect. *Gideon v. Wainwright* (1963) and later decisions required that indigent criminal defendants be provided with legal counsel. The Court's decisions spurred state and local governments to increase their commitment to fund defense for the indigent. Because of that commitment, reflected in high levels of funding, the great majority of felony defendants now are represented by government-provided attorneys.[67] Certainly low-income defendants are in a far better position than they were prior to 1963.

But funding of counsel has never been fully adequate. It has become less adequate with rapid growth in the number of criminal cases during a period when there is little political support for assistance to criminal defendants. As a result, according to one federal judge, "perfunctory representation of indigent criminal defendants is the order of the day in American courts."[68] Thus the Court has achieved considerable change in state and local policies, but that change falls short of what many people saw as the promise of the *Gideon* decision.

State legislatures and governors engage in direct defiance of the Court's decisions more often than do Congress and the president. This difference may result chiefly from the sheer number of states rather than from differences in the behavior of state and federal officials. Still, it suggests that the Court may face special difficulties when it seeks to bring about fundamental changes in state policies.

Yet resistance to the Court by state governments should not be exaggerated. Undoubtedly, their most frequent response to the Court's decisions is compliance. And much of what governors and legislatures do to limit the Court's impact, such as their reinstatement of the death penalty, is an effort to maintain the policies they want within the constraints of the Court's rulings.

Two Policy Areas

Patterns of response to the Court's decisions by the other two branches of government can be examined more closely with a look at two areas in which there has been a good deal of interaction between the Court and other policy makers.

Civil Rights Statutes.   Beginning in 1957, Congress adopted a series of statutes that prohibited discrimination along racial and other lines. The most important were the Civil Rights Act of 1964, which dealt with discrimination in employment and other fields, and the Voting Rights Act of 1965. Both statutes have been amended since then to broaden their impact. The Supreme Court has issued a number of major decisions and even more minor ones interpreting their provisions.

Democrats controlled the House from 1964 through 1994, and they enjoyed a Senate majority for all but six of those years.[69] Through the mid-1980s the Court generally gave broad interpretations to the civil rights laws, a stance that was consistent with the majority view in Congress. But Congress did override some decisions that narrowed the reach of the laws. The Pregnancy Discrimination Act of 1978 overturned a 1976 decision that exclusion of pregnancy from programs providing pay to disabled workers did not violate the Civil Rights Act of 1964.[70] Congress in 1988 reversed *Grove City College v. Bell* (1984), which had limited the reach of several statutes prohibiting discrimination by recipients of federal funds. And even with Republican control of the Senate, Congress amended the Voting Rights Act in 1982 to reverse a 1980 decision that established a heavy burden of proof for people trying to prove racial discrimination in election rules.[71]

In comparison with its predecessors, the Rehnquist Court has given narrower interpretations to civil rights laws. This stance aroused opposition from Congress in the early 1990s. The Civil Rights Act of 1991 overrode eight different Rehnquist Court decisions, most of them on employment discrimination. But since 1995, with Republican majorities in both houses, Congress has had little to complain about in the Court's decisions on the civil rights laws.

The Reagan and Bush adminstrations were less favorable than Congress to broad interpretation of the civil rights laws, and this stance shaped legislative response to the Court's decisions. The reversal of *Grove City* was delayed by President Reagan's opposition, and ultimately it was enacted through an override of his veto. The Civil Rights Act of 1991 became law only after President George Bush had vetoed an earlier version. Congress would have done even more to reverse conservative decisions under a Democratic president. But presidents can do much more to block action than to bring it about, and even with a Democratic president in the late 1990s the Court's narrow readings of civil rights laws were secure.

Abortion. After the Supreme Court struck down state prohibitions of abortion in *Roe v. Wade* (1973), most states enacted laws to regulate abortion.[72] Many of these laws were neutral regulations that would clearly be acceptable to the Court, such as a requirement that abortions be performed by licensed physicians. But many other state laws were motivated by the goal of limiting the Court's impact by making abortions more difficult to obtain. Some states adopted several different statutes of this type. Rhode Island sought to nullify the Court's decision altogether with a new statute.

Groups that opposed legal restrictions on abortion regularly challenged restrictive state laws. In a series of decisions from 1976 to 1986, the Court struck down a number of these laws as inconsistent with *Roe*. But the Court did uphold federal and state restrictions on the funding of abortion in the Medicaid program for low income people. (Several state courts, however, struck down state funding restrictions on the basis of provisions in state constitutions.)

As new appointments made the Court more conservative, its support for the principles of the *Roe* decision weakened. Many people interpreted the Court's decision in *Webster v. Reproductive Health Services* (1989) to mean that the Court would now allow substantial restrictions on abortion or even overturn *Roe* in an appropriate case. Consequently, legislators and interest groups in nearly every state sought new legislation that heavily restricted abortion. In the two years after *Webster,* the great majority of these efforts failed, but Pennsylvania enacted major restrictions on abortion, and Utah, Louisiana, and Guam prohibited abortions under most circumstances. In contrast, Connecticut and Maryland passed statutes protecting the right to abortion under state law.

The Court's decision in *Planned Parenthood v. Casey* (1992), which reaffirmed *Roe* for the most part, made it clear that the Court would strike down state prohibitions of abortion. But the decision also encouraged states to adopt restrictions that might be consistent with the Court's new rules for regulation of abortion. Since 1992 a number of the states have adopted laws requiring parental consent or notification in most instances before young women obtain abortions. Many states have required waiting periods between arranging for an abortion and obtaining it, and some have established special regulations for abortion clinics. During the rest of the 1990s the Court said little about what kinds of regulations were acceptable under *Casey*. But in *Stenberg v. Carhart* (2000) it stuck down a Nebraska law that contained another type of regulation, one prohibiting a method of abortion labeled "partial-birth abortion" by pro-life groups. Thirty other states had similar prohibitions, and the Court's ruling seemed to cover all or nearly all those laws. Following a well-established pattern in this field, legislators immediately began to draft new laws that might meet the Court's objections to the existing ones.

At the federal level, the Reagan and Bush administrations established restrictions on the availability of abortion in some areas of federal activity, such as the military. In the early 1990s, Congress took steps to overturn some of these restrictions, but President Bush used the veto power to block these initiatives. One example involved the "gag rule," a set of regulations by the Department of Health and Human Services that broadly prohibited family planning clinics funded by the federal government from engaging in activities that encouraged or facilitated abortion. The Court upheld these regulations in *Rust v. Sullivan* (1991). Later that year Congress passed a bill intended to overturn the regulations, but President Bush vetoed it; he vetoed similar legislation in 1992.

Two days after he became president, Bill Clinton eliminated the regulations of family planning clinics along with several other restrictions on abortion. When the Court ruled in 1993 that abortion clinics could not use a civil rights law to sue people who engaged in protests that obstruct access to the clinics, the Clinton administration encouraged Congress to pass a statute aimed at curbing those protests.[73] Congress did so in 1994, allowing criminal prosecutions and civil lawsuits against those engaged in such activities as blockading abortion clinics. After Congress came under Republican control in 1995, Clinton used veto threats and actual vetoes to limit anti-abortion legislation.

The abortion issue illustrates the importance of legislative responses to the Court's decisions. Even a seemingly definitive ruling in *Roe v. Wade* did not prevent Congress and state legislatures from enacting laws limiting access to abortion, and legislatures have done a great deal to shape the law of abortion within the constraints of the Court's decisions. The issue also underlines the role of chief executives. Governors in some states have encouraged restrictions on abortion, while other governors have prevented their enactment. The difference in the actions of the Bush and Clinton administrations underlines the president's importance in influencing federal responses to the Court's abortion decisions.

Impact on Society

In the 1890s, federal judge Isaac Parker told a reporter that "murders are on the increase" and said that "I attribute the increase to the Supreme Court." [74] Today, commentators continue to blame the Court for problems of crime. In 1998 two scholars concluded that "*Miranda* may be the single most damaging blow inflicted on the nation's ability to fight crime in the last half century." [75] After a wave of well-publicized shootings at schools, two law professors wrote in 1999 that, by striking down a federal law against carrying guns in school zones, the Court "has unwittingly allowed guns to fall into the hands of these young murderers." [76] A month earlier a popular comic strip had offered a different diagnosis: "What would you get if you took God, the Bible, and prayer out of public schools?" "Senseless violence." [77]

These statements illustrate a widely shared belief that the Supreme Court's decisions have a powerful impact not just on other policy makers but on American society as a whole. People often blame the Court for what they see as undesirable effects on society, but the Court also receives considerable praise for improving society. The belief that the Court powerfully shapes society is reflected in the attention that interest groups, the mass media, and political leaders give to the Court. But just how powerful is the Court's impact? This is an important question, perhaps the most important one that we can ask about the Court.

A General View

Any government policy can have a wide range of effects on society, including some that are indirect and quite unexpected. Certainly this is true of Supreme Court decisions. Often it is difficult to distinguish between the Court's impact and that of other forces contributing to the same result. For this reason it is seldom possible to make firm judgments about the effects of the Supreme Court on society.

Still, there is reason to be skeptical when people assert that the Court has sweeping effects on American society. In reality, the effects of Supreme Court policies on society are constrained a great deal by the context in which those policies operate.

A major part of that context is governmental. The Supreme Court seldom issues directives to people or institutions outside government. Rather, its decisions establish legal rules to govern decisions within government. This means that the Court's impact on society is mediated by other public policy makers.

One reason, discussed earlier, is that the impact of decisions can be narrowed by policy makers who act to limit them. Those who ascribe enormous effects to the Court's decisions on school religious practices seem to assume that public schools actually ended prayer and Bible-reading exercises after the Court prohibited these practices. In reality, these practices remained widespread.

More broadly, the Court is seldom the only government agency that deals with a particular set of issues. Rather, in most areas the Court is one policy maker among many that render decisions and undertake initiatives. In environmental policy, for instance, Congress sets the basic legal rules, administrative agencies elaborate on these rules and apply them to specific cases, and lower courts resolve most disagreements over agency decisions. The Court's participation is limited to resolving a few of the legal questions that arise in the lower courts. The Court can still have considerable impact, but it can hardly determine the character of environmental policy by itself.

The Court's policies also operate within a context of nongovernmental action. Even the direct impact of most decisions depends largely on the responses of people outside government. Especially important are the actions of people and institutions that the Court gives greater freedom. These beneficiaries of the Court's policies may not take full advantage of the freedom that the Court provides them. One reason is that they may not be aware of favorable decisions. But even those who know about such decisions do not always act on them. For example, welfare recipients may not insist on their procedural rights because they do not want to alienate officials who hold power over them. The Court's decisions have allowed attorneys to engage in advertising, but only a minority of lawyers make use of this freedom, in part because many see advertising by lawyers as unprofessional.[78]

The broad impact of Supreme Court decisions on society is also limited by forces outside of government. Phenomena such as the crime rate and the quality of education are affected by family socialization, the mass media, and the economy. Those forces are likely to exert a much stronger impact on the propensity to commit crimes or the performance of students than does a Supreme Court policy. Moreover, any effects that the Court does have operate within the constraints of these forces. This limitation is common to all public policies, no matter which branch issues them. But the Supreme Court is in an especially weak position, because it has little control over the behavior of the private sector and because it seldom makes comprehensive policy in a particular area.

Despite all these limitations, Supreme Court decisions can and do have significant effects on society. Frequently they exert an impact by shaping government policies on major issues. In this way the Court helps to determine whether businesses merge and whether people are compensated for acts of discrimination. To take an example that was discussed earlier, the effects of the Court's decision on the hiring of replacement workers for strikers have been quite substantial.[79] In this instance, as in others, the Court did not act alone. But by helping to determine what other policy makers do, it makes a difference. The Court also has an effect by shaping the political process itself: for instance, its decisions on campaign finance and term limits for legislators affect who serves in government and thus what government does. The Court hardly plays a dominant role in American society, but it would be a mistake to dismiss it as irrelevant.[80]

Some Areas of Court Activity

We can gain a better sense of the Court's impact on society and the forces that determine that impact by looking at a few areas of the Court's activity. These examples demonstrate that the Court's impact is complex, highly variable, and sometimes quite difficult to measure.

Abortion. Prior to the Court's 1973 decisions in *Roe v. Wade* and *Doe v. Bolton,* two-thirds of the states allowed abortion only under quite limited circumstances, and all but four states had very substantial restrictions. With its decisions the Court disallowed nearly all significant legal restrictions on abortion. In every year since 1976, there have been more than one million legal abortions. In light of the sequence of events, it seems reasonable to conclude that the Court is responsible for the large numbers of legal abortions. But the reality is more complicated, and it is impossible to assess the Court's impact with any precision.[81]

As Figure 6-1 shows, the number of legal abortions increased by about 150 percent between 1972 and 1979. This massive change suggests that the Court made a great deal of difference. But the rate of increase was actually greater between 1969 and 1972. That increase reflected changes in state laws before and during that period, as some states relaxed their general prohibitions of abortion and a few eliminated most restrictions. If the Court had never handed down *Roe v. Wade,* it is likely that the abortion rate would have grown further as a result of increasing numbers of abortions in the states that already allowed it and continuing change in state laws. But it is impossible to know how state laws would have evolved and how the abortion rate would have changed if the Court had not intervened.

After the Court decided *Roe v. Wade,* other government policies shaped its impact. Decisions by the federal government and most states to fund abortions through Medicaid only under limited circumstances have affected the rate of abortion among low-income women. Decisions not to perform abortions in government-run medical facilities have also affected the abortion rate. The number of legal abortions is influenced by an array of other policies, from rules for medical clinics that receive federal money to state-mandated waiting periods before abortions can be performed. The Court influences these policies through its rulings on what kinds of restrictions on abortion are allowable, but that influence falls far short of full control.

The abortion rate is powerfully affected by conditions other than government policy, conditions that the Court affects very little.[82] Of course, the number of abortions results largely from the number of unintended pregnancies and from women's choices whether to seek abortions. Also important is the ability of women who want abortions to obtain them. Only a small minority of privately owned hospitals perform abortions. Urban areas generally have clinics that perform abortions, but many rural areas lack such clinics. In the 1980s and 1990s, the number of facilities that performed abortions declined substantially. These patterns reflect personal beliefs about abortion on the part of medical personnel as well as restrictive laws